PHILIP'S

MODERN SCHOOL ·ATLAS·

GEORGE PHILIP

In Association with Heinemann Educational

George Philip Ltd.
59 Grosvenor Street
London W1X 9DA

Heinemann Educational
Halley Court Jordan Hill
Oxford OX2 8EJ

ASTRONOMICAL GEOGRAPHY

THE SOLAR SYSTEM

The Solar System is a tiny part of one of the countless galaxies that make up the Universe. It consists of the Sun at the centre with nine planets and various moons, comets, dust particles and gases revolving around it. All the planets revolve around the Sun in the same direction, anti-clockwise when viewed from the Northern Heavens, and almost in the same plane.

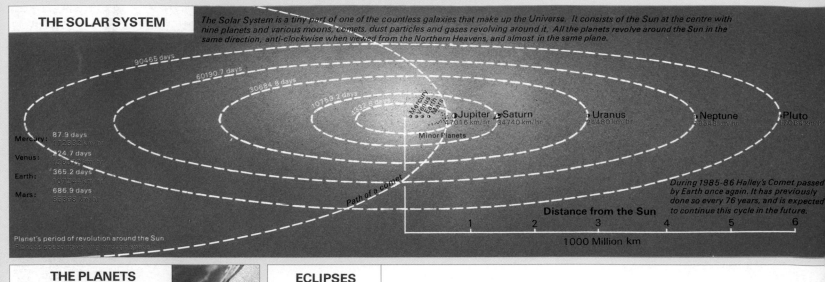

90465 days
60190.7 days
30684.8 days
10759.2 days
1332.6 days

Mercury · Venus · Earth · Mars

Jupiter   Saturn   Uranus   Neptune   Pluto
47016 km/hr 34740 km/hr   24480 km/hr   18481 km/hr   17064 km/hr

Minor Planets

Mercury: 87.9 days
           172332 km/hr
Venus: 224.7 days
           126072 km/hr
Earth: 365.2 days
           107244 km/hr
Mars: 686.9 days
           86868 km/hr

Path of a comet

During 1985-86 Halley's Comet passed by Earth once again. It has previously done so every 76 years, and is expected to continue this cycle in the future.

Distance from the Sun

Planet's period of revolution around the Sun
Planet's speed travelling through space.

1   2   3   4   5   6
1000 Million km

THE PLANETS IN RELATION TO THEIR SIZE

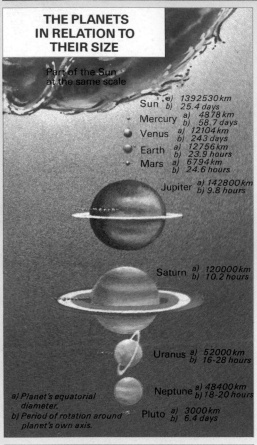

Part of the Sun at the same scale

Sun	a)	1392530km
	b)	25.4 days
Mercury	a)	4878 km
	b)	58.7 days
Venus	a)	12104 km
	b)	243 days
Earth	a)	12756 km
	b)	23.9 hours
Mars	a)	6794km
	b)	24.6 hours
Jupiter	a)	142800 km
	b)	9.8 hours
Saturn	a)	120000 km
	b)	10.2 hours
Uranus	a)	52000 km
	b)	16-28 hours
Neptune	a)	48400km
	b)	18-20 hours
Pluto	a)	3000 km
	b)	6.4 days

a) Planet's equatorial diameter.
b) Period of rotation around planet's own axis.

ECLIPSES

When the Moon passes between the Earth and the Sun it blots out the sunlight over part of the Earth's surface. This is called a partial eclipse of the Sun.

→ Direction of moon's orbit
← Direction of earth's orbit

When the Earth passes between the Moon and the Sun it casts a shadow over the whole surface of the Moon. This is a total eclipse of the Moon.

Partial eclipse

EARTH
MOON
SUN

MOON
EARTH
SUN

An eclipse of the Sun and of the Moon does not occur every month, because of the 5° difference between the plane of the Moon's orbit and the plane in which the Earth moves.

Total eclipse

TIDES

High Spring tide
Low Neap tide
Last quarter
New moon
Sun
High Spring tide
Full moon
Low Neap tide
First quarter

The rise and fall of the seas are due to the gravitational pull of the Moon. When the Sun and Moon pull in the same direction high tides result.

THE PHASES OF THE MOON

The Moon, like the planets, has no light of its own and shines only by reflecting sunlight.

Appearance of moon from earth

First Quarter 3
SUN LIGHT

4
2

EARTH
Night   Day
Full Moon   New Moon

5
6

Position of moon
Last Quarter 7
8
SUN LIGHT

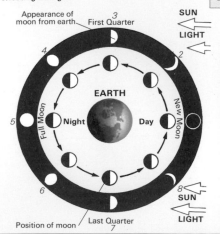

The Moon rotates on its own axis in just over 27 days, which is the same as its period of revolution around the Earth, so that it always presents the same face (hemisphere) to us. Because the Earth has moved on its own orbital plane around the Sun, while the Moon is revolving around it, the time from one full Moon to the next is 29½ days.

Crescent moon (2)	Half moon, first quarter (3)	The waxing moon (4)	Full moon (5)	The waning moon (6)	Half moon, last quarter (7)	The old moon (8)

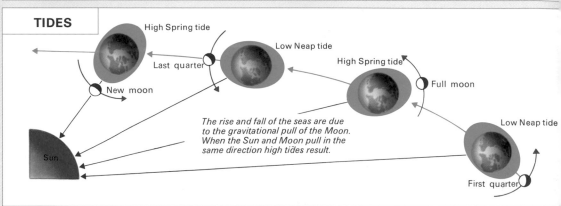

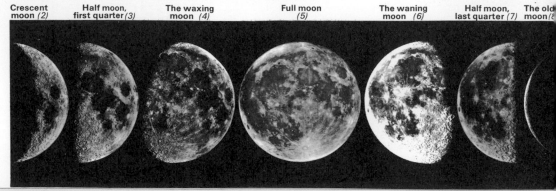

THE SEASONS

The earth revolves around the sun once a year in an anti-clockwise direction. The earth is tilted at an angle of 66½ degrees to the plane of its orbit and always points into space in the same direction. In June the northern hemisphere is tilted towards the sun and it is the northern summer — days are longer and it is generally warmer. The southern hemisphere is pointing away from the sun. It is cooler and the days are shorter — the southern winter. In December the reverse is the case.

Equinox — One of the two times in the year when day and night are of equal length, owing to the Sun being overhead at the Equator.

Solstice — One of the two times in the year, midway between the two equinoxes, when the Sun is overhead at one of the Tropics (Cancer or Capricorn) and is at its highest latitude from the Equator (23½° North or South).

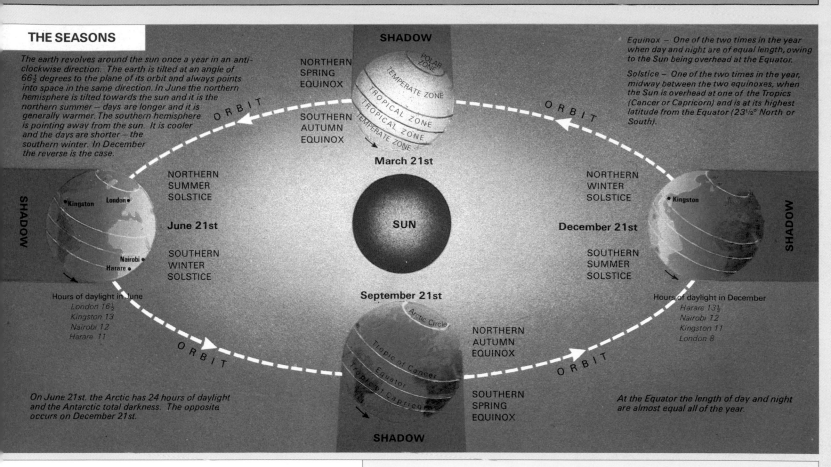

SHADOW

NORTHERN SPRING EQUINOX

POLAR ZONE
TEMPERATE ZONE
TROPICAL ZONE
TROPICAL ZONE
TEMPERATE ZONE

SOUTHERN AUTUMN EQUINOX

ORBIT

March 21st

NORTHERN SUMMER SOLSTICE

June 21st

SOUTHERN WINTER SOLSTICE

- Kingston
- London

- Nairobi
- Harare

SHADOW

SUN

ORBIT

NORTHERN WINTER SOLSTICE

December 21st

SOUTHERN SUMMER SOLSTICE

- Kingston

SHADOW

September 21st

Arctic Circle
Tropic of Cancer
Equator
Tropic of Capricorn

NORTHERN AUTUMN EQUINOX

SOUTHERN SPRING EQUINOX

SHADOW

ORBIT

Hours of daylight in June
London 16½
Kingston 13
Nairobi 12
Harare 11

On June 21st. the Arctic has 24 hours of daylight and the Antarctic total darkness. The opposite occurs on December 21st.

Hours of daylight in December
Harare 13½
Nairobi 12
Kingston 11
London 8

At the Equator the length of day and night are almost equal all of the year.

LENGTH OF DAY AND NIGHT ON THE EARTH

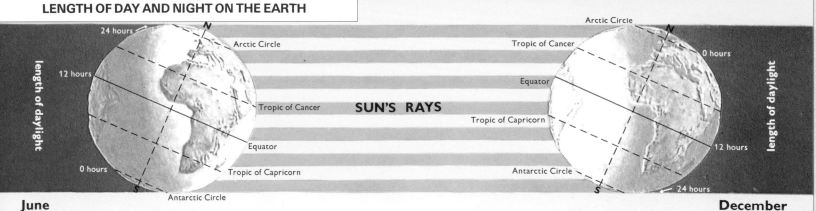

length of daylight

24 hours
12 hours
0 hours

Arctic Circle
Tropic of Cancer
Equator
Tropic of Capricorn
Antarctic Circle

SUN'S RAYS

Arctic Circle
Tropic of Cancer
Equator
Tropic of Capricorn
Antarctic Circle

0 hours
12 hours
24 hours

length of daylight

June

December

TIME

The Year — the time taken by the Earth to revolve around the Sun, or 365¼ days.

The Month — the approximate time taken by the Moon to revolve around the Earth. The twelve months of the year in fact vary from 28 (29 in a Leap Year) to 31 days.

The Week — an artificial period of 7 days, not based on astronomical time.

The Day — the time taken by the Earth to complete one rotation on its axis.

The Hour — 24 hours make one day. Usually the day is divided into hours A.M. (ante meridiem or before noon) and P.M. (post meridiem or after noon), although most timetables now use the 24-hour system, from midnight to midnight, for example, 1p.m. = 13.00 hours.

SUNRISE AND SUNSET

From the diagrams below it is possible to find out the time of sunrise or sunset on a given date and for latitudes between 60°N and 60°S.

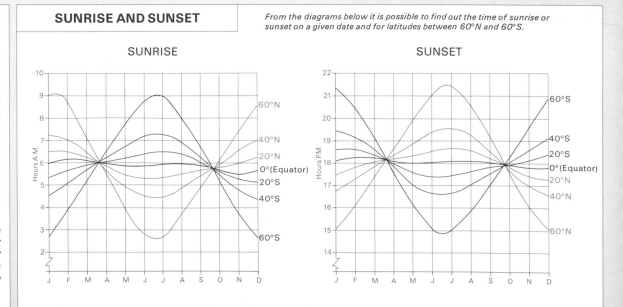

SUNRISE

Hours A.M.

60°N
40°N
20°N
0°(Equator)
20°S
40°S
60°S

J F M A M J J A S O N D

SUNSET

Hours P.M.

60°S
40°S
20°S
0°(Equator)
20°N
40°N
60°N

J F M A M J J A S O N D

PHILIP'S

MODERN SCHOOL ·ATLAS·

SETTLEMENTS

PARIS   Berne   Livorno   Brugge   Algeciras   *Fréjus*   Oberammergau   Thira

Settlement symbols and type styles vary according to the scale of each map and indicate the importance of towns on the map rather than specific population figures

∴ Ruins or Archæological Sites   ◡ Wells in Desert

ADMINISTRATION

———— International Boundaries

— — — International Boundaries (Undefined or Disputed)

—·····— Internal Boundaries

National Parks

Country Names

NICARAGUA

Administrative Area Names

KENT

CALABRIA

International boundaries show the *de facto* situation where there are rival claims to territory

COMMUNICATIONS

——— Principal Roads

——— Other Roads

-·-·- Trails and Seasonal Roads

⩤ Passes

✿ Airfields

——— Principal Railways

-·-·- Railways Under Construction

——— Other Railways

⊐---⊏ Railway Tunnels

········· Principal Canals

PHYSICAL FEATURES

⌇ Perennial Streams

-·-·- Intermittent Streams

⬭ Perennial Lakes

Intermittent Lakes

Swamps and Marshes

Permanent Ice and Glaciers

▲ 8848 Elevations in metres

▼ 8050 Sea Depths in metres

1134 Height of Lake Surface Above Sea Level in metres

ELEVATION AND DEPTH TINTS

Height of Land Above Sea Level

in metres | 6000 | 4000 | 3000 | 2000 | 1500 | 1000 | 400 | 200 | 0

in feet | 18 000 | 12 000 | 9000 | 6000 | 4500 | 3000 | 1200 | 600

Land Below Sea Level

Depth of Sea

in feet | 6000 | 12 000 | 15 000 | 18 000 | 24 000 | in feet

in metres | 0 | 200 | 2000 | 4000 | 5000 | 6000 | 8000 | in metres

Some of the maps have different contours to highlight and clarify the principal relief features

KEY TO COLOUR CODING

The atlas is divided into four sections for ease of use.

- BRITISH ISLES
- EUROPE, ASIA, OCEANIA, AFRICA, NORTH AMERICA & SOUTH AMERICA
- THE WORLD
- INDEX

© 1992 George Philip Limited, London
Eighty-eighth Edition

ISBN 0 540 05669 3 Paperback Edition
ISBN 0 540 05668 5 Hardback Edition

Edited by B.M. Willett, B.A., Cartographic Editor, George Philip Limited

Printed in Great Britain by Butler and Tanner Limited, Frome

CONTENTS

Publisher's Note   The maps of the Soviet Union and Yugoslavia show the situation at the time of going to press in December, 1991. Extra maps of the Republics and Nationalities of the Soviet Union and the Republics and Ethnic Groups of Yugoslavia are provided on p.161.

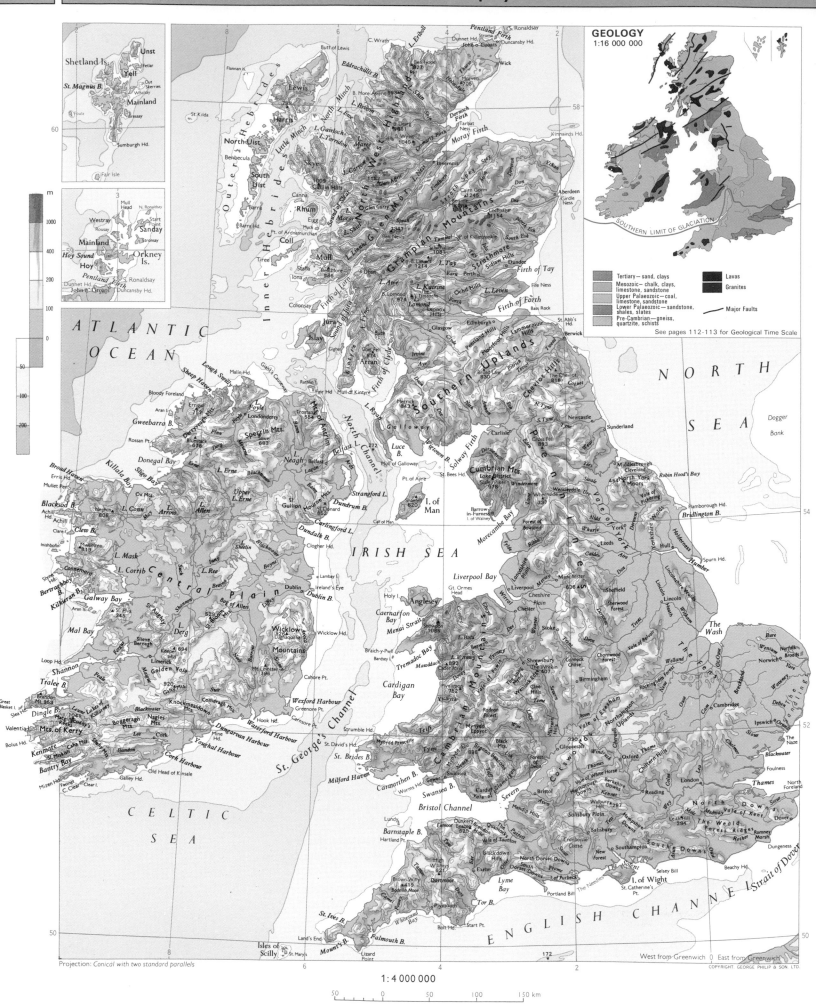

GEOLOGY
1:16 000 000

SOUTHERN LIMIT OF GLACIATION

Tertiary — sand, clays
Mesozoic — chalk, clays, limestone, sandstone
Upper Palaeozoic — coal, limestone, sandstone
Lower Palaeozoic — sandstone, shales, slates
Pre-Cambrian — gneiss, quartzite, schists

Lavas
Granites

Major Faults

See pages 112-113 for Geological Time Scale

Shetland Is.

Orkney Is.

ATLANTIC OCEAN

NORTH SEA

Dogger Bank

IRISH SEA

I. of Man

CELTIC SEA

St. GEORGE'S CHANNEL

Central Plain

Grampian Mountains

Southern Uplands

Cumbrian Mts.
Lake District

Pennines

Cambrian Mountains

North Downs

South Downs

The Weald

ENGLISH CHANNEL   Strait of Dover

Projection: Conical with two standard parallels

1:4 000 000

50   0   50   100   150 km

West from Greenwich   0   East from Greenwich

COPYRIGHT GEORGE PHILIP & SON LTD.

The DISTRICTS of Northern Ireland have been numbered and can be identified by reference to this table.

1	Londonderry	14	Craigavon
2	Limavady	15	Armagh
3	Coleraine	16	Newry & Mourne
4	Ballymoney	17	Banbridge
5	Moyle	18	Down
6	Larne	19	Lisburn
7	Ballymena	20	Antrim
8	Magherafelt	21	Newtownabbey
9	Cookstown	22	Carrickfergus
10	Strabane	23	North Down
11	Omagh	24	Ards
12	Fermanagh	25	Castlereagh
13	Dungannon	26	Belfast

ORKNEY

Kirkwall

HIGHLAND

SHETLAND

Lerwick

WESTERN ISLES

Stornoway

ATLANTIC

OCEAN

HIGHLAND

Inverness GRAMPIAN

Aberdeen

SCOTLAND

TAYSIDE

Dundee

FIFE
Glenrothes

CENTRAL
Stirling

Edinburgh
LOTHIAN
Glasgow

STRATHCLYDE

Newtown
St. Boswells

BORDERS

NORTH

DUMFRIES
AND
GALLOWAY Dumfries

NORTHUMBERLAND
Morpeth

Newcastle
TYNE AND
WEAR

SEA

Carlisle

Durham

DURHAM

CUMBRIA

CLEVELAND
Middlesbrough

Northallerton

NORTH
YORKSHIRE

LANCASHIRE
Preston

HUMBERSIDE
Beverley

WEST
YORKSHIRE Wakefield

Lifford
DONEGAL Londonderry

Antrim

NORTHERN
IRELAND
Tyrone

Belfast

Down

Fermanagh

Sligo
LEITRIM Monaghan Armagh

SLIGO

MAYO
Castlebar

Carrick-on-Shannon
MONAGHAN
Cavan
CAVAN

LOUTH
Dundalk

ROSCOMMON
Longford
LONGFORD
Roscommon
Mullingar
WESTMEATH

MEATH

ISLE OF
MAN

Douglas

IRISH SEA

GREATER
MANCHESTER
MERSEYSIDE Manchester
Liverpool

SOUTH
YORKSHIRE Barnsley

ENGLAND
Lincoln

Chester
CHESHIRE
DERBYSHIRE

NOTT-
INGHAM-
SHIRE LINCOLNSHIRE
Matlock
Nottingham

GALWAY
Galway

IRELAND

OFFALY
Tullamore

KILDARE
Naas

Dublin
Dublin

CLARE
Ennis

Limerick

LAOIS
Port Laoise

TIPPERARY

Kilkenny
KILKENNY

Carlow
CARLOW

WICKLOW
Wicklow

Caernarfon
GWYNEDD

Mold
CLWYD

Shrewsbury
SHROPSHIRE

Stafford
STAFFORD-
SHIRE

WEST
MIDLANDS
Birmingham
WARWICK-
SHIRE Warwick

Leicester
LEICESTERSHIRE

NORTH-
AMPTON-
SHIRE Northampton

CAMBRIDGE-
SHIRE

NORFOLK
Norwich

LIMERICK

Tralee

KERRY

LIMERICK

WATERFORD Waterford

WEXFORD

Clonmel

Wexford

WALES

POWYS

Llandrindod
Wells

DYFED

Carmarthen

HEREFORD
AND
WORCESTER Worcester

Gloucester
GLOUCESTER-
SHIRE

Oxford
OXFORDSHIRE

Bedford
BEDFORD-
SHIRE

Cambridge

SUFFOLK
Ipswich

Hertford
HERTFORD-
SHIRE

BUCK-
INGHAM-
SHIRE
Aylesbury

ESSEX
Chelmsford

CORK

Cork

WEST
GLAMORGAN
Swansea MID
GLAMORGAN
Cardiff
SOUTH
GLAMORGAN

GWENT
Cwmbran

Bristol

AVON

BERKSHIRE
Reading

GREATER
LONDON
Kingston

Maidstone

St. GEORGE'S Channel

North Channel

CELTIC

SEA

DEVON
Exeter

SOMERSET
Taunton

WILTSHIRE
Trowbridge

HAMPSHIRE
Winchester

WEST
SUSSEX
Chichester

SURREY

KENT

EAST
SUSSEX
Lewes

DORSET
Dorchester

Newport
ISLE OF
WIGHT

CORNWALL
Truro

ENGLISH CHANNEL

FRANCE

West from Greenwich 0 East from Greenwich
COPYRIGHT. GEORGE PHILIP & SON. LTD.

○ Norwich	Administrative headquarters
MERSEYSIDE	Metropolitan counties
Antrim	Former Northern Ireland counties

1:4 000 000

50 0 50 100 150 km

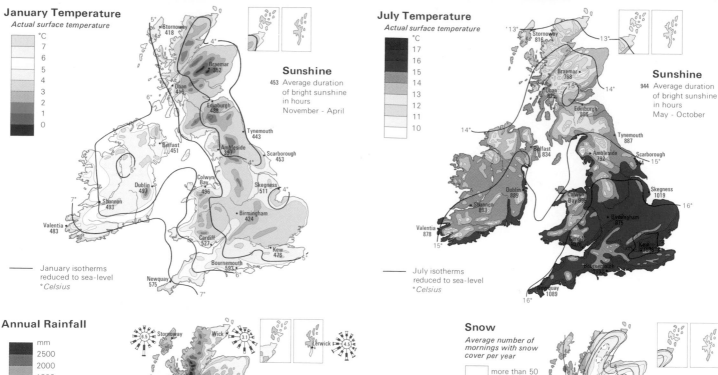

January Temperature
Actual surface temperature

°C
7
6
5
4
3
2
1
0

Stornoway 418
Braemar 352
Oban 416
Edinburgh 488
Tynemouth 443
Belfast 451
Ambleside 397
Scarborough 453
Colwyn Bay 496
Dublin 497
Skegness 511
Shannon 493
Birmingham 424
Valentia 483
Cardiff 527
Kew 476
Bournemouth 593
Newquay 575

Sunshine
453 Average duration of bright sunshine in hours
November – April

January isotherms reduced to sea-level
°*Celsius*

July Temperature
Actual surface temperature

°C
17
16
15
14
13
12
11
10

Stornoway 816
Braemar 768
Oban 825
Edinburgh 806
Tynemouth 887
Belfast 834
Ambleside 792
Scarborough 944
Dublin 889
Skegness 1019
Shannon 883
Colwyn Bay 995
Birmingham 878
Valentia 878
Cardiff
Kew
Bournemouth 1183
Newquay 1089

Sunshine
944 Average duration of bright sunshine in hours
May – October

July isotherms reduced to sea-level
°*Celsius*

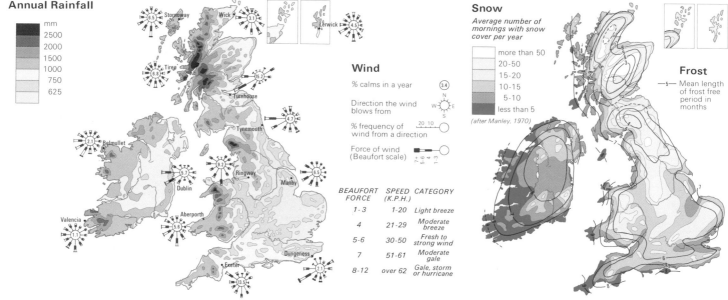

Annual Rainfall

mm
2500
2000
1500
1000
750
625

Stornoway
Wick
Lerwick
Tiree
Turnhouse
Tynemouth
Belmullet
Ringway
Dublin
Manby
Valencia
Aberporth
Dungeness
Exeter

Wind

% calms in a year   (3.4)

Direction the wind blows from

% frequency of wind from a direction   20 10

Force of wind (Beaufort scale)

BEAUFORT FORCE	SPEED (K.P.H.)	CATEGORY
1 - 3	1-20	Light breeze
4	21-29	Moderate breeze
5 - 6	30-50	Fresh to strong wind
7	51-61	Moderate gale
8 - 12	over 62	Gale, storm or hurricane

Snow
Average number of mornings with snow cover per year

more than 50
20-50
15-20
10-15
5-10
less than 5

(after Manley, 1970)

Frost
—5— Mean length of frost free period in months

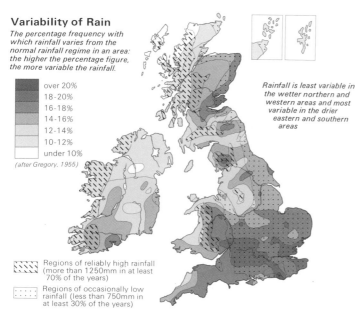

Variability of Rain
The percentage frequency with which rainfall varies from the normal rainfall regime in an area: the higher the percentage figure, the more variable the rainfall.

over 20%
18-20%
16-18%
14-16%
12-14%
10-12%
under 10%

(after Gregory, 1955)

Rainfall is least variable in the wetter northern and western areas and most variable in the drier eastern and southern areas

Regions of reliably high rainfall (more than 1250mm in at least 70% of the years)

Regions of occasionally low rainfall (less than 750mm in at least 30% of the years)

COPYRIGHT. GEORGE PHILIP & SON, LTD.

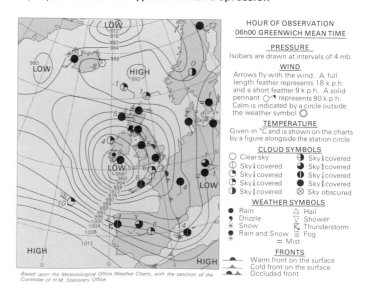

Synoptic Chart for a Typical Winter Depression

HOUR OF OBSERVATION
06h00 GREENWICH MEAN TIME

PRESSURE
Isobars are drawn at intervals of 4 mb.

WIND
Arrows fly with the wind. A full length feather represents 18 k.p.h. and a short feather 9 k.p.h. A solid pennant represents 90 k.p.h. Calm is indicated by a circle outside the weather symbol ◯

TEMPERATURE
Given in °C and is shown on the charts by a figure alongside the station circle.

CLOUD SYMBOLS
◯ Clear sky
◖ Sky ½ covered
◐ Sky ¾ covered
◕ Sky ¾ covered
◑ Sky ⅛ covered
◒ Sky ⅜ covered
● Sky ⅝ covered
◉ Sky ⅞ covered
⊗ Sky obscured

WEATHER SYMBOLS
● Rain
, Drizzle
✳ Snow
✱ Rain and Snow
△ Hail
▽ Shower
К Thunderstorm
≡ Fog
= Mist

FRONTS
Warm front on the surface
Cold front on the surface
Occluded front

Based upon the Meteorological Office Weather Charts, with the sanction of the Controller of H.M. Stationery Office

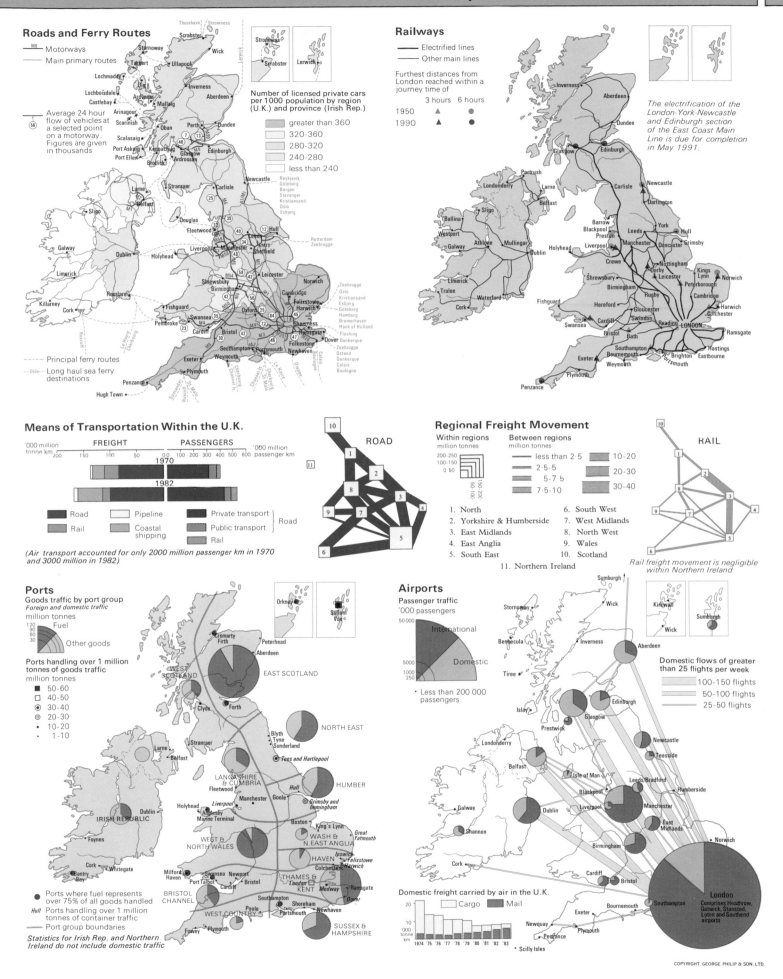

Roads and Ferry Routes

— M6 — Motorways
——— Main primary routes

⑤⑥ Average 24 hour flow of vehicles at a selected point on a motorway. Figures are given in thousands

Number of licensed private cars per 1000 population by region (U.K.) and province (Irish Rep.)

greater than 360
320-360
280-320
240-280
less than 240

- - - - Principal ferry routes
- - Oslo - - Long haul sea ferry destinations

Railways

——— Electrified lines
——— Other main lines

Furthest distances from London reached within a journey time of

	3 hours	6 hours
1950	▲	●
1990	▲	●

The electrification of the London-York-Newcastle and Edinburgh section of the East Coast Main Line is due for completion in May 1991.

Means of Transportation Within the U.K.

'000 million tonne km

FREIGHT — PASSENGERS

'000 million passenger km

1970
1982

Road
Rail
Pipeline
Coastal shipping

Private transport
Public transport
Rail
} Road

(Air transport accounted for only 2000 million passenger km in 1970 and 3000 million in 1982)

ROAD

Regional Freight Movement

Within regions million tonnes
200-250
100-150
0 50
50-100
150-200

Between regions million tonnes
——— less than 2·5
——— 2·5-5
——— 5-7·5
——— 7·5-10
10-20
20-30
30-40

1. North
2. Yorkshire & Humberside
3. East Midlands
4. East Anglia
5. South East
6. South West
7. West Midlands
8. North West
9. Wales
10. Scotland
11. Northern Ireland

RAIL

Rail freight movement is negligible within Northern Ireland

Ports

Goods traffic by port group
Foreign and domestic traffic
million tonnes
120
90
60
30
Fuel
Other goods

Ports handling over 1 million tonnes of goods traffic
million tonnes
■ 50-60
□ 40-50
◉ 30-40
◎ 20-30
• 10-20
· 1-10

● Ports where fuel represents over 75% of all goods handled
Hull Ports handling over 1 million tonnes of container traffic
——— Port group boundaries

Statistics for Irish Rep. and Northern Ireland do not include domestic traffic

Airports

Passenger traffic
'000 passengers
50 000
5000
1000
250
International
Domestic

· Less than 200 000 passengers

Domestic flows of greater than 25 flights per week
100-150 flights
50-100 flights
25-50 flights

Domestic freight carried by air in the U.K.
20
10
'000 tonne km
Cargo
Mail
1974 '75 '76 '77 '78 '79 '80 '81 '82 '83

London Comprises Heathrow, Gatwick, Stansted, Luton and Southend airports

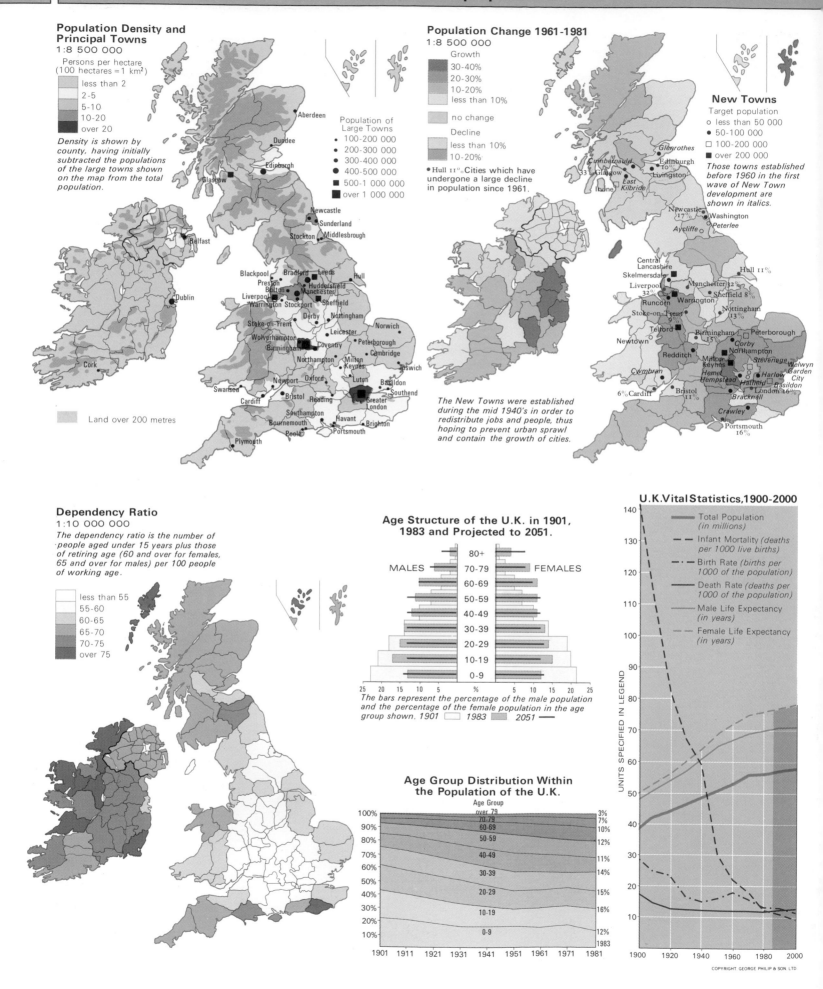

Population Density and Principal Towns
1:8 500 000

Persons per hectare
(100 hectares = 1 km²)

less than 2
2–5
5–10
10–20
over 20

Density is shown by county, having initially subtracted the populations of the large towns shown on the map from the total population.

Population of Large Towns
- 100–200 000
- 200–300 000
- 300–400 000
- 400–500 000
■ 500–1 000 000
■ over 1 000 000

Land over 200 metres

Population Change 1961–1981
1:8 500 000

Growth
30–40%
20–30%
10–20%
less than 10%

no change

Decline
less than 10%
10–20%

● Hull 11% Cities which have undergone a large decline in population since 1961.

The New Towns were established during the mid 1940's in order to redistribute jobs and people, thus hoping to prevent urban sprawl and contain the growth of cities.

New Towns
Target population
○ less than 50 000
● 50–100 000
□ 100–200 000
■ over 200 000

Those towns established before 1960 in the first wave of New Town development are shown in italics.

Dependency Ratio
1:10 000 000

The dependency ratio is the number of people aged under 15 years plus those of retiring age (60 and over for females, 65 and over for males) per 100 people of working age.

less than 55
55–60
60–65
65–70
70–75
over 75

Age Structure of the U.K. in 1901, 1983 and Projected to 2051.

MALES   FEMALES

80+
70–79
60–69
50–59
40–49
30–39
20–29
10–19
0–9

25 20 15 10 5   %   5 10 15 20 25

The bars represent the percentage of the male population and the percentage of the female population in the age group shown. 1901 ☐ 1983 ▨ 2051 —

Age Group Distribution Within the Population of the U.K.

Age Group
over 79 — 3%
70–79 — 7%
60–69 — 10%
50–59 — 12%
40–49 — 11%
30–39 — 14%
20–29 — 15%
10–19 — 16%
0–9 — 12%

1901 1911 1921 1931 1941 1951 1961 1971 1981 1983

U.K. Vital Statistics, 1900–2000

— Total Population (in millions)
- - - Infant Mortality (deaths per 1000 live births)
-·-·- Birth Rate (births per 1000 of the population)
— Death Rate (deaths per 1000 of the population)
— Male Life Expectancy (in years)
- - - Female Life Expectancy (in years)

UNITS SPECIFIED IN LEGEND

1900 1920 1940 1960 1980 2000

COPYRIGHT GEORGE PHILIP & SON LTD

Agricultural Land Use Capability
1:10 000 000

NORTHERN IRELAND AND THE IRISH REPUBLIC
(Land Use Range)
- Wide
- Somewhat Limited
- Limited
- Very Limited
- Extremely Limited

GREAT BRITAIN
(Land Quality)
- First Class
- Good
- Good and Medium
- Medium
- Medium and Poor
- Poor
- Urban Areas

The land use capability classification assesses the value of land for agricultural purposes according to physical conditions and type of management.

Leading Agricultural Enterprises
1:10 000 000
- Crops
- Dairy
- Beef
- Sheep
- Pigs
- Horticulture
- Crofting

The leading enterprises shown on this map are those which use the most man-days in each district.

Principal Crops
Production ('000 tonnes)

Wheat	11 605
Barley	8879
Oats	556
Potatoes	6000
Sugar Beet	7980
Fruit	418
Hops	5

Yield of Selected Crops in the U.K.
tonnes/ha.
- 1939
- 1983

(WHEAT, BARLEY, OATS, SUGAR BEET, POTATOES)

Number and Size of Agricultural Holdings in the U.K.

Average Size of Holding (hectares)

	1940	1980
England and Wales	33.8	60.2
Scotland	81.8	96.2
Northern Ireland	13.7	24.2

- over 100 ha.
- 50-100 ha.
- 40-50 ha.
- 20-40 ha.
- 5-20 ha.
- 2-5 ha.
- under 2 ha.

(1940, 1950, 1960, 1970, 1980)

Self-Sufficiency of the U.K. in Agricultural Production
(home production given as a percentage of total consumption)

PRODUCT	1969	1977	1987
Wheat	42%	61%	79%
Barley	90%	121%	114%
Potatoes	91%	95%	95%
Sugar	33%	40%	53%
Cheese	45%	67%	67%
Butter	12%	40%	63%
Beef	77%	72%	99%
Pork	101%	62%	127%
Poultry	100%	100%	98%

Fishing
1:10 000 000

Quantity of fish landed by domestic vessels at major ports, (port districts in Scotland.)

- less than 10 000 tonnes
- 10-50 000 tonnes
- 50-100 000 tonnes
- over 100 000 tonnes

- Predominantly deep sea fish (demersal)
- Predominantly shallow water fish (pelagic)
- Predominantly shellfish

(Ullapool, Fraserburgh, Peterhead, Aberdeen, SCOTLAND, Ayr, Burtonport, Killybegs, Howth, Galway, WALES, Dunmore East, Castletownbere, Milford Haven, Newlyn, Falmouth, Plymouth, Brixham, ENGLAND, Lowestoft, Grimsby, Hull, Bridlington, Scarborough, Whitby, North Shields, Fleetwood)

Forestry
- Forested Areas
- Newly planted areas
- Restocking of existing areas

The graphs show the area of forest planted annually by the Forestry Commission.

(ha. 2000, 1000 — 1975, 1980, 1984 SCOTLAND)
(ha. 2000, 1000 — 1975, 1980, 1984 WALES)
(ha. 3000, 2000, 1000 — 1975, 1980, 1984 ENGLAND)

Area of Agricultural Land Under Selected Enterprises

TOTAL AREA
- Others 4%
- Rough Grazing 32%
- Arable 37%
- Permanent Pasture 27%

18 734 728 hectares

CEREALS
- Oats 3%
- Maize and Rye 1%
- Barley 54%
- Wheat 42%

3 960 569 hectares

HORTICULTURE
- Soft Fruit 8%
- Greenhouse Crops 6%
- Orchard Fruit 18%
- Vegetables 68%

222 024 hectares

OTHER CROPS
- Others 2%
- Turnips, Kale, Peas, Beans and other stock feeding crops 26%
- Rape 26%
- Sugar Beet 23%
- Potatoes 23%

842 339 hectares

Quantity of Fish Landed by British Vessels in all Fishing Areas
'000 tonnes
- Demersal Fish
- Pelagic Fish
- Shellfish

(1950, 1960, 1970, 1980, 1983)

Number and Size of Livestock Holdings in the U.K.
'000 holdings
- over 1000 head
- 500-1000 head
- 200-500 head
- 100-200 head
- 50-100 head
- 10-50 head
- under 10 head

(DAIRY CATTLE, BEEF CATTLE, PIGS, SHEEP)

COPYRIGHT. GEORGE PHILIP & SON. LTD

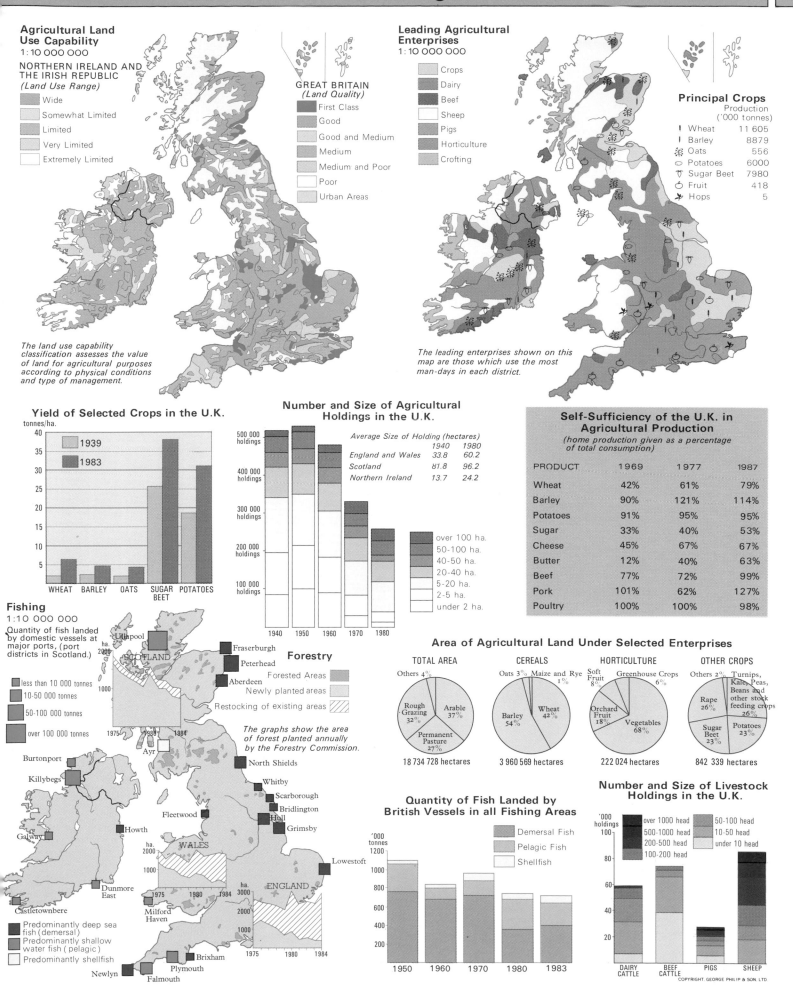

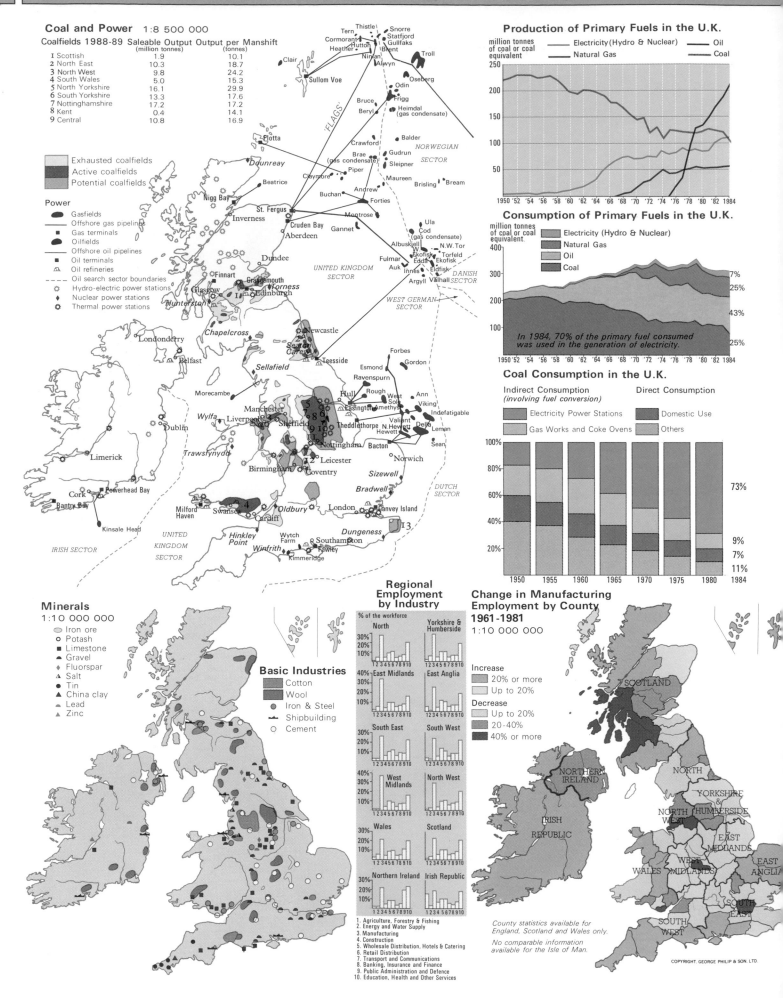

Coal and Power 1:8 500 000

Coalfields 1988-89 Saleable Output Output per Manshift

		(million tonnes)	(tonnes)
1	Scottish	1.9	10.1
2	North East	10.3	18.7
3	North West	9.8	24.2
4	South Wales	5.0	15.3
5	North Yorkshire	16.1	29.9
6	South Yorkshire	13.3	17.6
7	Nottinghamshire	17.2	17.2
8	Kent	0.4	14.1
9	Central	10.8	16.9

Exhausted coalfields
Active coalfields
Potential coalfields

Power

- Gasfields
- Offshore gas pipelines
- Gas terminals
- Oilfields
- Offshore oil pipelines
- Oil terminals
- Oil refineries
- Oil search sector boundaries
- Hydro-electric power stations
- Nuclear power stations
- Thermal power stations

Minerals 1:10 000 000

- Iron ore
- Potash
- Limestone
- Gravel
- Fluorspar
- Salt
- Tin
- China clay
- Lead
- Zinc

Basic Industries

- Cotton
- Wool
- Iron & Steel
- Shipbuilding
- Cement

Production of Primary Fuels in the U.K.

million tonnes of coal or coal equivalent

— Electricity (Hydro & Nuclear) — Oil
— Natural Gas — Coal

Consumption of Primary Fuels in the U.K.

million tonnes of coal or coal equivalent

- Electricity (Hydro & Nuclear) 7%
- Natural Gas 25%
- Oil 43%
- Coal 25%

In 1984, 70% of the primary fuel consumed was used in the generation of electricity.

Coal Consumption in the U.K.

Indirect Consumption *(involving fuel conversion)*
- Electricity Power Stations
- Gas Works and Coke Ovens

Direct Consumption
- Domestic Use
- Others

73%
9%
7%
11%

1950 1955 1960 1965 1970 1975 1980 1984

Regional Employment by Industry

% of the workforce

North, Yorkshire & Humberside, East Midlands, East Anglia, South East, South West, West Midlands, North West, Wales, Scotland, Northern Ireland, Irish Republic

1. Agriculture, Forestry & Fishing
2. Energy and Water Supply
3. Manufacturing
4. Construction
5. Wholesale Distribution, Hotels & Catering
6. Retail Distribution
7. Transport and Communications
8. Banking, Insurance and Finance
9. Public Administration and Defence
10. Education, Health and Other Services

Change in Manufacturing Employment by County 1961-1981 1:10 000 000

Increase
- 20% or more
- Up to 20%

Decrease
- Up to 20%
- 20-40%
- 40% or more

County statistics available for England, Scotland and Wales only.

No comparable information available for the Isle of Man.

COPYRIGHT. GEORGE PHILIP & SON. LTD.

EMPLOYMENT

Employment in the U.K. by Industry

Numbers employed '000

25000
20000
15000
10000
5000

1931 1941 1951 1961 1971 1981 1984

- 62% Services
- 7% Transport
- 26% Manufacturing
- 3% Mining & Energy Supply
- 2% Agriculture, Forestry & Fishing

Employment by County

£ Over 75% employed in Services

Over 30% employed in Manufacturing

Over 5% employed in Agriculture

County statistics available for England, Scotland and Wales only.

UNEMPLOYMENT

1:10 000 000

Unemployment Rate by County, 1985

- over 20%
- 16-20%
- 12-16%
- 8-12%
- less than 8%

The unemployment rate is the number of unemployed expressed as a percentage of the working population (employed labour force plus the unemployed)

Leisure

1:8 500 000

- National Parks National Park Direction Areas (Scotland)
- National Forest Parks
- Areas of Outstanding Natural Beauty (England & Wales) National Scenic Areas (Scotland)
- Coastal Conservation Zones (Scotland) Heritage Coasts (England & Wales)
- Long Distance Footpaths
- Navigable Waterways
- Canals

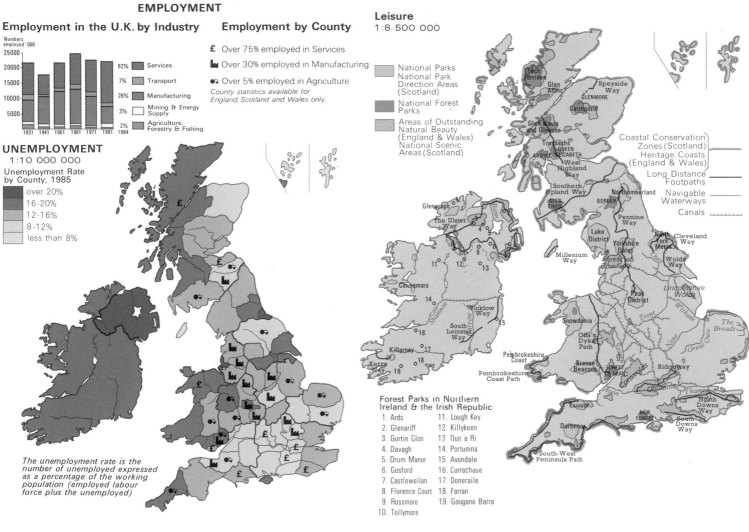

Forest Parks in Northern Ireland & the Irish Republic

1. Ards
2. Glenariff
3. Gortin Glen
4. Davagh
5. Drum Manor
6. Gosford
7. Castlewellan
8. Florence Court
9. Rossmore
10. Tollymore
11. Lough Key
12. Killykeen
13. Dun a Ri
14. Portumna
15. Avondale
16. Currachase
17. Doneraile
18. Farran
19. Gougane Barra

Top Ten Trading Partners with the U.K. by Value of Goods

IMPORTS

- West Germany : £11090 million
- U.S.A. : £9356 million
- Netherlands : £6147 million
- France : £5886 million
- Norway : £3853 million
- Italy : £3814 million
- Japan : £3768 million
- Belgium-Lux. : £3692 million
- Irish Republic : £2635 million
- Switzerland : £2491 million

EXPORTS

- U.S.A. : £10149 million
- West Germany : £7458 million
- France : £7082 million
- Netherlands : £6128 million
- Irish Republic : £3393 million
- Belgium-Lux. : £3052 million
- Italy : £2903 million
- Sweden : £2889 million
- Switzerland : £1549 million
- Saudi Arabia : £1387 million

Food and drink — Fuel — Manufactured goods
Raw materials — Machinery and equipment

U.K. Trade by Country Group and Commodity Type

(percentages are given by value of trade)

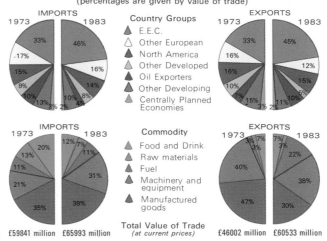

IMPORTS 1973 / 1983
33% / 46%
17% / 16%
15% / 14%
9% / 8%
10% / 4%
13% / 2%

Country Groups
- E.E.C.
- Other European
- North America
- Other Developed
- Oil Exporters
- Other Developing
- Centrally Planned Economies

EXPORTS 1973 / 1983
33% / 45%
16% / 12%
16% / 15%
10% / 5%
7% / 10%
15% / 11%
3% / 2%

IMPORTS 1973 / 1983
20% / 12% 7%
13% / 11%
11% / 31%
21% / 39%
35%

Commodity
- Food and Drink
- Raw materials
- Fuel
- Machinery and equipment
- Manufactured goods

EXPORTS 1973 / 1983
3% 7% / 7% 3%
3% / 22%
40% / 38%
47% / 30%

Total Value of Trade *(at current prices)*
£59841 million £65993 million   £46002 million £60533 million

Balance of Payments (£ million)

		1967	1977	1987
CREDITS	Visibles *(Exports)*	5241	31682	79422
	Invisibles	3310	21351	80010
	Total	8551	53033	159432
DEBITS	Visibles *(Imports)*	5840	34006	89584
	Invisibles	2992	19177	72352
	Total	8832	53183	161936
BALANCE		−281	−150	−2504

Visible trade involves transactions of goods while invisible trade involves transactions of money and services.

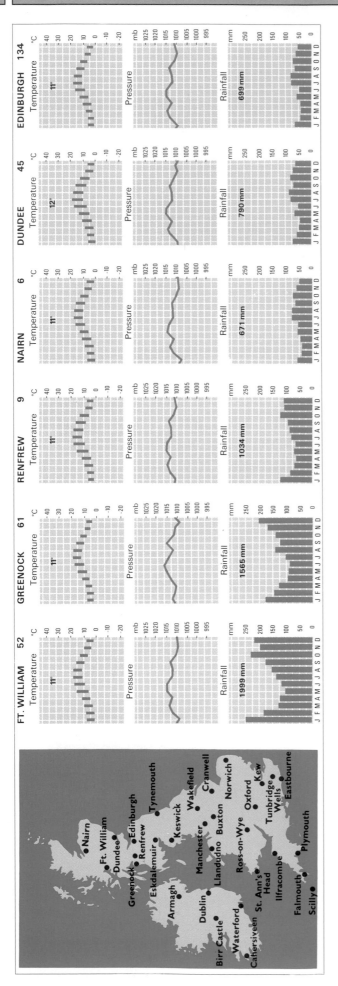

The climate graphs should be used in conjunction with the maps illustrating the climate of the British Isles on page 6. The stations have been selected to show climatic variations throughout the British Isles. On each graph the name of the station is followed by its height in metres above sea level, so that comparisons between stations can be made allowing for elevation. Temperature is shown by a bar, the top of the bar representing the mean monthly maximum and the bottom of the bar the mean monthly minimum temperature. A mid point between these is the mean monthly temperature; the mean annual range of temperature (in degrees Celsius) is given above the graph. The line on the pressure graphs shows the mean monthly pressure (in millibars and reduced to sea level). The rainfall graphs show the average monthly rainfall and above them is given the average total annual rainfall (in millimetres).

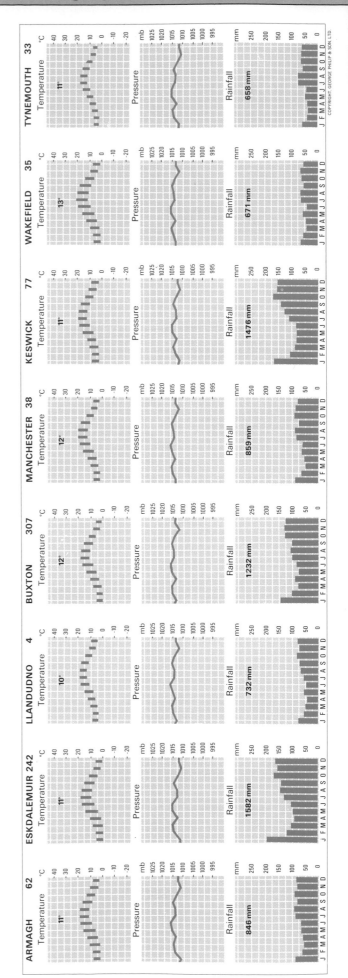

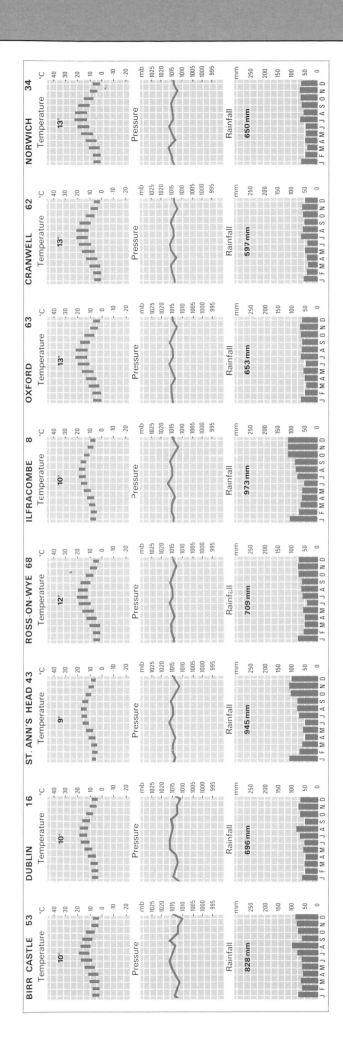

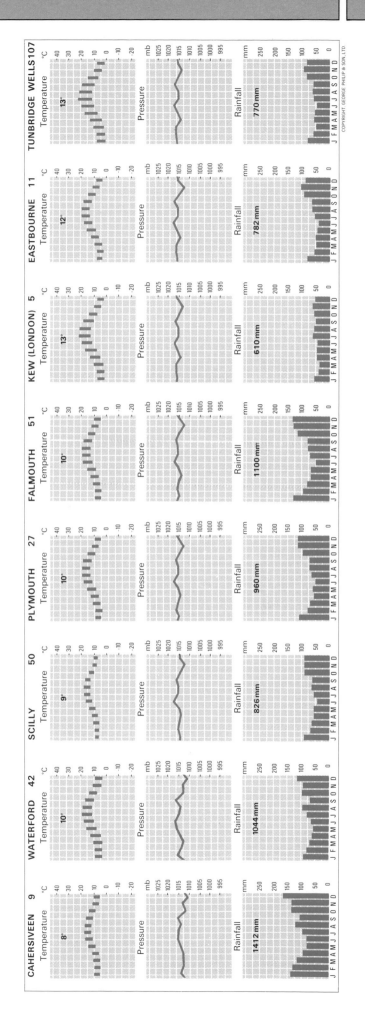

Projection: Conical with two
standard parallels

1:1 000 000

10   0   10   20   30   40 km

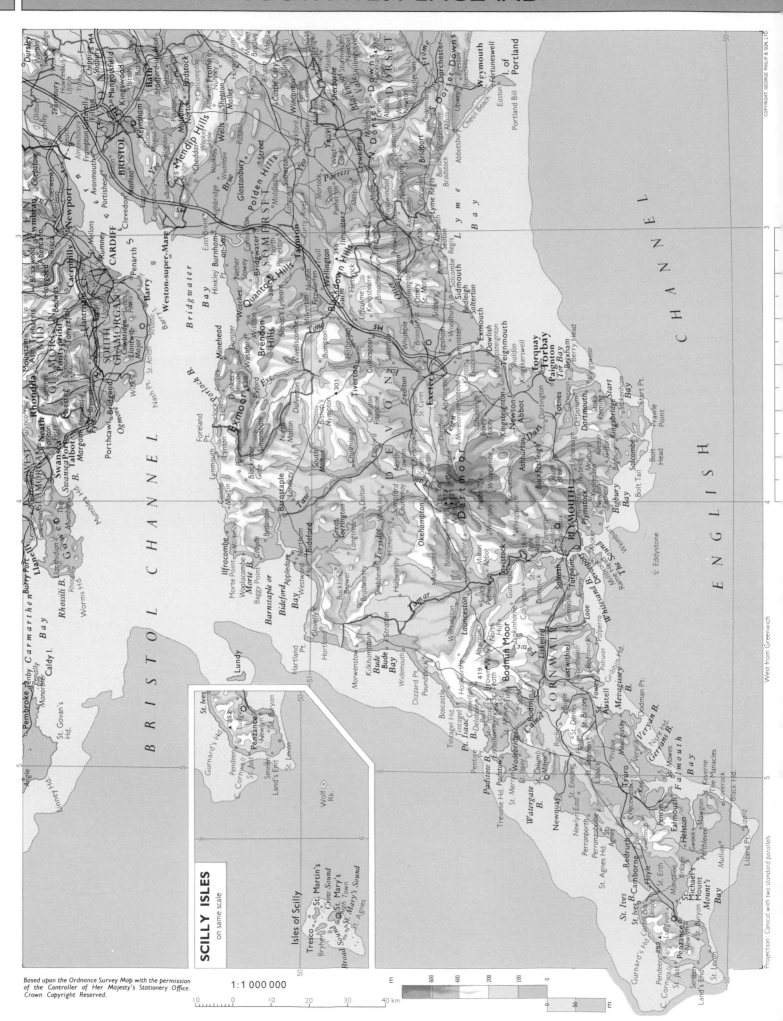

SCILLY ISLES
on same scale

1:1 000 000

West from Greenwich

Projection : Conical with two standard parallels

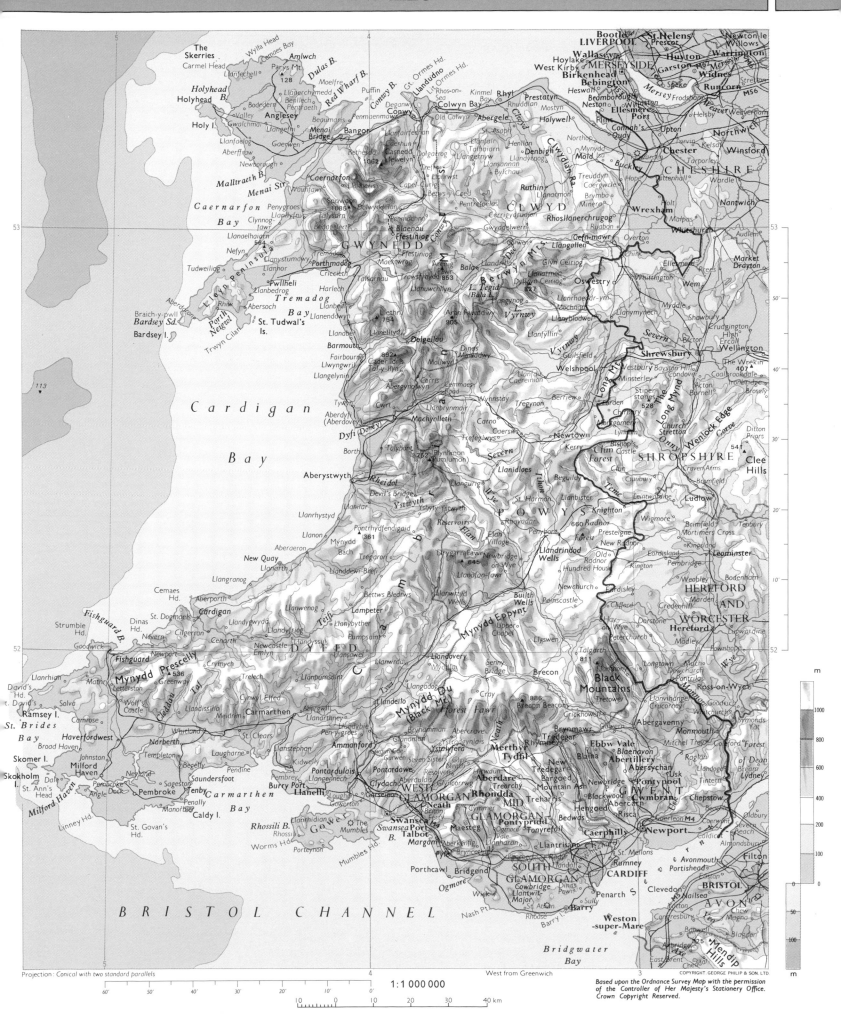

Projection : Conical with two standard parallels

Continuation
Northwards
on same scale

NORTH SEA

TYNE AND WEAR

BORDERS

NORTHUMBERLAND

HADRIAN'S WALL

TYNE AND WEAR

CLEVELAND

North York
Moors

Cleveland Hills

YORKSHIRE

Vale of Pickering

Bridlington
Bay

HUMBERSIDE

Holderness

LEEDS

WEST YORKSHIRE

KINGSTON-UPON-HULL

Humber

Mouth of the Humber

SOUTH YORKSHIRE

SHEFFIELD

Isle of Axholme

Scunthorpe

Grimsby

Cleethorpes

Spurn Hd.

LINCOLNSHIRE

Lincoln

Lincolnshire Wolds

DERBY

NOTTINGHAM

The Wash

NORFOLK

West from Greenwich

1:1 000 000

10   0   10   20   30   40 km

East from Greenwich

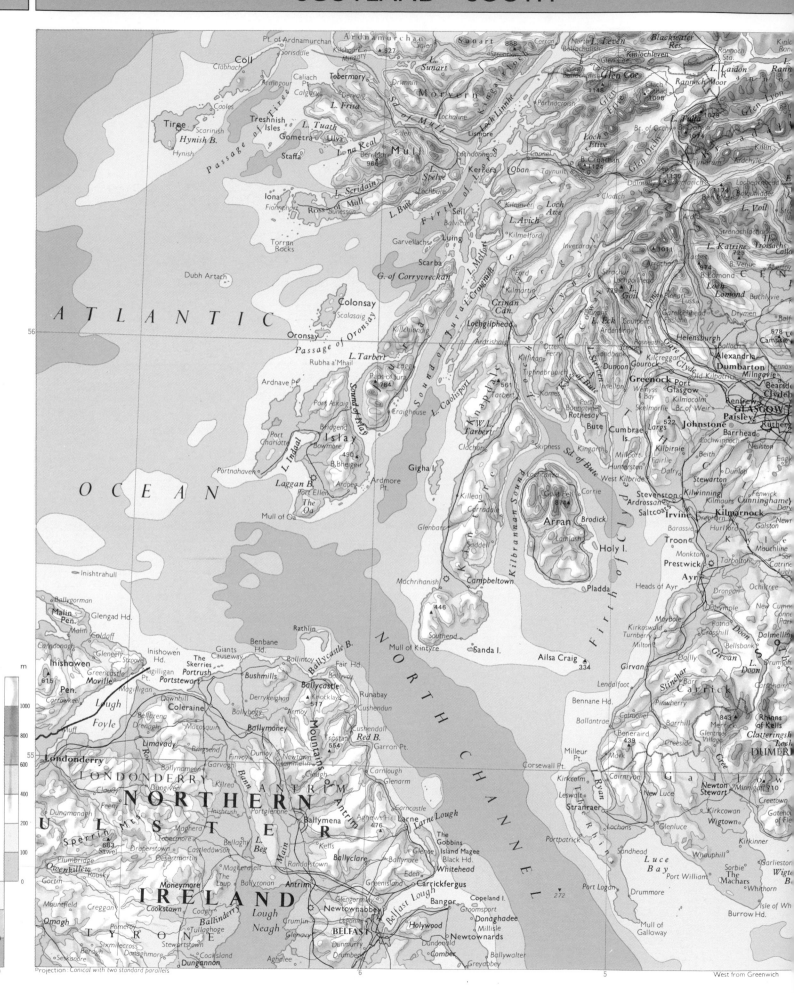

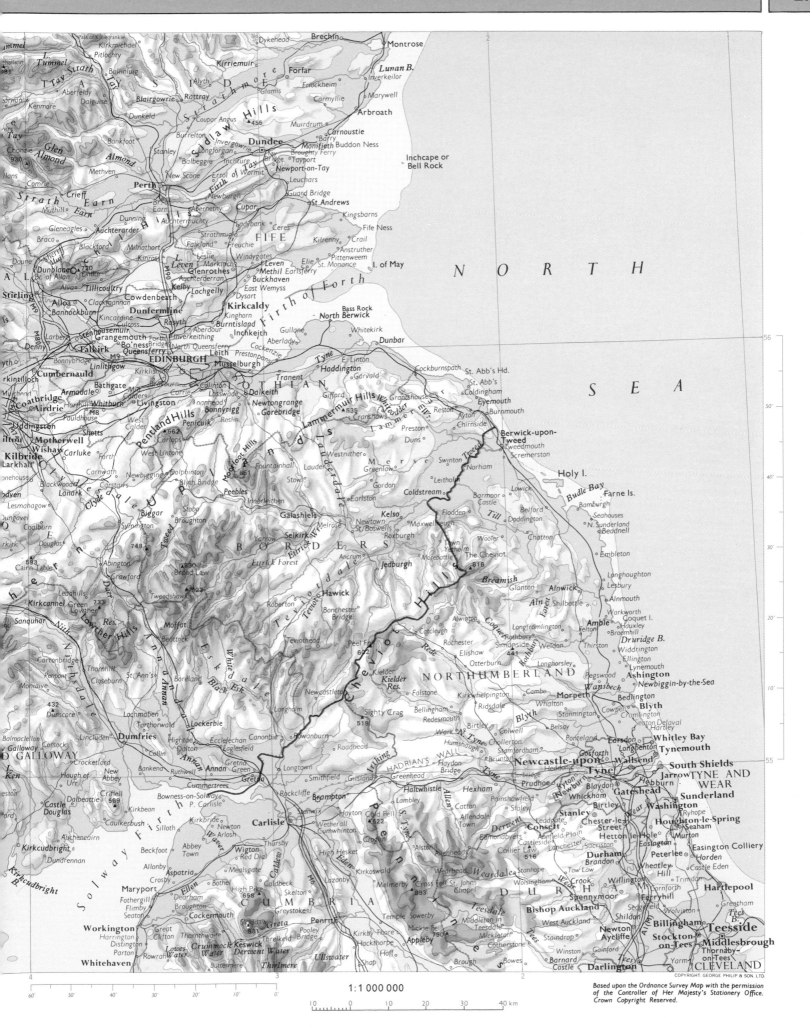

1:1 000 000

10   0   10   20   30   40 km

SHETLAND ISLANDS
on same scale

Hecma Ness
Haroldswick
Ramna Stacks
Point of Fethaland
Baltasound
Balta
Unst
Uyeasound
Mu Ness
Bluemull Sd.
Whale Firth
Gutcher
Cullivoe
The Faither
North Roe
Ronas Hill 450
Fetlar
Colgrave Sd.
Mid Yell
Yell
The Snap
Esha Ness
Hillswick
Sullom
Burravoe
Lunna Ness
St. Magnus Bay
SHETLAND
Skaw Taing
Out Skerries
Brae
Muckle Roe
Voe
Whalsay
Papa Stour
The Häa
Sd. of Papa
Sandness
S Nesting Bay
Walls
Vaila
Easter Skeld
Score Hd.
Lerwick
I. of Noss
Gruting
Scalloway
Bressay
Bard Hd.
Hamnavoe
West Burra
293
Bressay Sd.
Helli Ness
Kettla Ness
Hoswick
Mousa
St. Ninian's I.
Scousburgh
Fitful Hd.
Boddam
B. of Quendale
Sumburgh Hd.

Butt of Lewis
Port of Ness
South Dell
Ness
Borve
North Tolsta
Tolsta Hd.
Barvas
Carloway
Shawbost
291
Newmarket
Back
Broad Bay
Tiumpan Hd.
Gallan Hd.
Great Bernera
Uig
L. Roag
Callanish
Stornoway
Melbost
Eye Peninsula
Portaguiran
Bayble
Lewis
Lochs
Crossbost
Cramore
Chicken Hd.
Aird Brenish
575
Gisla
Loch Langavat
Balallan
L. Erisort
Park
Kintaravay
Gravir
Kebock Hd.
Scarp
Husinish
Husinish Pt.
N. Harris
Ardvourlie Castle
571
Beinn Mhor 799
L. Shell
W. L. Tarbert
Ardhasig
Torbert
L. Seaforth
Sd. of Shiant
Shiant Is
Taransay
Harris
WESTERN
Sd. of Taransay
Toe Hd.
B. L. Tarbert
Scalpay
Scarastavore
S. Harris
Leverburgh
Rodel
Renish Pt.
Rubha Hunish
ISLES
Haskeir Is.
Pabbay
Sd. of Pabbay
Berneray
Griminish Pt.
Sollas
Kilmaluag
Vaternish Pt.
Lochmaddy
North Uist
L. Maddy
Loch Snizort
Vaternish
Uig
Trotternish
Rona
Sound of Raasay
Paible
Clachan
Carinish
L. Eport
Eaval
347
Dunvegan Head
Stein
Monach Is.
Sound of Monach
Baleshare
Gramsdale
Grimsay
Ronay
Milovaig
Lephin
Roskhill
488
The Storr 719
Raasay
Benbecula
Wiay
Bagh nam Faoileann
Dunvegan
Portree
Ardivachar Pt.
L. Bee
Bracadale
Colbore
Scalpay
Howmore
South Uist
605 Hecla
L. Bracadale
Carbost
Drynoch
Minginish
Kyle of Lochalsh
Rubha Ardvule
620 B. Mhor
L. Eynort
Fernilea
Sligachan
Cuillin Hills 1009
Bla Bheinn 828
Daliburgh
Lochboisdale
L. Boisdale
Glenbrittle
Rubh'an Dunain
Soay Sd.
Soay
L. Scavaig
Elgol
L. Eishort
Broadford
Sound of Barra
Sd. of Eriskay
Eriskay
Canna
Cuillin Sound
Teangue
Armadale
Greian Hd.
Barra
Sanday
Sd. of Canna
Rhum 810
Pt. of Sleat
Mallaig
384
Castlebay
Bruernish Pt.
Kinloch
Vatersay
Eigg
Sandray
394
Pabbay
Sd. of Eigg
Mingulay
Muck
Sd. of Arisaig
Berneray
Barra Head
Shona
Moidart
Coll
Clabhach
Pt. of Ardnamurchan
Sorisdale
527
Kilchoan
Ardnamurchan
Salen
241
Caliach Pt.
Calgary
Tobermory
Dervaig
Arinagour
Tiree
Scarinish
Treshnish Isles
L. Tuath
Hynish B.
Hynish
Passage of Tiree

C. Wrath
L. Inchard
Kinloch
L. Laxford
Handa I.
Scourie
Eddrachillis Bay
Pt. of Stoer
Drumbeg
Quinag
Stoer
Assynt
847
Enard Bay
Lochinver
Elphin
Rhu Coigach
Summer Isles
Lurgainn
Ullapool
Greenstone Pt.
Gruinard B.
L. Broom
Coigac
Mellon Charles
Aultbea
L. Ewe
An Teallach 1062
L. na Sealga
Melvaig
Poolewe
Fionn Loch
Braemore
Henderson
Kerrysdale
Talladale 981
L. Maree
Slioch
Fannich
Longa I.
L. Gairloch
Gairloch
1053
Torridon
Kinlochewe
Fasag
Achnasheen
L. Torridon
Shieldaig
Rona
Applecross Forest
Lochcarron
Coulags
Applecross
Carron
Monar Forest 1052 L. Monar
Toscaig
Kishorn
Stromeferry
Sgurr na
1115
Mullardo
Crowlin Is.
Stromemore
Plockton
Carron
Kyle of Lochalsh
Kyleakin
L. Alsh
Dornie
Carn Eige 1183
Glen
Glenelg
Inverinate
A'Chralaig 1120
The Saddle 1010
Glen Shiel
L. Hourn
L. Cluanie
Quoich
Knoydart
Inver
1046
Ladhar B. 1013
Tomdoun
Glen Garry
L. Nevis
Arnisdale
Sgurr na Ciche 1040
L. Arkaig
Loch Morar
Culvain 883
Gairlochy
Caledonian Canal
Arisaig
Glenfinnan
Kinlocheil
882
L. Eil
Kinlochmoidart
Loch Shiel
Fort William
Ardgour
888
Ben Nev
Corran
Sunart
Strontian
North Ballachulish
L. Leven
Drimnin
Morvern
Kingairloch
Lochaline
L. Linnhe
Sd. of Mull
Lismore I.
Portnacroish
L. Etive

Outer Hebrides
Little Minch
Inner Hebrides
North Minch
Skye
Inner Sound
Sound of Sleat
Morar

m
1000
800
600
400
200
100
0
0
50
100
m

Projection: Conical with two standard parallels

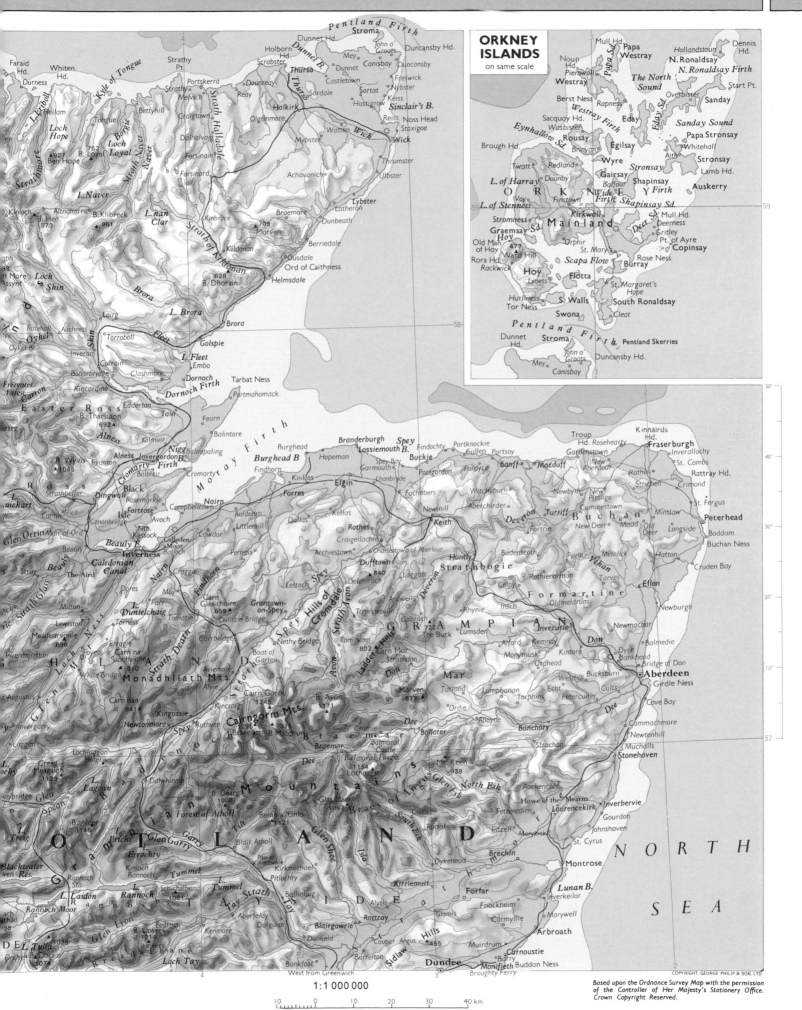

ORKNEY ISLANDS
on same scale

Orkney Islands inset labels: Mull Hd., Papa Westray, Hollandstoure, Dennis Hd., Noup Hd., N. Ronaldsay, N. Ronaldsay Firth, Westray, Papa Sd., Pierowall, Berst Ness, Rapness, The North Sound, Start Pt., Sacquoy Hd., Wasbister, Eynhallow Sd., Rousay, Eday, Sanday, Brough Hd., Brinyan, Egilsay, Sanday Sound, Papa Stronsay, Twatt, Redland, Wyre, Whitehall, L. of Harray, Dounby, Gairsay, Stronsay, L. of Stenness, Finstown, Shapinsay, Y Firth, Auskerry, Stromness, Kirkwall, Wide Firth, Shapinsay Sd., Lamb Hd., Graemsay Sd., Mainland, Deer Sd., Mull Hd., Hoy, Old Man of Hoy, Ward Hill, Orphir, St. Mary's, Deerness, Gritley, Rora Hd., Rackwick, Hoy, Elotta, Burray, Rose Ness, Copinsay, Hurliness, Tor Ness, S. Walls, Lyness, St. Margaret's Hope, South Ronaldsay, Swona, Cleat, Pentland Firth, Dunnet Hd., Stroma, Mey, John o' Groats, Canisby, Duncansby Hd., Pentland Skerries

Scale: 1:1 000 000

10 0 10 20 30 40 km

West from Greenwich

NORTH SEA

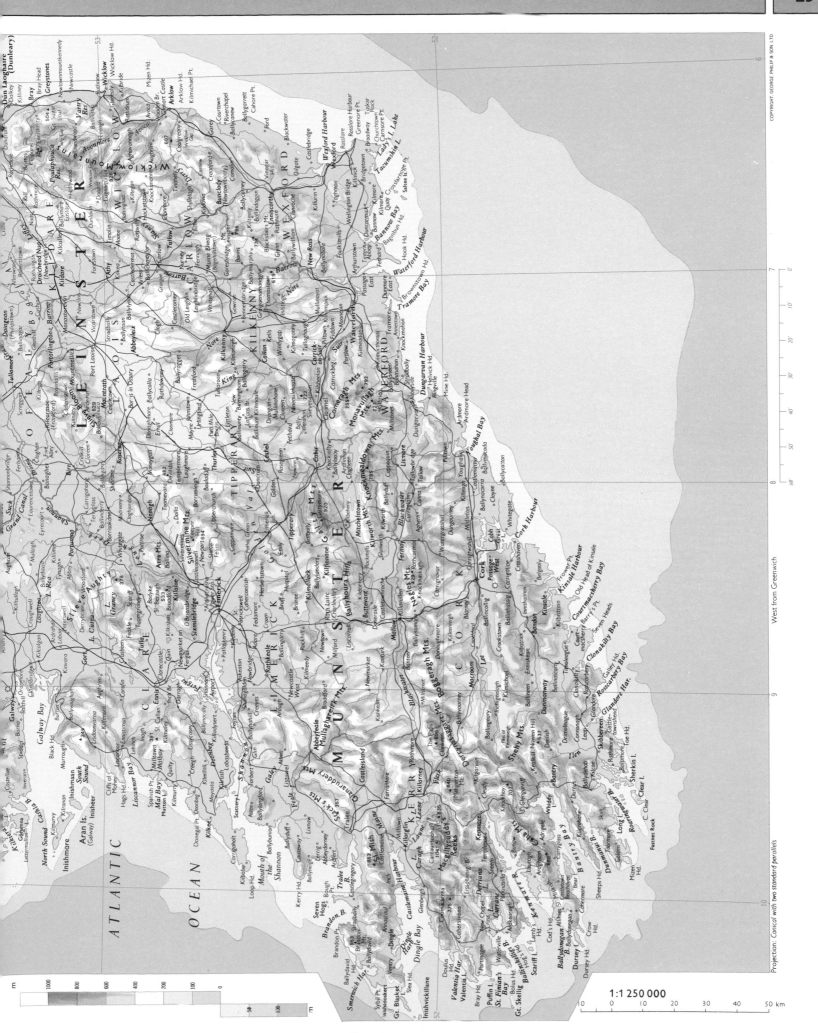

ATLANTIC

OCEAN

LEINSTER

MUNSTER

CORK

KERRY

CLARE

TIPPERARY

LIMERICK

WATERFORD

WEXFORD

WICKLOW

CARLOW

KILKENNY

KILDARE

LAOIS

OFFALY

GALWAY

Galway Bay

Dun Laoghaire
(Dunleary)

Wexford

Cork

Limerick

Projection: Conical with two standard parallels

West from Greenwich

1:1 250 000

10   0   10   20   30   40   50 km

m
1000 800 600 400 200 100 0

50
100
m

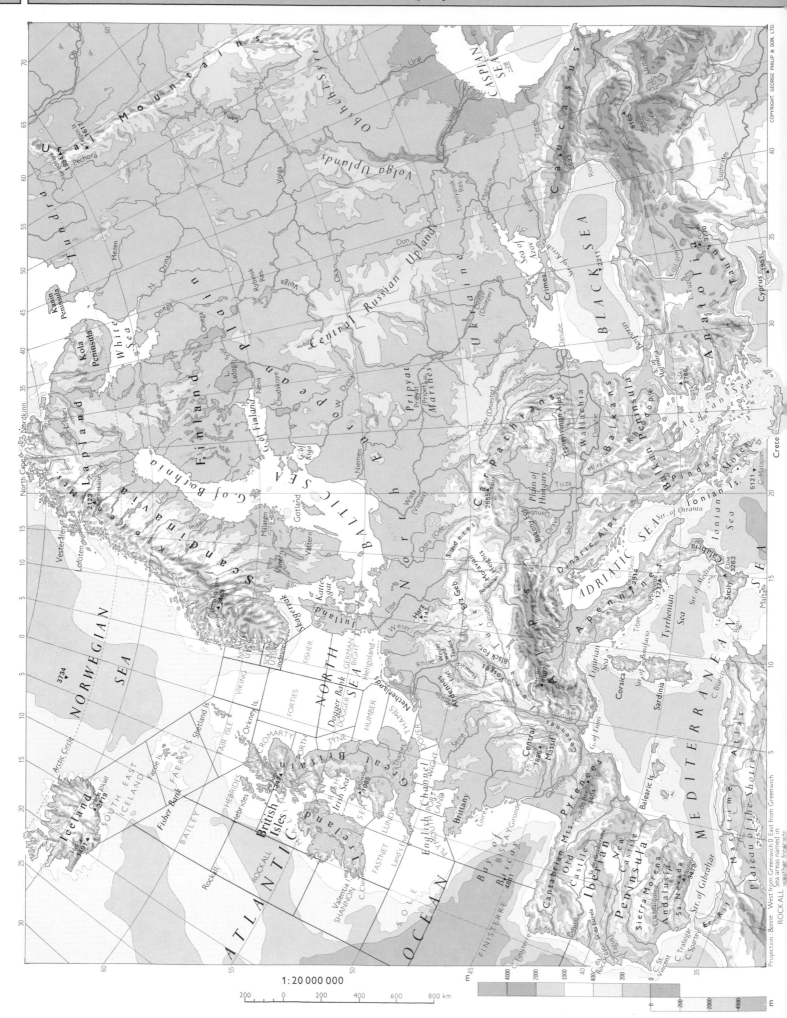

1:20 000 000

200 0 200 400 600 800 km

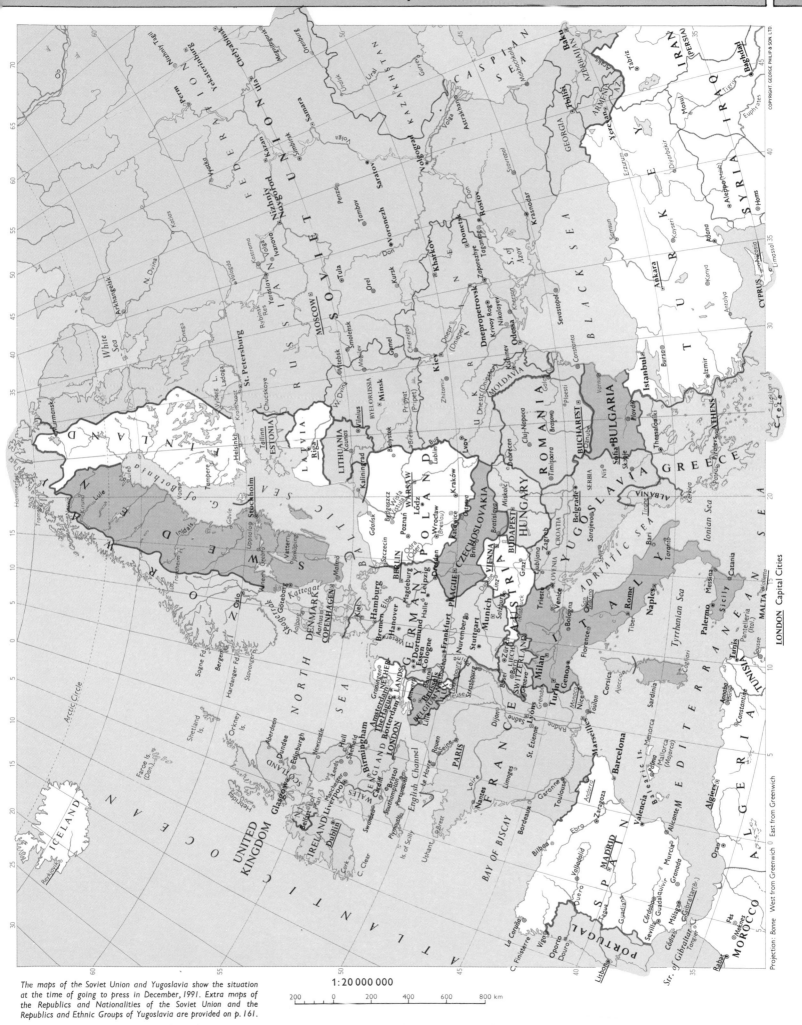

The maps of the Soviet Union and Yugoslavia show the situation at the time of going to press in December, 1991. Extra maps of the Republics and Nationalities of the Soviet Union and the Republics and Ethnic Groups of Yugoslavia are provided on p. 161.

1:20 000 000

200   0   200   400   600   800 km

LONDON Capital Cities

Projection: Bonne   West from Greenwich   0   East from Greenwich

COPYRIGHT GEORGE PHILIP & SON LTD.

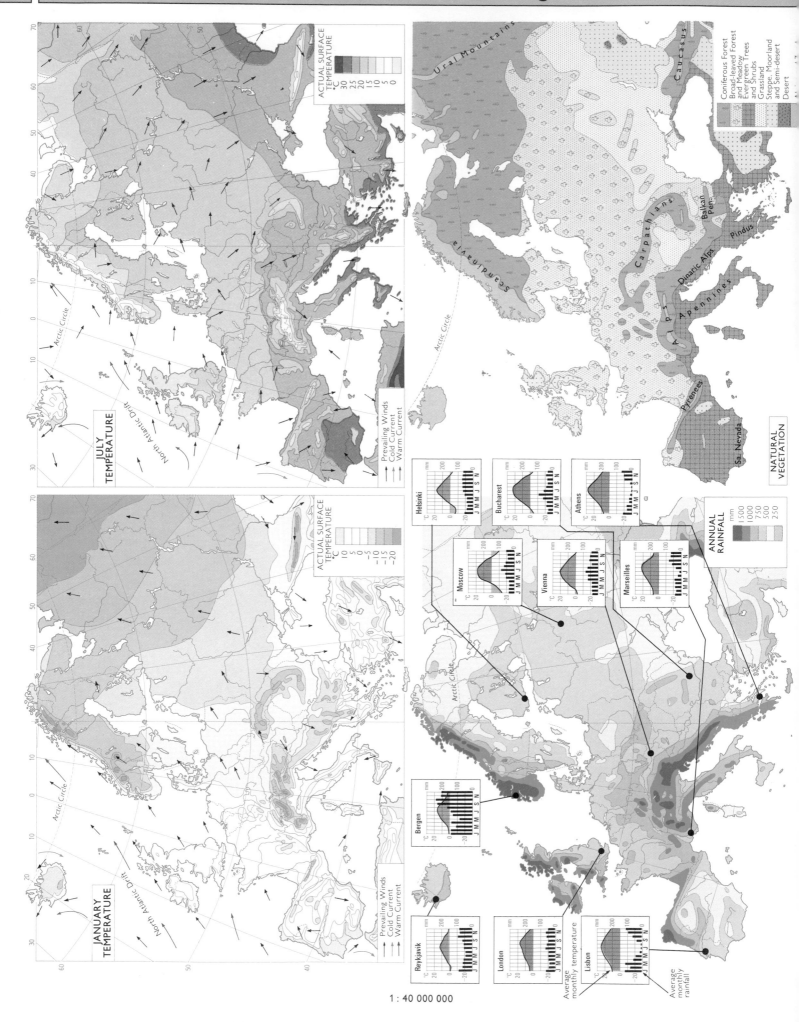

ACTUAL SURFACE
TEMPERATURE
°C
30
25
20
15
10
5
0

JULY
TEMPERATURE

North Atlantic Drift

Prevailing Winds
Cold Current
Warm Current

ACTUAL SURFACE
TEMPERATURE
°C
10
5
0
−5
−10
−15
−20

JANUARY
TEMPERATURE

North Atlantic Drift

Prevailing Winds
Cold Current
Warm Current

Ural Mountains

Scandinavia

Carpathians

Alps

Apennines

Dinaric Alps

Pindus

Balkan Pen.

Caucasus

Pyrenees

Sa. Nevada

NATURAL
VEGETATION

Coniferous Forest
Broad-leaved Forest
and Meadow
Evergreen Trees
and Shrubs
Grassland
Steppe, Moorland
and Semi-desert
Desert

Helsinki
Bucharest
Athens
Moscow
Vienna
Marseilles
Bergen
Reykjavik
London
Lisbon

Average
monthly temperature

Average
monthly rainfall

ANNUAL
RAINFALL
mm
1500
1000
750
500
250

Arctic Circle

1 : 40 000 000

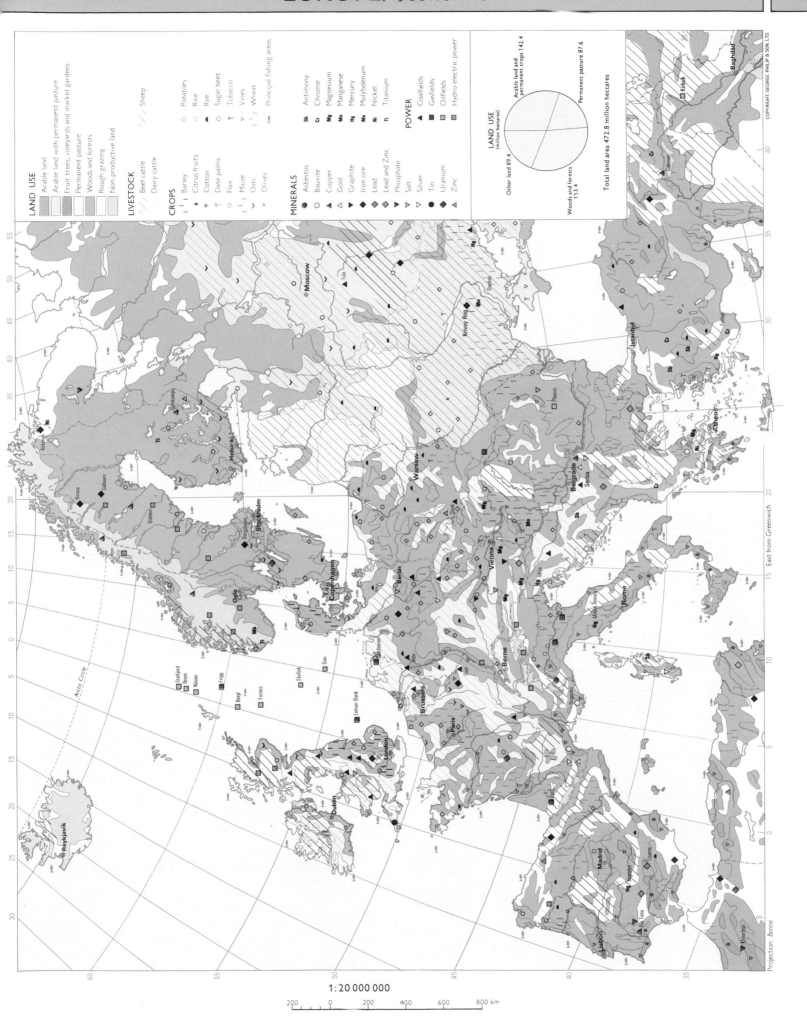

LAND USE

- Arable land
- Arable land with permanent pasture
- Fruit trees, vineyards and market gardens
- Permanent pasture
- Woods and forests
- Rough grazing
- Non-productive land

LIVESTOCK

- Beef cattle
- Dairy cattle
- Sheep

CROPS

Barley	Potatoes
Citrus fruits	Rice
Cotton	Rye
Date palms	Sugar beet
Flax	Tobacco
Maize	Vines
Oats	Wheat
Olives	Principal fishing areas

MINERALS

- Asbestos
- Bauxite
- Copper
- Gold
- Graphite
- Iron ore
- Lead
- Lead and Zinc
- Phosphate
- Salt
- Silver
- Tin
- Uranium
- Zinc

- **Sb** Antimony
- **Cr** Chrome
- **Mg** Magnesium
- **Mn** Manganese
- **Hg** Mercury
- **Mo** Molybdenum
- **Ni** Nickel
- **Ti** Titanium

POWER

- Coalfields
- Gasfields
- Oilfields
- Hydro electric power

LAND USE
(million hectares)

- Other land 89.4
- Arable land and permanent crops 142.4
- Permanent pasture 87.6
- Woods and forests 153.4

Total land area 472.8 million hectares

Moscow
Tula
Krivoy Rog — Mn
Donbas
Istanbul
Cr
Sh
Sh
Hg
Cr
Warsaw
Mg
Silesia
Mn
Belgrade
Serbia
Cr
Athens
Ni
Mg
Mg
Berlin
Vienna
Mg
Hg
Mg
Mo
Mg
Salzburg
Ruhr
Berne
Saar
Rome
Hg Mica Armani
Hg
Brussels
Briquettes
Paris
London
Dublin
Helsinki
Ti
Oslo
Mo
Stockholm
Bergslagen
Copenhagen
Kiruna
Ni
Gällivare
Boliden
Reykjavik
Madrid
Lisbon
Huelva
Rio Tinto
Minas
Almadén
Ploiesti
Galatz
Kirkuk
Baghdad
Kristiansund
Dnipro
Stanford
Brent
Ninian
Frigg
Beryl
Forties
Ekofisk
Dan
Leman Bank

Arctic Circle

East from Greenwich

Projection: Bonne

1 : 20 000 000

200   0   200   400   600   800 km

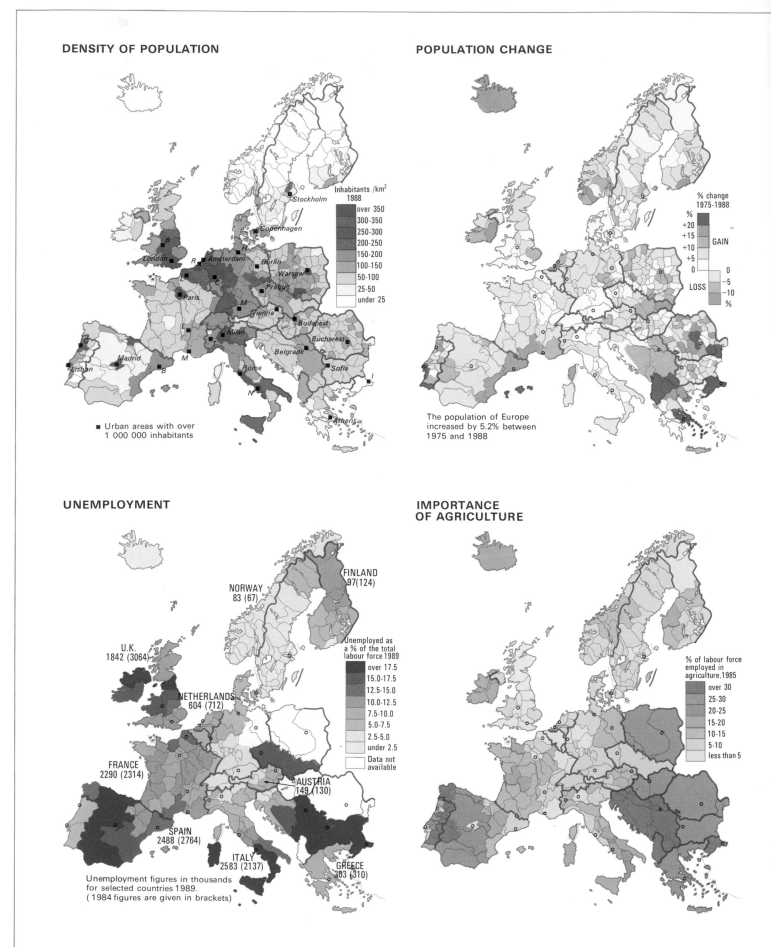

DENSITY OF POPULATION

Inhabitants /km²
1988

- over 350
- 300-350
- 250-300
- 200-250
- 150-200
- 100-150
- 50-100
- 25-50
- under 25

Stockholm
Copenhagen
B
London
R Amsterdam Berlin
Warsaw
C
Prague
Paris
M
Vienna
Budapest
L
Milan
Bucharest
O
Madrid
M
Belgrade
Lisbon
B
Rome
Sofia
M
N
I
Athens

■ Urban areas with over
1 000 000 inhabitants

POPULATION CHANGE

% change
1975-1988

%
+20
+15 GAIN
+10
+5
0 0
-5
LOSS
-10
%

The population of Europe
increased by 5.2% between
1975 and 1988

UNEMPLOYMENT

FINLAND
97(124)

NORWAY
83 (67)

U.K.
1842 (3064)

NETHERLANDS
604 (712)

Unemployed as
a % of the total
labour force 1989

- over 17.5
- 15.0-17.5
- 12.5-15.0
- 10.0-12.5
- 7.5-10.0
- 5.0-7.5
- 2.5-5.0
- under 2.5
- Data not available

FRANCE
2290 (2314)

AUSTRIA
149 (130)

SPAIN
2488 (2764)

ITALY
2583 (2137)

GREECE
303 (310)

Unemployment figures in thousands
for selected countries 1989.
(1984 figures are given in brackets)

IMPORTANCE
OF AGRICULTURE

% of labour force
employed in
agriculture,1985

- over 30
- 25-30
- 20-25
- 15-20
- 10-15
- 5-10
- less than 5

*The maps of the Soviet Union and Yugoslavia show the situation
at the time of going to press in December, 1991. Extra maps of
the Republics and Nationalities of the Soviet Union and the
Republics and Ethnic Groups of Yugoslavia are provided on p.161.*

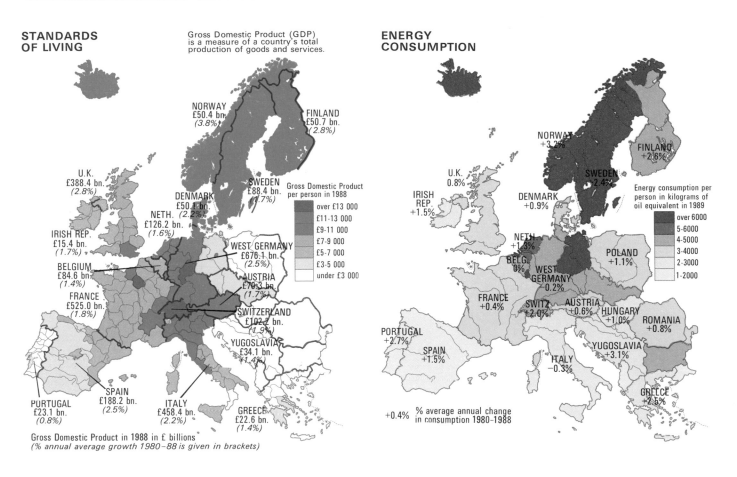

STANDARDS OF LIVING

Gross Domestic Product (GDP) is a measure of a country's total production of goods and services.

NORWAY £50.4 bn. (3.8%)

FINLAND £50.7 bn. (2.8%)

U.K. £388.4 bn. (2.8%)

DENMARK £50.1 bn. (2.2%)

SWEDEN £88.4 bn. (1.7%)

NETH. £126.2 bn. (1.6%)

Gross Domestic Product per person in 1988

- over £13 000
- £11-13 000
- £9-11 000
- £7-9 000
- £5-7 000
- £3-5 000
- under £3 000

IRISH REP. £15.4 bn. (1.7%)

WEST GERMANY £676.1 bn. (2.5%)

BELGIUM £84.6 bn. (1.4%)

AUSTRIA £70.3 bn. (1.7%)

FRANCE £525.0 bn. (1.8%)

SWITZERLAND £102.2 bn. (1.9%)

YUGOSLAVIA £34.1 bn. (1.4%)

SPAIN £188.2 bn. (2.5%)

PORTUGAL £23.1 bn. (0.8%)

ITALY £458.4 bn. (2.2%)

GREECE £22.6 bn. (1.4%)

Gross Domestic Product in 1988 in £ billions
(% annual average growth 1980-88 is given in brackets)

ENERGY CONSUMPTION

NORWAY +3.2%

FINLAND +2.6%

U.K. 0.8%

IRISH REP. +1.5%

DENMARK +0.9%

SWEDEN +2.4%

Energy consumption per person in kilograms of oil equivalent in 1989

- over 6000
- 5-6000
- 4-5000
- 3-4000
- 2-3000
- 1-2000

NETH. +1.3%

BELG. 0%

WEST GERMANY −0.2%

POLAND +1.1%

FRANCE +0.4%

SWITZ. +2.0%

AUSTRIA +0.6%

HUNGARY +1.0%

ROMANIA +0.8%

PORTUGAL +2.7%

SPAIN +1.5%

ITALY −0.3%

YUGOSLAVIA +3.1%

GREECE +2.5%

+0.4% % average annual change in consumption 1980-1988

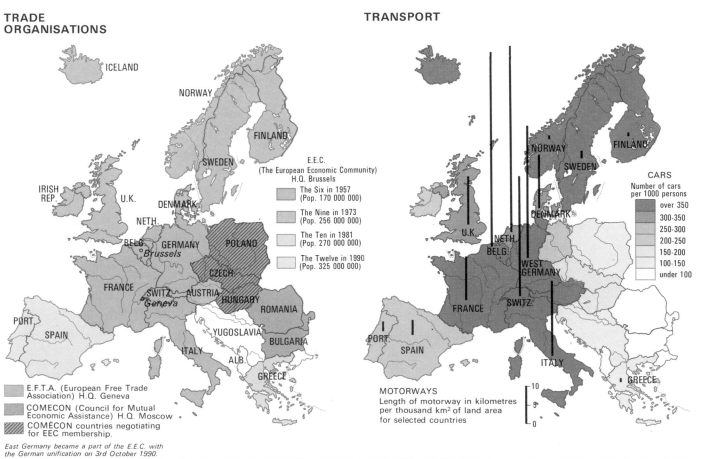

TRADE ORGANISATIONS

ICELAND

NORWAY

FINLAND

SWEDEN

IRISH REP.

U.K.

DENMARK

NETH.

E.E.C. (The European Economic Community) H.Q. Brussels

- The Six in 1957 (Pop. 170 000 000)
- The Nine in 1973 (Pop. 256 000 000)
- The Ten in 1981 (Pop. 270 000 000)
- The Twelve in 1990 (Pop. 325 000 000)

BELG. GERMANY
Brussels

POLAND

CZECH.

FRANCE

SWITZ. AUSTRIA
Geneva

HUNGARY

ROMANIA

PORT.

SPAIN

YUGOSLAVIA

BULGARIA

ITALY

ALB.

GREECE

- E.F.T.A. (European Free Trade Association) H.Q. Geneva
- COMECON (Council for Mutual Economic Assistance) H.Q. Moscow
- COMECON countries negotiating for EEC membership.

East Germany became a part of the E.E.C. with the German unification on 3rd October 1990.

TRANSPORT

NORWAY

FINLAND

SWEDEN

DENMARK

U.K.

NETH.

BELG.

WEST GERMANY

CARS
Number of cars per 1000 persons

- over 350
- 300-350
- 250-300
- 200-250
- 150-200
- 100-150
- under 100

FRANCE

SWITZ.

PORT.

SPAIN

ITALY

GREECE

MOTORWAYS
Length of motorway in kilometres per thousand km² of land area for selected countries

10
5
0

EUROPE: *statistics*

	Population								Land			Agriculture		
	Total	Density	Birth Rate	Death Rate	Life Expectancy	Growth 1965-80	Growth 1980-88	Urban	Area	Arable	Forest	Agricultural Population	Index of Production	Food Intake
	th.	persons per km²	per th. popn.	per th. popn.	yrs.	av. % per annum	av. % per annum	%	th. km²	th. km²	th. km²	% of total popn.	1979-81 = 100	calories per day
Albania	3145	117	26	6	72	2.5	2.1	35	27	7	11	51	111	2726
Austria	7563	91	12	11	74	0.3	0	57	83	15	32	7	105	3428
Belgium *	9867	329	12	11	75	0.3	0	97	30	8	7	2	116	3679
Bulgaria	8995	81	13	12	72	0.5	0.2	70	111	41	39	13	103	3663
Czechoslovakia	15610	125	14	11	71	0.5	0.3	68	125	51	46	10	125	3465
Denmark	5133	122	12	12	76	0.5	0	86	42	26	5	5	120	3633
Finland	4944	16	12	10	76	0.3	0.4	60	305	24	232	9	103	3122
France	55873	102	14	9	77	0.7	0.5	74	546	195	147	6	104	3336
Germany, East	16665	157	13	13	73	−0.2	−0.1	78	106	49	30	9	116	3791
Germany, West	61049	250	11	11	75	0.3	−0.1	86	244	75	73	4	112	3528
Greece	10030	77	11	10	76	0.7	0.5	61	131	39	26	26	104	3688
Hungary	10604	115	12	13	70	0.4	−0.1	59	92	53	17	13	105	3569
Iceland	249	3	17	7	77	0.8	1.1	90	100	0.1	1	8	106	3142
Ireland	3574	52	17	9	74	1	0.6	58	69	10	3	15	105	3632
Italy	57470	196	10	9	77	0.6	0.2	68	294	122	67	8	100	3523
Luxembourg *	371	143	12	10	74	0.9	0.2	83	3	0.6				
Malta	345	1150	15	8	73	0.2	−0.9	87	0.3	0.1	0	4	111	2682
Netherlands	14760	434	13	8	77	0.9	0.5	88	34	9	3	4	115	3326
Norway	4205	14	14	11	77	0.6	0.3	74	308	9	83	6	112	3223
Poland	37873	124	16	10	72	0.8	0.8	61	305	147	87	23	109	3336
Portugal	10162	111	12	9	74	0.6	0.3	32	92	28	36	19	107	3151
Romania	23052	100	16	11	70	1	0.4	49	230	107	63	23	114	3373
Spain	38997	78	11	8	77	1	0.5	77	499	204	157	12	114	3359
Sweden	8357	20	13	12	77	0.5	0.1	84	412	30	280	4	93	3064
Switzerland	6545	164	12	9	77	0.5	0.3	61	40	4	11	5	111	3437
United Kingdom	57019	236	14	11	75	0.2	0.2	92	242	70	23	2	106	3256
Yugoslavia	23552	92	15	9	72	0.9	0.7	48	255	78	93	25	103	3563
U.S.S.R.	285659	13	20	10	69	0.9	0.9	68	22272	2325	9440	15	118	3440

* Many figures for Luxembourg included in Belgium.

Population. This is the United Nation's estimate for the mid-year 1988 (thousands)

Population Density. This is the quoted population total divided by the quoted land area (persons per square kilometre).

Birth Rates and Death Rates. These are the registered or United Nation's estimated rates per thousand population.

Life Expectancy. This figure indicates the number of years that a child born today can expect to live if the levels of death of today last throughout its life. The figure is the average of that for men and women. The figure for women is usually higher than that for men (U.K. Male 75, female 78 years).

Population Growth. This shows the average annual percentage change in population for two periods, 1965–1980 and 1980–1988.

Urbanization. This is the percentage of the total population living in urban areas. The definition of urban is that of the individual nation and usually includes quite small towns.

Land Area. This is the total area of the country minus the area covered by major lakes and rivers (thousand square kilometres).

Arable Land and Permanent Crops. This excludes fallow land but includes temporary pasture (thousand square kilometres).

Forest and Woodland. This includes natural and planted woodland and land recently cleared of timber which will be replanted (thousand square kilometres).

Agricultural Population. This is the percentage of the economically active population working in agriculture. It also includes those people working in forestry, hunting and fishing.

Index of Agricultural Production. The base period for this index is 1979–1981 and it shows the level of production in each country in 1988 in comparison with that of the earlier period. Only edible crops and meat are included.

Food Intake. The figures are the average intake per person in calories per day for the year 1986.

Imports US$ per capita	Exports US$ per capita	Primary % of age group	Secondary % of age group	Popn. per doctor	Consumption in kg of oil equiv. per capita	Consumer Price Index 1980 = 100	G.N.P. US$ per capita	Growth per capita % per year 1965-88	Part formed by Agric. %	Part formed by Indust. %	end 1987 US$ millions	as % of G.N.P.	
	159	96	70		1178		900						Albania
4315	3592	100	79	388	3465	133	11980	3.1	3	37	302	0.2	Austria
8371	8407	96	96	331	4844	146	11480	2.6	2	31	592	0.4	* Belgium
1843	1915	100	100	277	4705		6295	3.1	15	62			Bulgaria
1554	1477	97	37	277	4954	111	8280	2.3	7	61			Czechoslovakia
4936	4811	98	100	399	3887	165	14930	1.9	5	29	922	0.9	Denmark
4017	4053	100	100	443	5581	170	14470	3.2	7	35	610	0.6	Finland
2819	2561	100	95	320	3729	172	12790	2.7	4	31	6959	0.7	France
1727	1792	100	78	439	6031		9800	3	13	66			Germany, East
3724	4812	97	72	377	4531	122	14400	2.5	2	38	4700	0.4	Germany, West
1347	649	100	88	351	1971	416	4020	3.1	16	29	23120	0.1	Greece
929	903	98	70	307	3062	184	2240	3.8	15	40	18957	79	Hungary
6321	5719	99	95	435	6884	1050	20160	2.4	10	16			Iceland
3809	4468	100	96	676	2503	195	6120	2	10	37	57	0.2	Ireland
2127	2029	97	76	234	2676	222	10350	2.7	4	34	2615	0.4	Italy
		100	74	552	11330	142	22600	1.7	3	29			* Luxembourg
3299	1751	97	75	879	1501	103	5050	2.7	4	29			Malta
6187	9293	100	100	450	5198	135	11860	2.1	4	30	2231	1	Netherlands
5369	5101	98	97	451	8932	192	17190	3.5	4	35	988	1	Norway
286	322	100	80	487	3386	928	1930	3.4	13	49	42135	58	Poland
1322	902	100	52	412	1322	381	2830	3.2	9	40	18245	63	Portugal
496	544	97	79	567	3464		5200	4.3	15		6662	5	Romania
1257	874	100	98	317	1939	214	6010	2.3	6	37			Spain
4861	5303	99	83	387	6453	177	15500	1.8	3	35	1534	0.9	Sweden
7725	6930	100		696	4105	128	21330	1.4	2	21	615	0.3	Switzerland
2708	2300	100	85	611	3805	160	10420	1.7	2	38	2615	0.3	United Kingdom
533	494	95	82	549	2115	2891	2480	3.7	11	43	23518	41	Yugoslavia
336	378	100	99	270	5006	108	7120	2.5	20	45			U.S.S.R.

Andorra, Land 0.5/Popn. 51; Faeroe Is. 1.4/46; Gibraltar 0.01/30; Liechtenstein 0.2/28; Monaco 0.0015/27; San Marino 0.06/23; Svalbard 62/4.

Trade. The trade figures are for the year 1988. The total trade figures have been divided by the population and are a measure of the country's external trade (U.S. $ per capita).

Education. The ages of primary school are taken to be 6–11 years and secondary school 12–17 years. The percentage of total school age group in this type of education is shown.

Energy. All forms of energy have been converted to their equivalent in oil. Firewood and other traditional forms used in developing countries are not included and so the energy consumption in those countries is understated (kilograms of oil equivalent per capita).

Consumer Price Index. The base year is 1980 which is 100 and the level of consumer prices in 1987 or 1988 are shown in relation to the base year. It is a measure of inflation.

G.N.P. (Gross National Product) This figure is an estimate of the average production per person measured in U.S. dollars and for 1988. The G.N.P. measures the value of goods and services produced in a country, plus the balance, positive or negative, of income from abroad, for example investments, interest on capital, money returned from foreign labour, etc. The rate of change is the average annual percentage change during the period 1965–1988 in the G.N.P. The G.D.P. (Gross Domestic Product) is the G.N.P. minus the foreign balances. The adjoining two columns show the percentage contribution to the G.D.P. made by the agricultural and mining and manufacturing sectors.

Loans and Debts. This figure in millions of U.S. dollars shows the external public debt ar the end of 1988. This is then shown as a percentage of the annual G.N.P. The figures in red show official development assistance made by the developed countries and also as a percentage of the donor country's G.N.P.

To convert from square kilometres (km²) to square miles multiply by 0.39
To convert from kilograms to pounds multiply by 2.2

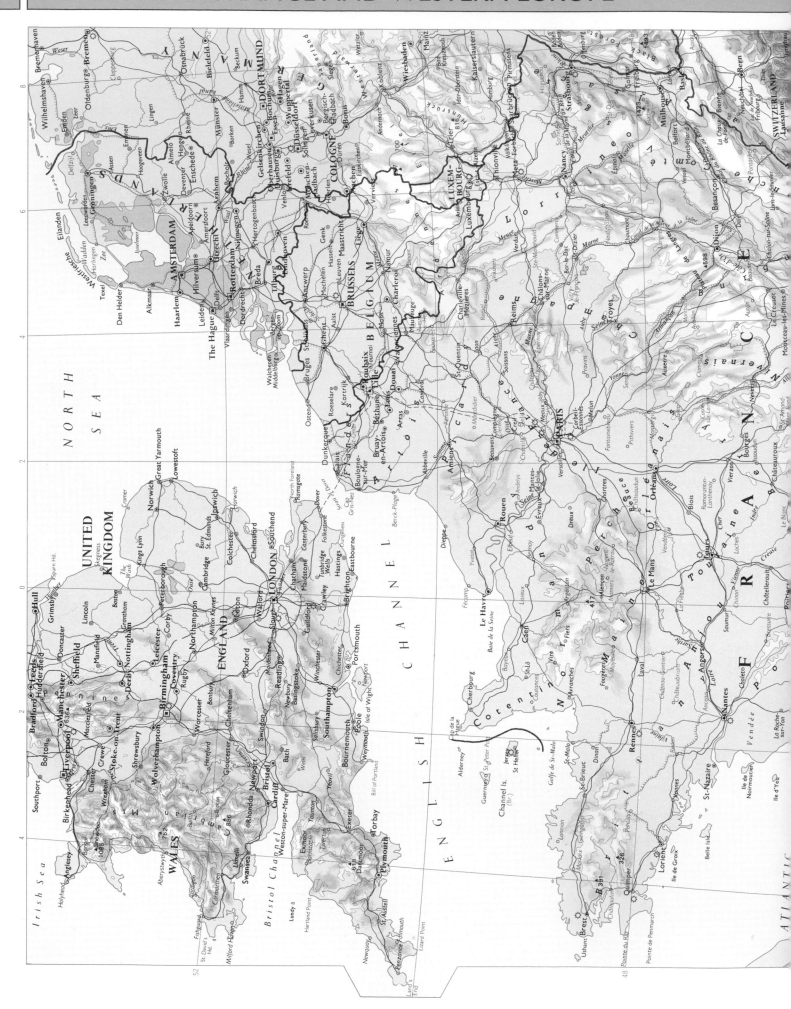

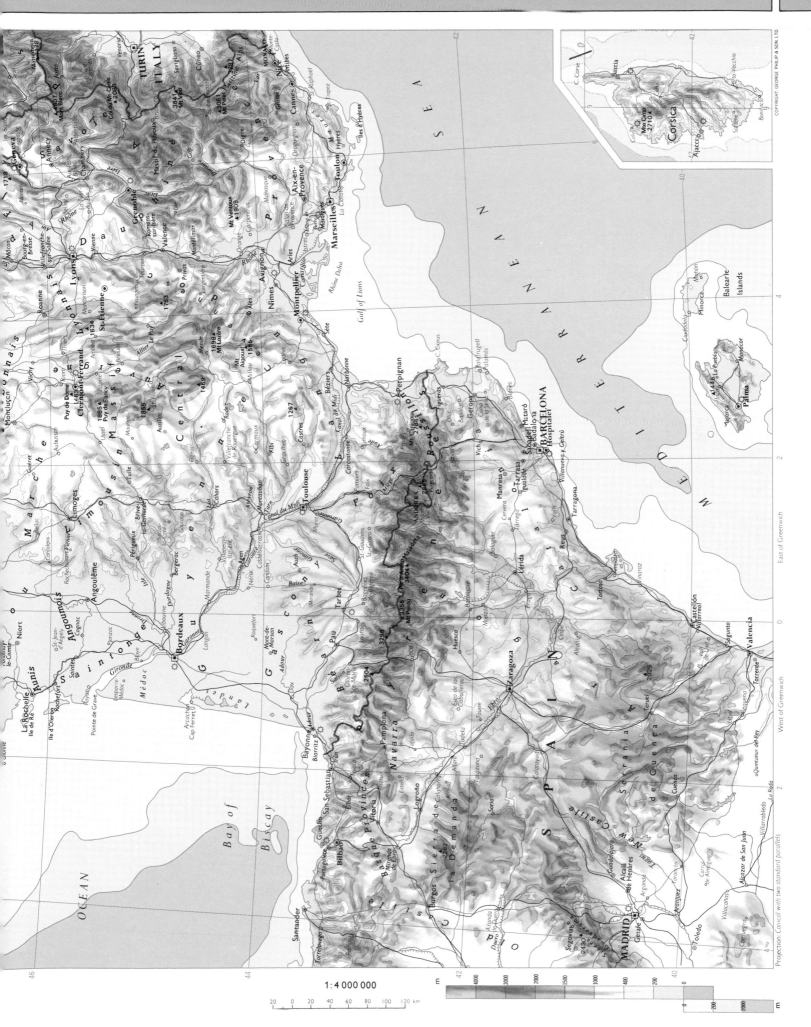

1 : 4 000 000

20   0   20   40   60   80   100   120 km

Projection: Conical with two standard parallels

4000   3000   2000   1500   1000   400   200   0

m

0   200   2000

m

Projection: Conical with two standard parallels

East from Greenwich

COPYRIGHT. GEORGE PHILIP & SON. LTD.

1:2 000 000

10 0 10 20 30 40 50 60 70 80 km

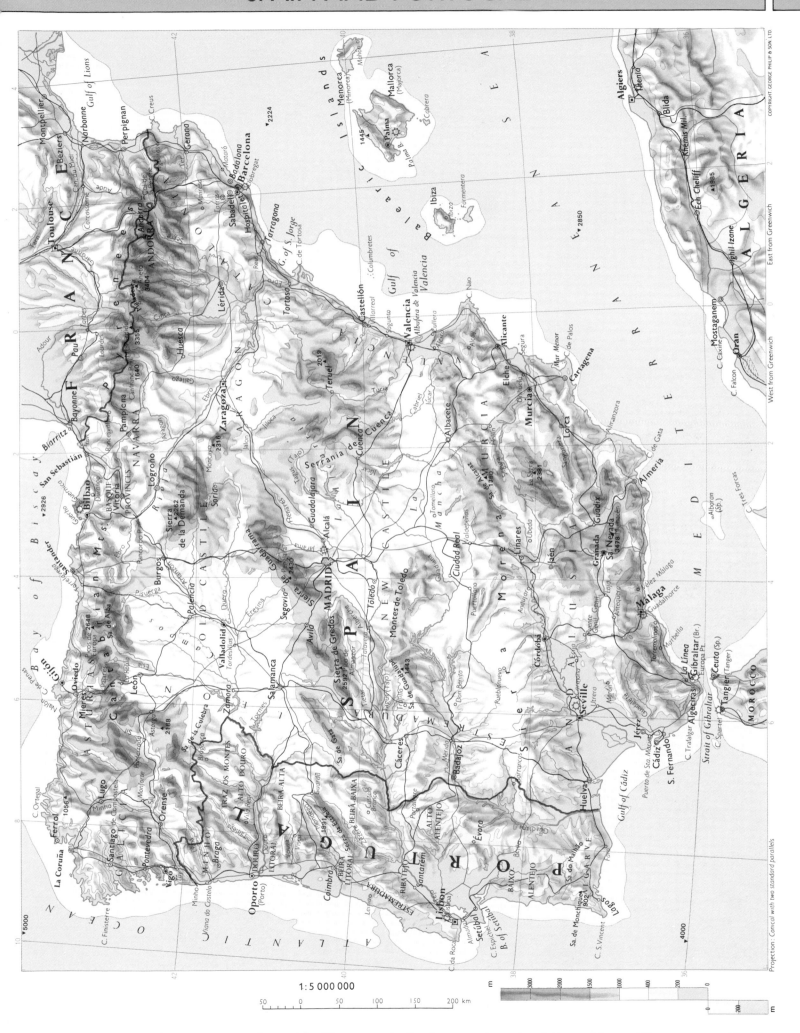

1 : 5 000 000

Projection: Conical with two standard parallels

The maps of the Soviet Union and Yugoslavia show the situation at the time of going to press in December, 1991. Extra maps of the Republics and Nationalities of the Soviet Union and the Republics and Ethnic Groups of Yugoslavia are provided on p. 161.

Projection: Conical with two standard parallels.

West from Greenwich   0   East from Greenwich

1:10 000 000

100   0   100   200   300   400 km

Division between Greeks and Turks
in Cyprus; Turks to the North.

MALTA
1:1 000 000

0   10 km

S.E. EUROPE
POLITICAL
1:25 000 000

Projection: Conical with two standard parallels

The maps of the Soviet Union and Yugoslavia show the situation at the time of going to press in December, 1991. Extra maps of the Republics and Nationalities of the Soviet Union and the Republics and Ethnic Groups of Yugoslavia are provided on p.161.

SOVIET
UNION

Transylvania

R O M A N I A

Szeged
Hódmezővásárhely
Arad
Alba-Iulia
Sfântu Gheorghe
Carpathians
Focşani
Galati
Izmail
Sasyk

Szekszárd
Baja
Deva
Sibiu
Braşov
(Oraşul Stalin)
Braila
Tulcea

Pécs
Subotica
Timişoara
Kikinda
Transylvanian *Alps*
Red
Tower P.
350
Mt. Negoiu
2635
Mt. Omu
2507
Buzau
Buzău
Danube

Sombor
Zrenjanin
(Petrovgrad)
Peleaga
2509
Paringul Mare
2518
Rimnicu Vilcea
Tirgovişte
Ploeşti
Bucharest
(Bucureşti)
Constanţa

Osijek
Novi Sad
Drava
Pancevo
Tirgu-Jiu
Piteşti
Argeş
Dâmboviţa
Ialomita

Belgrade
(Beograd)
Smederevo
Orşova
Iron Gate
Turnu-
Severin
Jiu
Olt
Slatina
Craiova
Danube
Călăraşi
Dobrogea
Trajan's
Wall

Tuzla
Bosna
Sava
Morava
Vedea
Olt
Giurgiu
Siliştra
Tutrakan
C. Kaliakra

GOSLAVIA
Kragujevac
Cacak
Timok
Vidin
Oryakhovo
Somovit
Svishtov
Ruse (Ruschuk)
Dobrich
(Tolbukhin)

Sarajevo
Krusevac
Niš
2168
Pleven
Sumen
(Kolarovgrad)
Varna

Mostar
Drina
Leskovac
Uzna Morava
Dragoman
Sofia
Vezhen
2198
Gabrovo
Shipka P.
Sliven
Burgas
BLACK
SEA

2522
Durmitor
Kosovska
Mitrovica
Iskar
Pristina
Pernik
BULGARIA
Trajan's Gate
Stara Zagora
Yambol

MONTENEGRO
Pec
Sara Gora
Kumanovo
Kyustendil
Maritsa
Pazardzhik
Plovdiv
Musala
2925
Khaskovo
Arda
Istranca
1018
C. Igneada

Titograd
(Podgorica)
Prizren
2496
Skopje
 Rhodope
Mountains
Edirne
TURKEY
Bosporus

Shkodër
White Drin
Tetovo
Korab
2764
Solunska
2540
Prilep
Struma
Vardar
Mesta
Dhidhimotikhon
Istanbul
Üsküdar

Bojana
Drin
MACEDONIA
Bitola
(Monastir)
Petrich
DONI
Xánthi
Komotini
THRACE
Ergene
Sea of Marmara
Marmara
Imrali
Bursa
2543

Durrës
Tirane
Elbason
2559
Ohridsko L.
Prespa
Florina
Edhessa
Dojran
Seres
A
C
Dráma
Kaválla
Alexandroúpolis
Enez
G. of Saros
Gelibolu
(Gallipoli)
Bandirma

Brindisi
Shkumbin
Berat
Tomorrit
2480
Kastoria
Veroia
Thessaloniki
C. Platí
1127 Thásos
Samothráki
1600
Gökçeada
Çanakkale
Dardanelles
(Hellespont)
Troy
Ida 1766
Balikesir
2181

Lecce
Galatina
Vijosë
Sazan
Vlorë
Korçë
Kozáni
Aliákmon
G. of
Thessaloniki
G. of Toronaíos
Singitikós G.
Mt. Áthos
2033
C. Planka
Límnos
Bozca Ada
Ayvalik
Edremit
2308
TURKEY
Anatolia

C. Otranto
C. St. Maria
di Leuca
Smolikas
2637
Olympus
2917
Ossa
1978
Píndus
Mts.
C. Psevdhókavos
Áyios
Evstrátios
C. Burun
Lésvos
968
Mitilini

Kérkira
(Corfu)
Ioánnina
Trikkala
Larisa
Píion
1575
Iliodhrómia
N. Sporades
Skíros
C. Kafirévs
Khíos
(Chios)
Manisa
Turgutlu
Izmir
(Smyrna)
2157
Alaşehir

EPIRUS
Árta
THESSALY
Vólos
G. of Vólos
Menderes

Préveza
Amfilokhía
Lamía
P. of Thermopylae
Gióna
2510
Dhirfis
1743
Évvoia
(Euboea)
Khalkis
Athens
(Athinai)
Piraievs
(Piraeus)
Andros
Ándros
Tínos
Mikonos
Ikaria
Samos
Aydin
Levkás
(Sta. Maura)
Kefallinía
(Cephalonia)
Mesolóngion
G. of Patrai
Gulf of Corinth
Parnassós
2457
1398
C. Kafirévs
Ermoúpolis
Síros
Rinia
Páros
Náxos
1001
Fournoí
G. of Kerme
2294
Ródhos

Zákinthos
Zákinthos
Argostólion
Pátrai
2224
Killíni
2376
Corinth
Mycenae
Alyíon
G. of Aíyina
Kéa
Kíthnos
Sérifos
KIKLADHES
Sífnos
Sikinos
Thíra
Amorgós
Astipálaia
Kálimnos
Kos
G. of
Mandalya
Ródhos
(Rhodes)
4486

Pírgos
Olympia
Návplion
Idhra
Tripolis
Spárti
Kalamáta
Paikon
Mílos
(Cyclades)
Tílos
1215

Kiparissía G.
G. of Argolís
5121
Páyetos Mts.
Yíthion
G. of Lakonía
C. Malea
Kithira
(Cerigo)
Karpáthos
1216

ÍONIAN
SEA
Andikíthira
C. Spátha
Khanión B.
Soúdhas B.
Khania
Lévka Óri
2452
CRETE
Rethimnon
C. Dia
Iráklion
(Candia)
Knossos
Metabéllou B.
Dhíkti
2148
Kásos

RRANEAN
SEA
C. Lithinon
Mt. Idhi
2456

1:5 000 000

50   0   50   100   150   200 km

CENTRAL
EUROPE
POLITICAL
1:25 000 000

The maps of the Soviet Union and Yugoslavia show the situation
at the time of going to press in December, 1991. Extra maps of
the Republics and Nationalities of the Soviet Union and the
Republics and Ethnic Groups of Yugoslavia are provided on p. 161.

1:5 000 000

50   0   50   100   150   200 km

COPYRIGHT GEORGE PHILIP & SON LTD.

ICELAND
At the same scale as main map

The maps of the Soviet Union and Yugoslavia show the situation at the time of going to press in December, 1991. Extra maps of the Republics and Nationalities of the Soviet Union and the Republics and Ethnic Groups of Yugoslavia are provided on p.161.

The maps of the Soviet Union and Yugoslavia show the situation at the time of going to press in December, 1991. Extra maps of the Republics and Nationalities of the Soviet Union and the Republics and Ethnic Groups of Yugoslavia are provided on p.161.

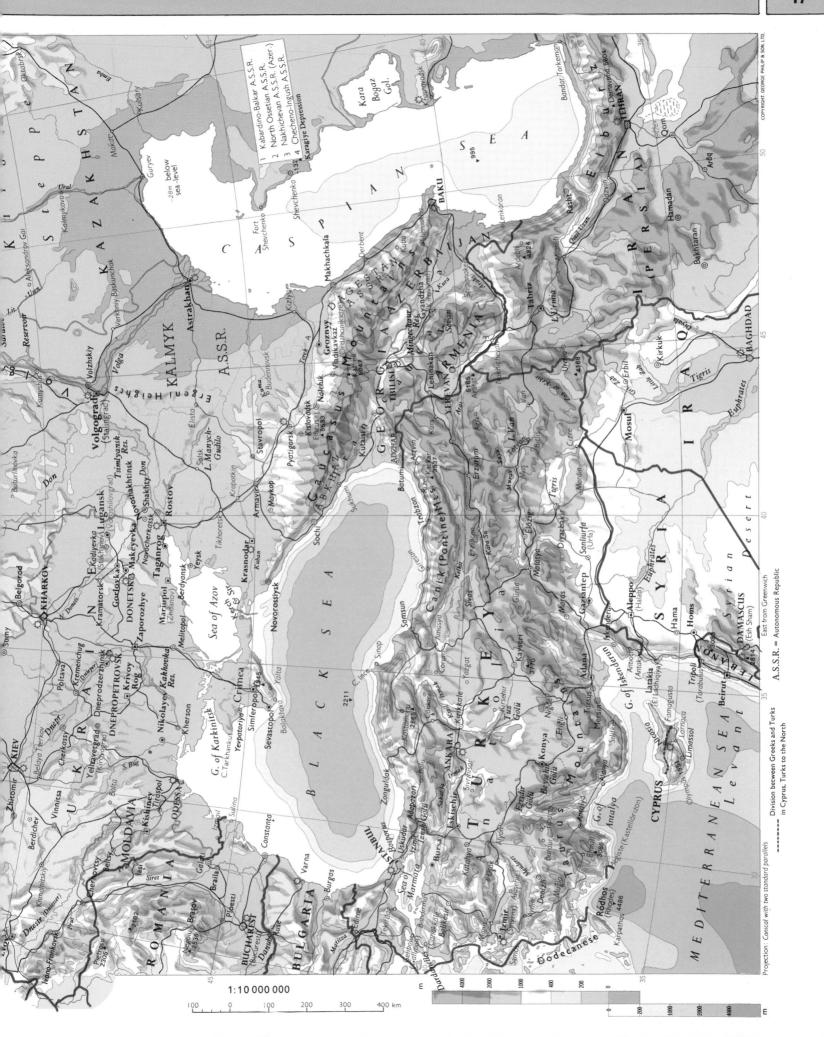

Kara
Bogaz
Gol.

Dermavend 5604

TEHRAN

Qom

Ardq

C A S P I A N   S E A

995

Shevchenko

Fort
Shevchenko

−28m
below
sea-level

Guryev

1 Kabardino-Balkar A.S.S.R.
2 North Ossetian A.S.S.R.
3 Nakhichevan A.S.S.R. (Azer.)
4 Checheno-Ingush A.S.S.R.
Karagiye Depression

Bandar Torkeman

Gorgan

E l b u r z

M t s.

Rasht

Qazvin

I   R   A   N

(P E R S I A)

Hamadan

Bakhtaran

BAKU

Lenkoran

Makhachkala

Derbent

Kuba

Shemakha

A Z E R B A I J A N

Gyandzha

Mingechaur
Res.

Tabriz

L. Urmia

Ardbil

4824

Oazl Uzun

KAZAKHSTAN

Embo
Okjabrsk

Pkulsary

Makat.

Aleksandrov Gai

Kalmykovo

Ural

Uzen

Lit.

Sarpa

Reservoir

Kuybyshev

Astrakhan

KALMYK   A.S.S.R.

Ergeni Heights

Volgograd
(Stalingrad)

Elista

Grozny

Ordzhonikidze

Vladikavkaz

D A G E S T A N
A.S.S.R.

Kizlyar

Budennovsk

Terek 4

Nalchik

Elbrus
5633

C a u c a s u s   M o u n t a i n s

A B K H A Z I A

Sukhumi

GEORGIA

TBILISI

Leninakan

Agri

Ararat
5185

YEREVAN

ARMENIA

Sevan
L. Sevan

Stepanakert

Nakhichevan

4168

Van

L. Van

Kura

Aras

Erzurum

Kars

Kelkit

K Z L Z L   Irmak

BAGHDAD

Kirkuk

I   R   A   Q

Mosul

Erbil

Tigris

Little Zab

Great Zab

Euphrates

VOLGA

Kamyshin

Volzhskiy

Volga

Don

L. Manych
Gudilo

Salsk

Tsimlyansk
Res.

Shakhty

Novoshakhtinsk

Rostov

Novocherkassk

Tikhoretsk

Kropotkin

Armavir

Maykop

Stavropol

Pyatigorsk

Kislovodsk

Kuraisin

ADZHAR

Batumi

Rize

Trabzon

C a n i k (P o n t i n e)   M t s.

Giresun

Samsun

Sinop

C. Ince

2211

Ordu

Sivas

Erzincan

Tunceli

Elazig

Malatya

Diyarbakir

Kara Su

Tigris

Mardin

Cizre

Sanliurfa
(Urfa)

Gaziantep

Maras

Aleppo
(Halab)

S Y R I A

Hama

Homs

DAMASCUS
(Esh Sham)

LEBANON

Beirut

Tripoli
(Tarabulus)

Latakia
(El Ladhiqiya)

Iskenderun

Antakya
(Antioch)

G. of Iskenderun

Adana

Tarsus

Mersin

T a u r u s   M o u n t a i n s

Konya

Nigde

Kayseri

ANKARA

T U R K E Y

A n a t o l i a

2865

Eregli

Tuz
Golu

Aksaray

Kirsehir

Kirikkale

Yozgat

Corum

Amasya

Tokat

Sakarya

Zonguldak

Bolu

Eskisehir

Bursa

ISTANBUL

Uskudar

Adapazari

Bosporus

Sea of
Marmara

Izmit

Canakkale

Dardanelles

Gallipoli
(Gelibolu)

Bandirma

Balikesir

Izmir

Manisa

Aydin

Denizli

Mugla

Isparta

Beysehir
Golu

Egridir
Golu

Burdur

Afyon

Kutahya

3086

Antalya

G. of
Antalya

Alanya

3770

Olympus

Kastellorizon

Kas

CYPRUS

Nicosia

Famagusta

Larnaca

Limassol

M E D I T E R R A N E A N   S E A

L e v a n t

Rodhos
(Rhodes)

4486

Dodecanese

Karpathos

Samos

Kos

Syrian
Desert

S y r i a n   D e s e r t

3608

2814

KHARKOV

Belgorod

Sumy

Poltava

Kremenchug

Kharkov

Kramatorsk

Ekadiyevka
(Stakhanov)

Lugansk
(Voroshilovgrad)

Gorlovka

Makeyevka

DONETSK

Taganrog

Zaporozhye

Z. Donets

U K R A I N E

Z. Bug

Melitopol

Berdyansk

Mariupol
(Zhdanov)

Krivoy
Rog

DNEPROPETROVSK

Dnepr

Dneprodzerzhinsk

Nikolayev

Kherson

Kakhovka
Res.

Sea of Azov

Kerch

Yeysk

Krasnodar

Kuban

Novorossiysk

Sochi

B L A C K   S E A

Crimea

Simferopol

Sevastopol

Yalta

1545

Balaklava

G. of Karkinitsk

C. Tarkhankut

Yevpatoriya

KIEV

Zhitomir

Berdichev

Vinnitsa

Cherkassy

Belaya Tserkov

Bolta

Kishinev

MOLDAVIA

Tiraspol

Chernovtsy

Ivano-Frankovsk

Khmelnitskiy

Kirovograd

Yelizavetgrad
(Kirovograd)

Dnestr (Dniester)

Pru

Galati

Braila

Siret

Ploesti

BUCHAREST
(Bucuresti)

R O M A N I A

2543
2535

Brasov

Danube

Ruse

Constanta

Sulina

Izmail

Reni

B U L G A R I A

Varna

Burgas

Danube

Maritsa

Edirne

Tekirdag

Samsun

ROSTOV

Kuybyshev

Kumyshy

Kalmykovo

Copyright: George Philip & Son, Ltd.

1:10 000 000

100   0   100   200   300   400 km

m   4000   2000   1000   400   200   0

East from Greenwich

Projection: Conical with two standard parallels

Division between Greeks and Turks
in Cyprus, Turks to the North

A.S.S.R. = Autonomous Republic

45   40   35   30   35

SOVIET UNION

RUSSIAN FED.
1. Daghestan A.S.S.R.
2. Kabardino–Balkar A.S.S.R.
3. Mari A.S.S.R.
4. Mordovian A.S.S.R.
5. North Ossetian A.S.S.R.
6. Tatar A.S.S.R.
7. Udmurt A.S.S.R.
8. Chuvash A.S.S.R.
9. Checheno–Ingush A.S.S.R.
AZERBAIJAN
10. Nakhichevan A.S.S.R.
GEORGIA
11. Abkhaz A.S.S.R.
12. Adzhar A.S.S.R.

Projection: Conical Orthomorphic with two standard parallels

East from Greenwich

*The maps of the Soviet Union and Yugoslavia show the situation
at the time of going to press in December, 1991. Extra maps of
the Republics and Nationalities of the Soviet Union and the
Republics and Ethnic Groups of Yugoslavia are provided on p. 161.*

Boundaries of
A.S.S.R.
(Autonomous
Republics)

1 : 20 000 000

200   0   200   400   600   800 km

COPYRIGHT. GEORGE. PHILIP & SON. LTD.

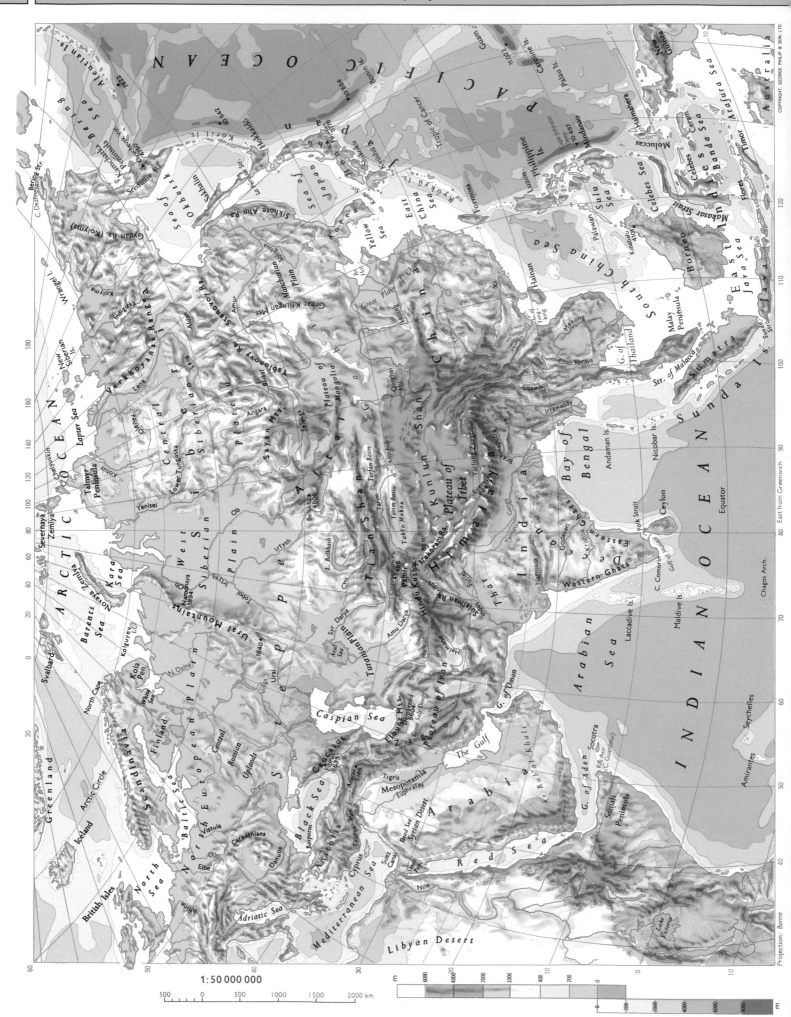

ASIA: *physical*

COPYRIGHT. GEORGE PHILIP & SON. LTD.

P A C I F I C   O C E A N

ARCTIC OCEAN

INDIAN OCEAN

Projection: Bonne

1:50 000 000

500   0   500   1000   1500   2000 km

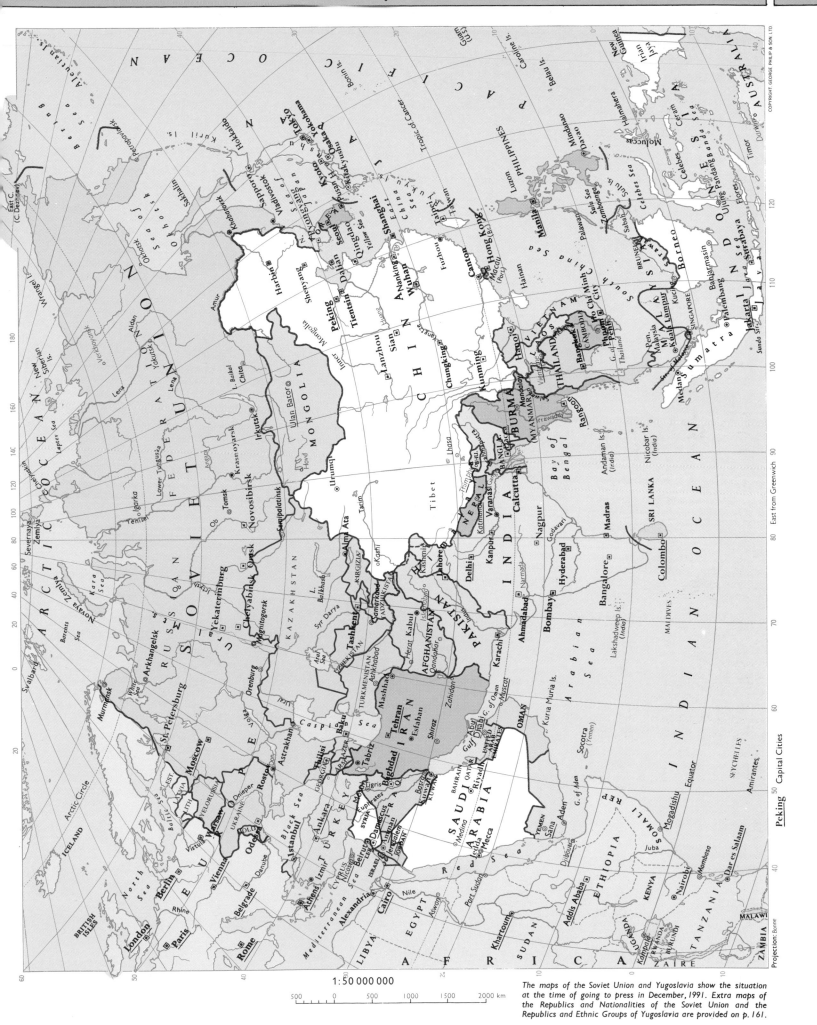

1:50 000 000

500   0   500   1000   1500   2000 km

Peking ▪ 50 Capital Cities

The maps of the Soviet Union and Yugoslavia show the situation at the time of going to press in December, 1991. Extra maps of the Republics and Nationalities of the Soviet Union and the Republics and Ethnic Groups of Yugoslavia are provided on p.161.

COPYRIGHT GEORGE PHILIP & SON LTD.

Projection: Bonne

East from Greenwich

ASIA: *climate and natural vegetation*

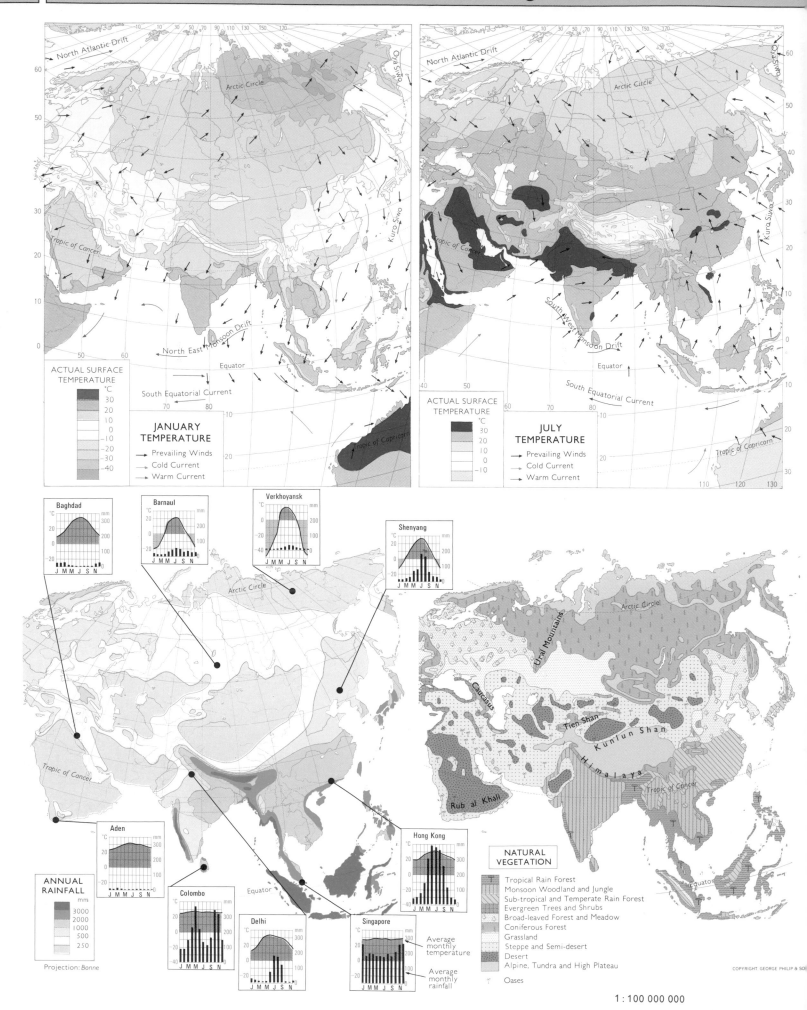

ACTUAL SURFACE
TEMPERATURE
°C
30
20
10
0
-10
-20
-30
-40

JANUARY
TEMPERATURE

→ Prevailing Winds
→ Cold Current
→ Warm Current

ACTUAL SURFACE
TEMPERATURE
°C
30
20
10
-10

JULY
TEMPERATURE

→ Prevailing Winds
→ Cold Current
→ Warm Current

Baghdad

Barnaul

Verkhoyansk

Shenyang

Aden

ANNUAL
RAINFALL

mm
3000
2000
1000
500
250

Colombo

Delhi

Hong Kong

Singapore

Average
monthly
temperature

Average
monthly
rainfall

NATURAL
VEGETATION

Tropical Rain Forest
Monsoon Woodland and Jungle
Sub-tropical and Temperate Rain Forest
Evergreen Trees and Shrubs
Broad-leaved Forest and Meadow
Coniferous Forest
Grassland
Steppe and Semi-desert
Desert
Alpine, Tundra and High Plateau

Oases

Projection: Bonne

1 : 100 000 000

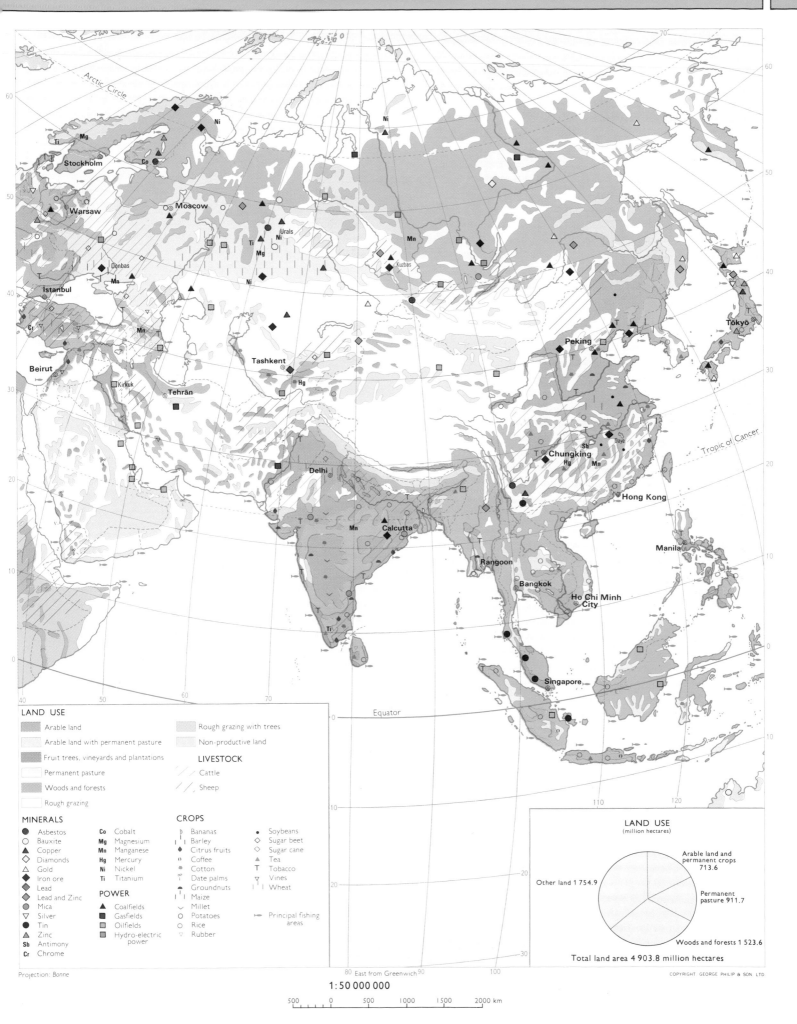

LAND USE

- Arable land
- Arable land with permanent pasture
- Fruit trees, vineyards and plantations
- Permanent pasture
- Woods and forests
- Rough grazing
- Rough grazing with trees
- Non-productive land

LIVESTOCK

- ⫽ Cattle
- ⫻ Sheep

MINERALS

- ● Asbestos
- ○ Bauxite
- ▲ Copper
- ◇ Diamonds
- △ Gold
- ◆ Iron ore
- ◆ Lead
- ◆ Lead and Zinc
- ● Mica
- ▽ Silver
- ● Tin
- △ Zinc
- **Sb** Antimony
- **Cr** Chrome
- **Co** Cobalt
- **Mg** Magnesium
- **Mn** Manganese
- **Hg** Mercury
- **Ni** Nickel
- **Ti** Titanium

POWER

- ▲ Coalfields
- ■ Gasfields
- ■ Oilfields
- ■ Hydro-electric power

CROPS

- ⅅ Bananas
- | | Barley
- ◆ Citrus fruits
- ⊕ Coffee
- ⁂ Cotton
- ⁘ Date palms
- | | Groundnuts
- | | | Maize
- ⌣ Millet
- ○ Potatoes
- ○ Rice
- ▽ Rubber
- • Soybeans
- ◇ Sugar beet
- ◇ Sugar cane
- ⬠ Tea
- ▽ Tobacco
- T Tobacco
- ▽ Vines
- | | | Wheat
- ⊷ Principal fishing areas

LAND USE
(million hectares)

- Other land 1 754.9
- Arable land and permanent crops 713.6
- Permanent pasture 911.7
- Woods and forests 1 523.6

Total land area 4 903.8 million hectares

Projection: Bonne

East from Greenwich

1:50 000 000

500 0 500 1000 1500 2000 km

COPYRIGHT GEORGE PHILIP & SON LTD

	Population								Land			Agriculture		
	Total	Density	Birth Rate	Death Rate	Life Expectancy	Growth 1965-80	Growth 1980-88	Urban	Area	Arable	Forest	Agricultural Population	Index of Production	Food Intake
	th.	persons per km²	per th. popn.	per th. popn.	yrs.	av. % per annum	av. % per annum	%	th. km²	th. km²	th. km²	% of total popn.	1979-81 = 100	calories per day
Afghanistan	15513	24	48	22	37	2.4	2.6	22	648	81	19	57	99	2055
Bangladesh	115244	130	42	12	51	2.7	2.8	13	134	92	21	71	109	1927
Burma (Myanmar)	40162	61	31	10	60	2.3	2.2	24	658	101	324	49	146	2609
Cambodia	7869	45	41	17	48	0.3	2.9	12	177	31	134	71	173	2276
China	1083889	116	21	7	70	2.2	1.2	38	9326	970	1166	70	140	2630
Cyprus	686	76	19	8	76		1.1	53	9	2	1	22	96	3378
Hong Kong	5674	5674	13	5	76	2.1	1.5	93	1	0.1	0.1	1	60	2859
India	813990	274	32	11	58	2.3	2.1	27	2973	1689	671	68	133	2238
Indonesia	174832	97	27	11	61	2.3	2.1	27	1812	212	1215	51	138	2579
Iran	48555	30	43	12	63	3.2	3	53	1636	148	180	30	121	3313
Iraq	17657	41	43	8	64	3.4	3.6	72	434	55	19	23	136	2932
Israel	4444	222	23	7	76	2.8	1.7	91	20	4	1	5	115	3061
Japan	122433	330	11	6	78	1.2	0.6	77	371	47	251	8	102	2864
Jordan	3937	41	46	7	66	2.6	3.7	66	97	4	0.7	7	158	2991
Korea, North	21877	182	29	5	69	2.7	2.5	67	120	24	90	36	132	3151
Korea, South	42593	435	16	6	70	1.9	1.4	69	98	21	65	28	112	2907
Laos	3879	17	41	16	49	1.4	2.4	17	231	9	130	73	132	2391
Lebanon	2827	283	29	8	67	1.6	−0.01	83	10	3	0.8	11	129	2995
Malaysia	16921	51	29	6	70	2.5	2.6	40	329	44	196	35	165	2730
Mongolia	2086	1	39	8	64	3	2.9	51	1565	13	152	33	119	2807
Nepal	18053	132	40	15	51	2.4	2.7	9	137	23	23	92	125	2052
Pakistan	105677	136	33	8	55	3.1	3.1	31	779	208	31	51	140	2315
Philippines	59686	200	33	8	64	2.9	2.4	41	298	79	110	48	109	2372
Saudi Arabia	14016	7	42	8	64	4.6	3.7	75	2150	12	12	42	332	3004
Singapore	2639	4398	20	5	73	1.6	1.1	100	0.6	0.03	0.03	1	91	2840
Sri Lanka	16565	255	21	6	71	1.8	1.5	21	65	19	18	52	100	2401
Syria	11667	63	44	7	65	3.4	3.6	51	184	56	5	26	126	3260
Taiwan	19673	547	16	5	73		1.5	72	36	9	2	26	104	
Thailand	54469	106	22	7	65	2.7	1.9	21	512	201	144	66	120	2331
Turkey	53772	70	28	8	64	2.4	2.3	47	771	279	202	51	119	3229
Vietnam	66682	205	32	10	66	3.1	2.6	21	325	65	130	63	136	2297
Yemen, North	8742	45	48	16	46	2.8	2.7	23	195	14	16	65	132	2318
Yemen, South	2339	7	47	16	51	2	2.9	42	333	1	15	34	108	2299
U.S.S.R. †														
Oceania														
Australia	16506	2	15	7	76	1.8	1.4	86	7618	471	1060	6	114	3326
New Zealand	3623	14	17	8	75	1.3	1	84	269	5	73	10	93	3463
Papua New Guinea	3804	8	35	12	54	2.3	2.7	15	452	4	383	70	121	2205

† See statistics table for Europe.

Population. This is the United Nation's estimate for the mid-year 1988 (thousands)

Population Density. This is the quoted population total divided by the quoted land area (persons per square kilometre).

Birth Rates and Death Rates. These are the registered or United Nation's estimated rates per thousand population.

Life Expectancy. This figure indicates the number of years that a child born today can expect to live if the levels of death of today last throughout its life. The figure is the average of that for men and women. The figure for women is usually higher than that for men (U.K. Male 75, female 78 years).

Population Growth. This shows the average annual percentage change in population for two periods, 1965–1980 and 1980–1988.

Urbanization. This is the percentage of the total population living in urban areas. The definition of urban is that of the individual nation and usually includes quite small towns.

Land Area. This is the total area of the country minus the area covered by major lakes and rivers (thousand square kilometres).

Arable Land and Permanent Crops. This excludes fallow land but includes temporary pasture (thousand square kilometres).

Forest and Woodland. This includes natural and planted woodland and land recently cleared of timber which will be replanted (thousand square kilometres).

Agricultural Population. This is the percentage of the economically active population working in agriculture. It also includes those people working in forestry, hunting and fishing.

Index of Agricultural Production. The base period for this index is 1979–1981 and it shows the level of production in each country in 1988 in comparison with that of the earlier period. Only edible crops and meat are included.

Food Intake. The figures are the average intake per person in calories per day for the year 1986.

| Trade | | Education | | Health | Energy | Consumer Price Index | G.N.P. | | G.D.P. | | Loans & Debt | | |
| Imports | Exports | Primary | Secondary | | | | | Growth per capita | Part formed by Agric. | Part formed by Indust. | | | |
US$ per capita	US$ per capita	% of age group	% of age group	Popn. per doctor	Consumption in kg of oil equiv. per capita	1980 = 100	US$ per capita	% per year 1965-88	%	%	end 1987 US$ millions	as % of G.N.P.	
91	36	18	6	6419	71				69	14			Afghanistan
150	62	60	18	6731	47	199	160	0.3	47	13	9432	49	Bangladesh
16	5	100	24	3743	73	190	200	2.3	51	10	4386	46	Burma (Myanmar)
					59				41	17			Cambodia
40	36	100	42	1000	525		290	5.2	31	49	27919	7	China
		99	90	746	1599	148	6260		7	16	1439	35	Cyprus
8541	8543	100	69	1075	1525	180	8070	6.2	0	29			Hong Kong
23	15	92	35	2521	208	201	300	1.8	30	30	41694	16	India
83	98	100	41	9464	216	199	450	4.5	26	33	47562	59	Indonesia
377	417	100	18	2780	955				26	36			Iran
420	511	99	52	1806	732				18	46			Iraq
3217	1907	99	79	345	1965	46447	6800	2.5	5	21	26332	87	Israel
1192	1870	100	96	663	3232	116	15760	4.2	3	41			Japan
684	236	99	79	1139	750	134	1560		9	28	3585	67	Jordan
				420	2165								Korea, North
961	1107	94	95	1166	1475	160	2690	6.4	11	43	23907	14	Korea, South
18	8	94	19	1362	37		170				833	165	Laos
665	209	100	56	667	871				9	12	496		Lebanon
739	1055	100	54	1935	771	130	1810	4.1	20	31	19377	56	Malaysia
		100	92	104	1181								Mongolia
32	8	79	25	30230	23	204	160	0.5	57	14	1060	34	Nepal
55	39	52	24	2941	207	129	350	2.5	23	28	13072	37	Pakistan
120	95	100	68	6700	241	289	590	1.7	24	33	23710	60	Philippines
1460	1650	71	44	688	3292	95	6200	4	4	50			Saudi Arabia
12308	10834	100	71	1309	4436	118	7940	7.2	1	38			Singapore
126	84	100	66	5516	160	234	400	3	27	27	3956	56	Sri Lanka
218	116	100	60	1309	900	538	1640	3.3	27	19	4678	24	Syria
1754	2721	100	95	1016	73	174			6	40			Taiwan
238	214	99	29	6294	330	139	850	3.9	17	23	17685	31	Thailand
263	190	100	44	1381	763	528	1210	2.6	17	36	30697	42	Turkey
28	16	100	43	995	88		300		29	17			Vietnam
150	2	79	15	6268	100		590		28	17	2166	39	Yemen, North
620	175	66	19	4344	707		420		16	23	1689	171	Yemen, South
													† U.S.S.R.
													Oceania
1776	1532	100	96	436	4821	176	11100	1.8	4	33	501	0.3	Australia
2002	1982	100	84	576	4211	245	7750	0.9	8	31	84	0.5	New Zealand
321	308	60	11	6160	229	158	700	0.8	34	26	2218	64	Papua New Guinea

Bahrain, Land 0.6/Popn. 445; Bhutan 47/1370; Brunei 5.3/235; Kuwait 17.8/1919; Macau 0.02/429; Maldives 0.3/200; Oman 212.5/1402; Qatar 11/332; U.A.E. 83.6/1500.
American Samoa 0.2/36; Cocos Is. 0.01/0.6; Cook Is. 0.2/20; Fed. States of Micronesia 0.7/90; Fiji 18.3/722; Fr. Polynesia 3.7/179; Guam 0.6/128; Kiribati 0.7/66; Nauru 0.02/8; New Caledonia 18.8/158;
Niue I. 0.26/2; Norfolk I. 0.036/2; Northern Marianas 0.5/17; Palau 0.5/12; Samoa 2.9/163; Solomon Is. 27.5/293; Tokelau 0.01/2; Tonga 0.7/100; Tuvalu 0.2/8; Vanuatu 14.8/150; Wallis & Futuna 0.2/14.

Trade. The trade figures are for the year 1988. The total trade figures have been divided by the population and are a measure of the country's external trade (U.S. $ per capita).

Education. The ages of primary school are taken to be 6–11 years and secondary school 12–17 years. The percentage of total school age group in this type of education is shown.

Energy. All forms of energy have been converted to their equivalent in oil. Firewood and other traditional forms used in developing countries are not included and so the energy consumption in those countries is understated (kilograms of oil equivalent per capita).

Consumer Price Index. The base year is 1980 which is 100 and the level of consumer prices in 1987 or 1988 are shown in relation to the base year. It is a measure of inflation.

G.N.P. (Gross National Product) This figure is an estimate of the average production per person measured in U.S. dollars and for 1988. The G.N.P. measures the value of goods and services produced in a country, plus the balance, positive or negative, of income from abroad, for example investments, interest on capital, money returned from foreign labour, etc. The rate of change is the average annual percentage change during the period 1965–1988 in the G.N.P. The G.D.P. (Gross Domestic Product) is the G.N.P. minus the foreign balances. The adjoining two columns show the percentage contribution to the G.D.P. made by the agricultural and mining and manufacturing sectors.

Loans and Debts. This figure in millions of U.S. dollars shows the external public debt ar the end of 1988. This is then shown as a percentage of the annual G.N.P. The figures in red show official development assistance made by the developed countries and also as a percentage of the donor country's G.N.P.

To convert from square kilometres (km²) to square miles multiply by 0.39
To convert from kilograms to pounds multiply by 2.2

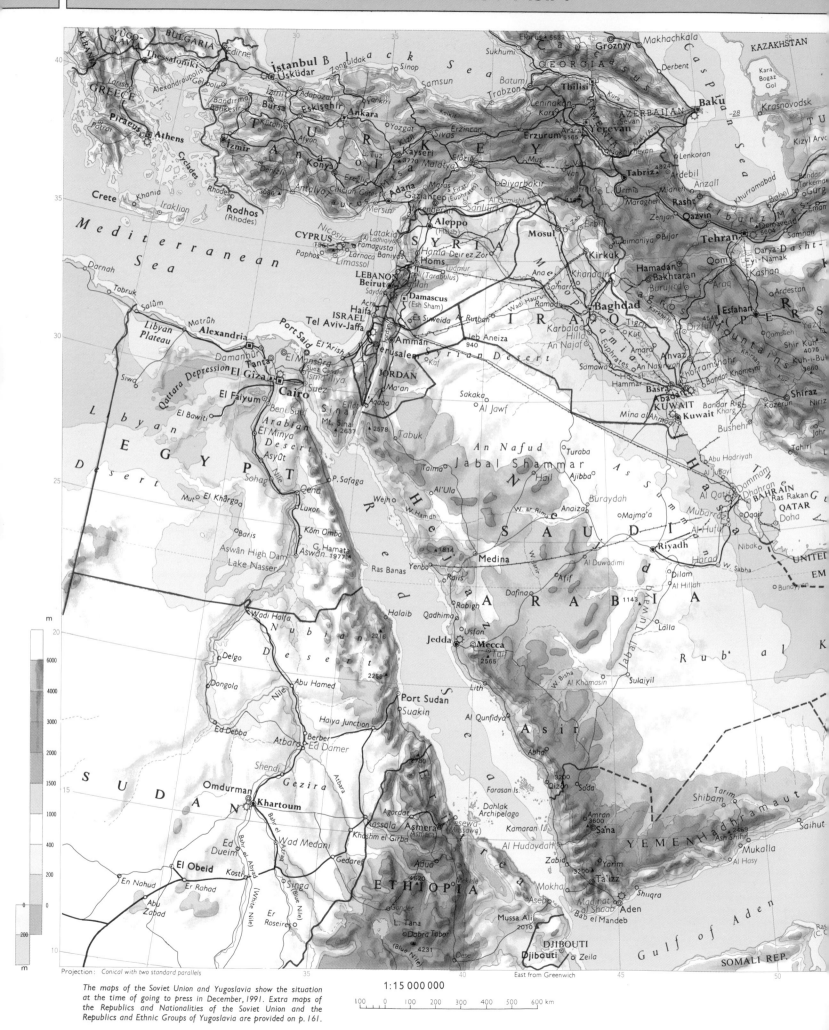

Projection: Conical with two standard parallels

The maps of the Soviet Union and Yugoslavia show the situation at the time of going to press in December, 1991. Extra maps of the Republics and Nationalities of the Soviet Union and the Republics and Ethnic Groups of Yugoslavia are provided on p.161.

1:15 000 000

100   0   100   200   300   400   500   600 km

SOVIET
UNION
UZBEKISTAN
MENISTAN

Samarkand
Amu Darya
Bukhara
TADZHIKISTAN
Dushanbe
CHINA

Kara Kum
Ashkhabad
Chardzhou
Kholm
Kerkio
Termez
Pamir
Kashmir
Srinagar

Nishapur
Mary
Kushka
Kunduz
Chitral
Gilgit

Mashhad
Kabul
Jalalabad
Peshawar
Rawalpindi
Jammu

Herat
Khyber Pass
Kohat
Sialkot

AFGHANISTAN
Ghazni
Banu
Lahore

Daulatabad
3787
Qandahar
Sandeman
Multan

Farah
Girishk
Helmand
Bolan Pass
Bahawalpur

Zabul
Quetta
Registan
Nushki
Kalat
Sukkur

Kerman
Saguch
3994
Zahidan
Larkana
Nawabshah

Saidabad
4419
Ladis
Kuh-i-Taftan
4042

Bam
Khanu
Bampur
Hyderabad

Minab
Faruch
Pasni
Karachi

Kuhran
2163

Str. of Hormuz
2057
Sharja

Abu Dhabi
Gulf of Oman
As Sohar
Matrah
Muscat

Al Khabura
Ras al Hadd
Tropic of Cancer

J. ash Sham
3019

Sur
2161
Batha

Dawwah
Al Masira

Al Khalari
Ras al Madraka

Gulf of Masira

Dhofar
Sauqra Bay

1678
Kuria Muria
Is.

Salala
Marbat

Arabian
Sea

BEIRUT
(Bayrut)
Djounie
(Juniyah)
J. Sannin
2628
Ba'labakk
(Baalbek)

Bikfaiya
Zahlah
Anti Lebanon
2462

LEBANON
Aley
Zabdani

Sayda
(Sidon)
Bisri
Jezzine
Khirbat Qanafar
Damascus
(Esh Sham)
Dareiya

Nabatiyé
el Tahta
Litani
Hermon
2814
Qatana
Kiswe

Tyre
(Sur)
Al Khiyam
Qiryat
Shemona

Tibnin
SYRIA

Nahariya
Me'ona
1208
Al Qunaytirah
Sanamein

Acre
GALILEE
Tsefat
(Safad)
Capernaum
Izr'a

B. of Haifa
Kinneret
(Sea of
Galilee)
-209

Haifa
Qiryat Yam
Qiryat Ata
Migdal
Tiberias

Tirat
Karmel
546
Nazareth
Samar
Dara

Daliyat el Karmel
515
Afula
Arab

Caesarea
Taiyiba
Irbid
Ramtha

Megiddo
Plain of Esdraelon

Pardes Hanna
Umm
el Fahm
Janin
Beit Shean

Hadera
SAMARIA
Yabis
1198
Jebel 'Ajlun
1247
Al Mafraq

Netanya
Anabta
Tubas
Ajlun
Jarash

Tul Karm
940
881
Well
Nablus
Zarqa

Ra'anana
Damiya
Az Zarqa

Herzliya
Kefar Sava
Shilo
1113
As Salt

TEL AVIV-
JAFFA
Petah Tiqva
Ramat Gan
1016
Amman

Bat Yam
Holon
Damiya

Rishon Le-Zion
Lod (Lydda)
Jericho
JORDAN

Ashdod
Ramla
Ram Allah
Hussein

Yavne
Rehovot
Gedera
Qumran

Soreq
Ma'daba

Jerusalem
Bethlehem
802

Ashqelon
JUDAEA
Madaba

Qiryat
Gat
1020
Hebron
(El Khalil)

Gaza
(Ghazzah)
Shiqma
Az Zahiriya
Dhiban

Gaza
Strip
Heidan

Khan Yunis
Mishmar
Ha Negev
Murb

Rafah
Masada
Al Mazra

Habesor
716
Al Karak

Beersheba
Arad
Dimona

EGYPT
Qatana

THE HOLY LAND

– – – Armistice boundaries between Arab States
and Israel, 1949-1974
– – – – – –

1:1 500 000

10   0   10   20   30   40   50 km

Socotra (Yemen)
The Brothers

NEGEV
Qeziot

East from Greenwich   35

COPYRIGHT. GEORGE PHILIP & SON. LTD.

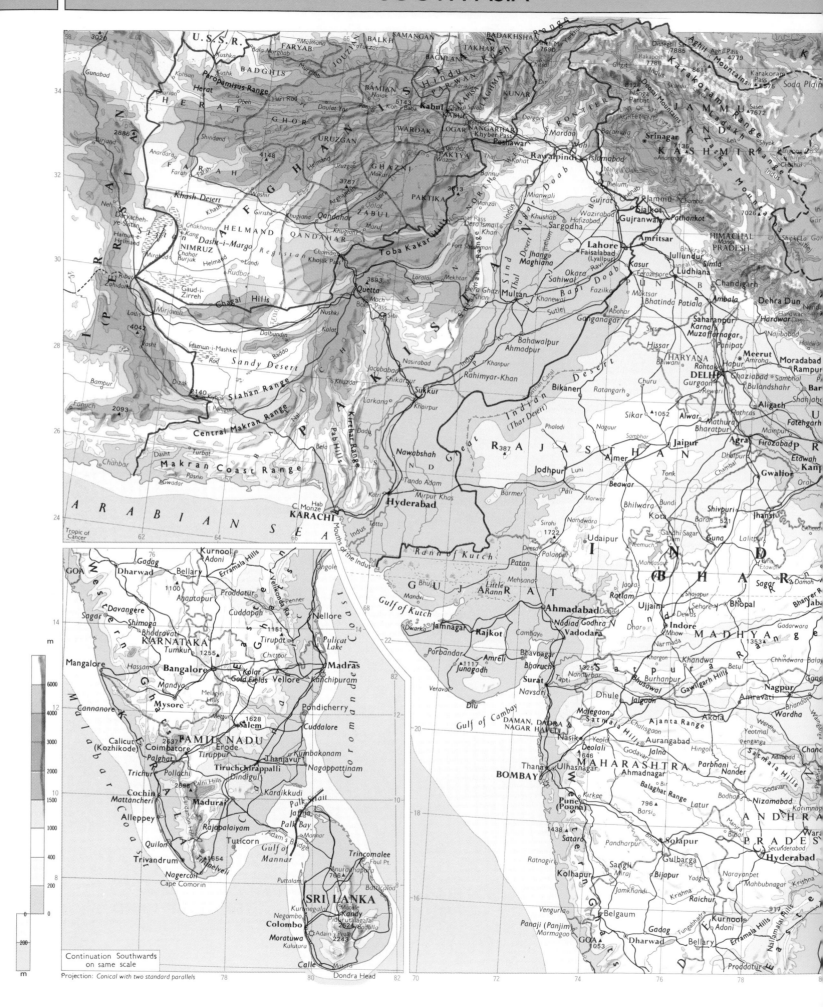

1:10 000 000

100   0   100   200   300   400 km

82   East from Greenwich   84   86   88   90   92   94   96

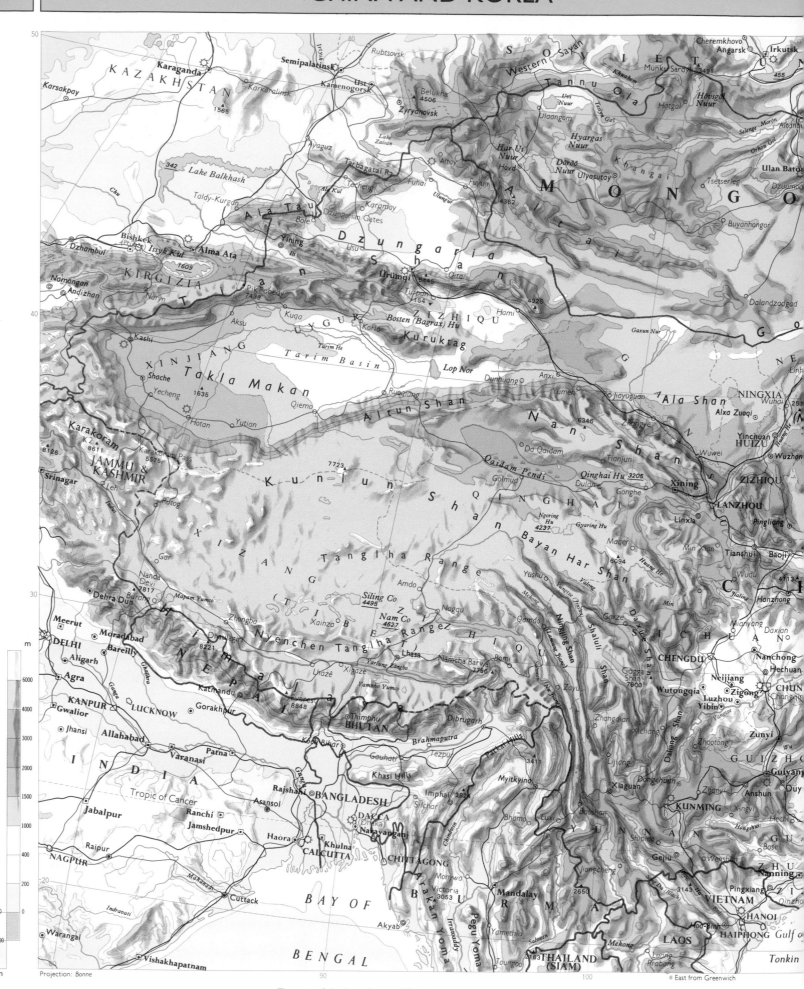

Projection: Bonne

● East from Greenwich

Lake Baykal
Ulan Ude
Yablonovyy Range
Chita
Nerchinsk
Borzya
Manzhouli
Hulun Nur
Cheybalsan
Kerülen
Buir Nur
Abagnar Qi
Dzamin Uud
Erenhot
Saynshand
 I O N
Amur
Svobodny
Blagoveshchensk
Aihui
Chegdomyn
Amur
Aleksandrovsk
C. Terpeniya
Poronaysk
Komsomolsk
Sakhalin
Yuzhno-Sakhalinsk
Khabarovsk
Birobidzhan
Bikin
L. Bolon
Orogen Zizhiqi
Nenjiang
Bei'an
Yichun
Hegang
Jiamusi
Shuangyashan
Butha Qi
Qiqihar
Anda
Suihua
Songhua
Mishan
Wakkanai
La Perouse Str.
Horqin Youyi
Qianqi
Tao'an
HARBIN
Jixi
Lake
Khanka
Asahigawa
Otaru
Hokkaido
SAPPORO
Kushiro
2290
Tonglido
1949
CHANGCHUN
Shuangliao
Siping
Liaoyuan
Songhua
Lake
Yanji
Mudanjiang
Ussuriysk
Vladivostok
Nakhodka
Hakodate
Tsugaru Strait
Aomori
Hachinohe
Morioka
Chifeng
Fuxin
FUSHUN
SHENYANG
Yonghas
Chongjin
Akita
Sado
Niigata
Koriyama
Utsunomiya
Hohhot
Jining
Zhangjiakou
Xuanhua
Chaoyang
Liaoyang
Benxi(Mukden)
ANSHAN
Dandong
Yalu
NORTH
Hungnam
Wonsan
Kanazawa
Toyama
Sendai
Datong
Chengde
Jinzhou
Yingkou
Qinghuangdao
G. of
Liaodong
Haeju
Kaesong
SEOUL
TOKYO
KAWASAKI
YOKOHAMA
Yokosuka
Hamamatsu
Shizuoka
Fuji-san
3776
NAGOYA
KYOTO
PEKING
(Beijing)
Tangshan
Liaodong
Korea Bay
DALIAN
(Lüda)
YONGYANG
INCHON
SOUTH
3058
Baoding
TIENTSIN(Tianjin)
Cangzhou
G. of Chihli
(Bo Hai)
Yantai
Weihai
Ye Xian
Taejon
TAEGU
PUSAN
Masan
OSAKA
KOBE
Okayama
Sakai
Wakayama
HIROSHIMA
TAIYUAN
HEBEI
Shijiazhuang
Dezhou
Weifang
Huang He
YELLOW
SEA
Kwangju
1915
Shimonoseki
Marsuyama
Shikoku
Kochi
Yangquan
Yuci
Fenyang
JINAN
Zibo
QINGDAO
KITAKYUSHU
FUKUOKA
Sasebo
Kumamoto
Tongchuan
Luoyang
Handan
Anyang
Tai'an
Jining
Lianyungang
Cheju Do
1950
Nagasaki
Kyushu
Sanmenxia
ZHENGZHOU
Kaifeng
Xinxiang
Pingdingshan
HENAN
Shangqiu
Xuzhou
Qingjiang
Hongze
Hu
JIANGSU
Kagoshima
Nanyang
Shangshui
Bengbu
Tanega
Han Shui
Zhumadian
Huainan
NANKING
(Nanjing)
Hefei
ANHUI
Zhenjiang
Changzhou
Wuxi
Suzhou
Nantong
SHANGHAI
Dabie Shan
WUHAN
Tongling
Wuhu
Hangzhou Wan
Xiangfan
Yichang
Shashi
Huangshi
Anqing
Yangtze
Hangzhou
Shaoxing
Ningbo
Changde
Dongting
Hu
Tunxi
ZHEJIANG
Jinhua
EAST CHINA
SEA
Amami-ō-Shima
Yiyang
Nanchang
Poyang L.
Jingdezhen
Shangrao
Wenzhou
HUNAN
Changsha
Xiangtan
JIANGXI
Wu Shan
2120
Nanping
RYUKYU Islands
Shaoyang
Zhuzhou
Jian
Nanping
Okinawa
Hengyang
Ji'an
Ganjiang
Min
Sanming
Fuzhou
Naha
Guilin
Nan Ling
Shaoguan
Zhangzhou
FUJIAN
Quanzhou
Sakashima Gunto
Tropic of Cancer
Chilung
TAIPEI
Taichung
Chiai
Yu Shan
3997
TAIWAN
PACIFIC
Mei Xian
Wuzhou
GUANGDONG
Chao'an
Xiamen
(Amoy)
Tainan
KAOHSIUNG
Shantou
Maoming
CANTON
Guangzhou
Foshan
Jiangmen
HONG KONG (Br.)
Macau
(Port.)
OCEAN
Zhanjiang
Haikou
Hainan Str.
AINAN
1879
SOUTH CHINA
SEA
Batan Is.
Babuyan Is.

1:15 000 000

100 0 100 200 300 400 500 600 km

CHINA

NORTH KOREA

Mudanjiang
Spassk-Dalni
Dalnegorsk
Lake Khanka
Ussuriysk
Yanji
Vladivostok
Nakhodka
Chongjin
Petra Velikogo Bay
Tanchon

SOUTH KOREA

Samchok
Ullung Do
Pusan

KOREA STRAIT

Tsushima
Iki
Fukue

SEA OF JAPAN

SEA OF OKHOTSK

Rebun
Rishiri
Wakkanai
Teshio
Otoineppu
Monbetsu
Rumoi
Shibatsu
Kitami
Abashiri
Asahigawa
Daisetsu 2290
HOKKAIDO
Otaru
Iwamisawa
Obihiro
Kushiro
Setana
Sapporo
Tomakomai 2052
Okushiri
Mombetsu
Muroran
Urakawa
C. Erimo
Esashi
Hakodate
C. Yesan
Tsugaru Strait
C. Shiriya
Matsumae
Mutsu
Aomori
Hirosaki
Odate
Hachinohe
Noshiro
C. Ogai
Akita
Iwate 2041
Morioka
Miyako
Hanamaki
Kitakami
Ichinoseki
Sakata
Mogami
Tsuruoka
Ishinomaki
Yamagata
Yonezawa
Sendai
Niigata
Shibata
Fukushima
Sado
Nagaoka
Agano
Bandai 1819
Aizuwakamatsu
Koriyama
Tajima
Iwaki
Hitachi
Takada
Nikko
Utsunomiya
Nanao
Toyama Bay
Nagano
Maebashi Kiryu
Tochigi
Mito
Tsuchiura
Takaoka
Toyama
Takasaki
Kanazawa
Matsumoto
Ueda
Kawagoe
Omiya
Fukui
Takayama
Ontake 3063
Kofu
Kawaguchi
Ichikawa
Choshi
Kiso
TOKYO
Tsuruga
Gifu
Fuji-San 3776
Kawasaki
Chiba
C. Kyo Wakasa Bay
Biwa
Ogaki
Yokohama
Yokosuka
Maizuru
Otsu
Nagoya
Shimizu
Numazu
Izumo
Tottori
Kyoto
Yokkaichi
Shizuoka
Ito
Tateyama
Matsue
Yonago
Tsuyama
Amagasaki
Okazaki
O-Shima
C. Hino
Okayama
Himeji
Kobe
Tsu
Hamamatsu
Toyohashi
Hamada
Masuda
Kurashiki
Akashi
Osaka
Nara
Toyohashi
Ise-Wan
Hagi
Hiroshima
Fukuyama
Sakai
Kishiwada
Wakayama
Tokuyama
Kure
Takamatsu
Shimonoseki
Ube
Niihama
Tokushima
Kii Channel
Shingu
Suo Bay
Matsuyama
Fukuoka
Kitakyushu
SHIKOKU
Kochi
C. Shio
Sasebo
Kurume
Beppu
Yawatahama
Nagasaki
Omuta
Oita
Uwajima
C. Muroto
Kumamoto
Kuju 1787
Bungo Channel
C. Ashizuri
Amakusa
Yatsushiro
Nobeoka
Sendai
KYUSHU
Miyazaki
Kagoshima
Miyakonojo
Kanoya
Osumi Channel
Osumi Islands
Tanega
Kuchinoerabu-Jima
Yaku
Tokara Channel
Nakano
Suwanose

Oki Is.

Inland Sea

Tsushima Strait

Sikhote Alin

PACIFIC OCEAN

Hachijo
Aoga

Yaku
Tokara Ch.
Nakano
Suwanose
Tokuno
Okinoerabu
Amami
RYUKYU ISLANDS
Okinawa-Shoto
Okinawa
Kerama
Naha
7507
Yaeyama
Ishigaki
Miyako
Iriomote

Projection : Bonne

East from Greenwich

1 : 7 500 000

50 0 50 100 150 200 250 300 km

m
1500
1000
400
200 30
0
0
200
m

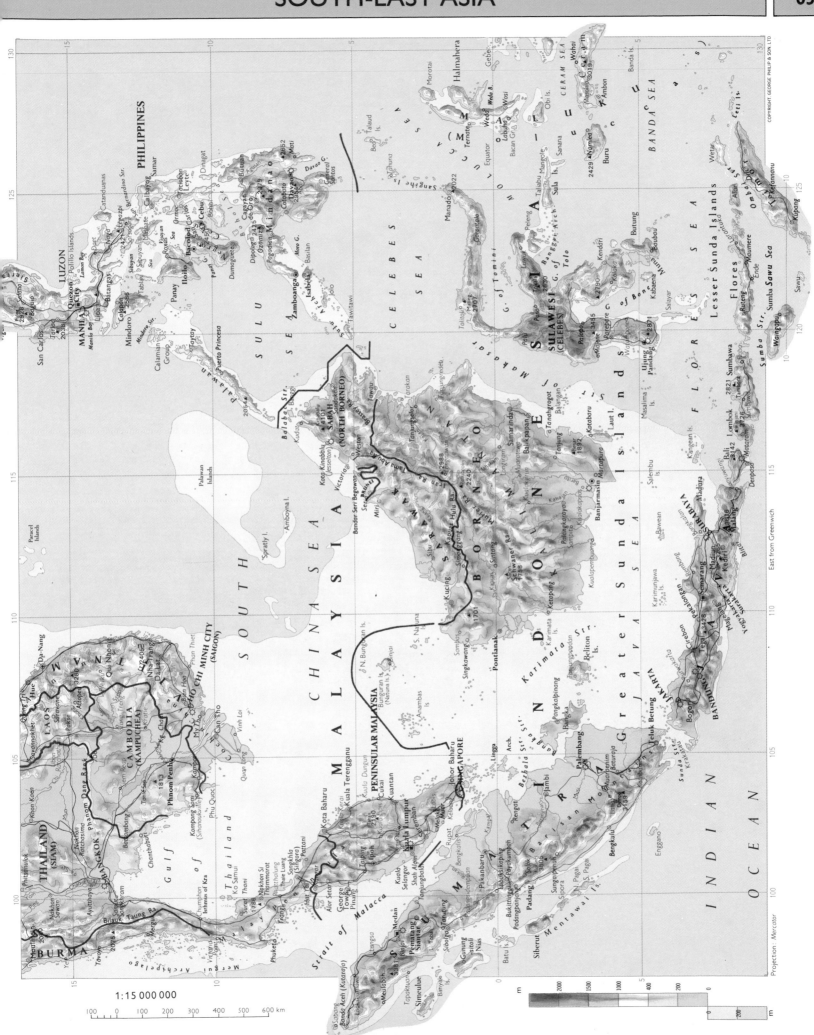

Projection: Mercator

1:15 000 000

100   0   100   200   300   400   500   600 km

PACIFIC OCEAN

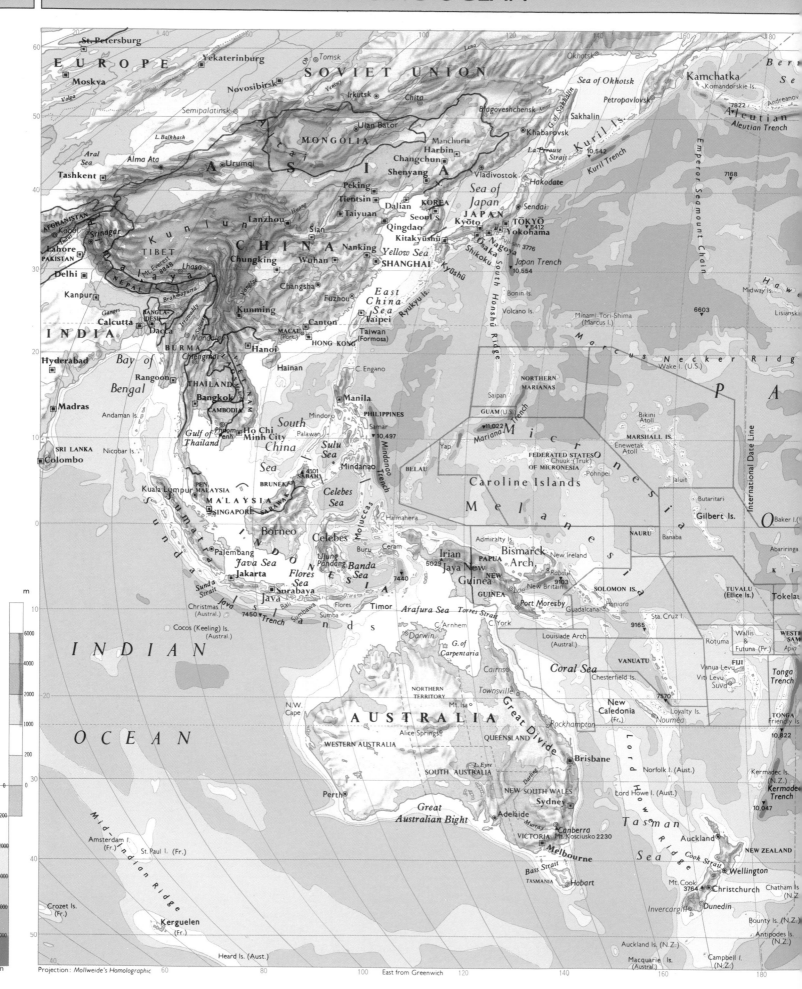

Projection: Mollweide's Homolographic   East from Greenwich

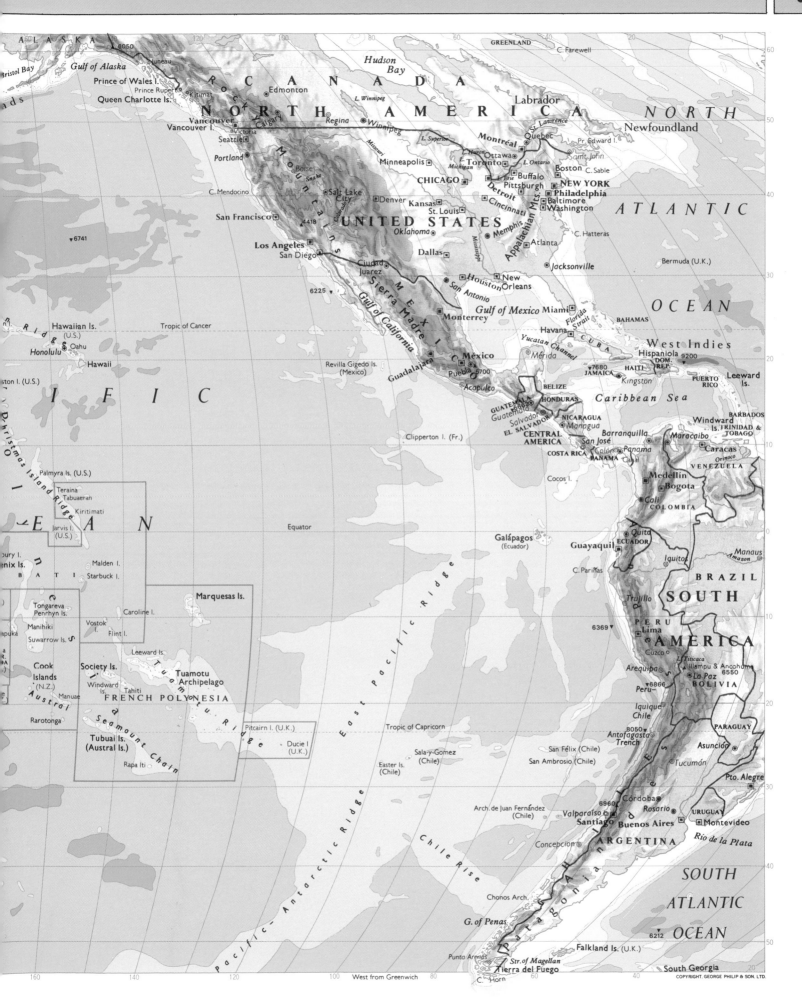

1:54 000 000

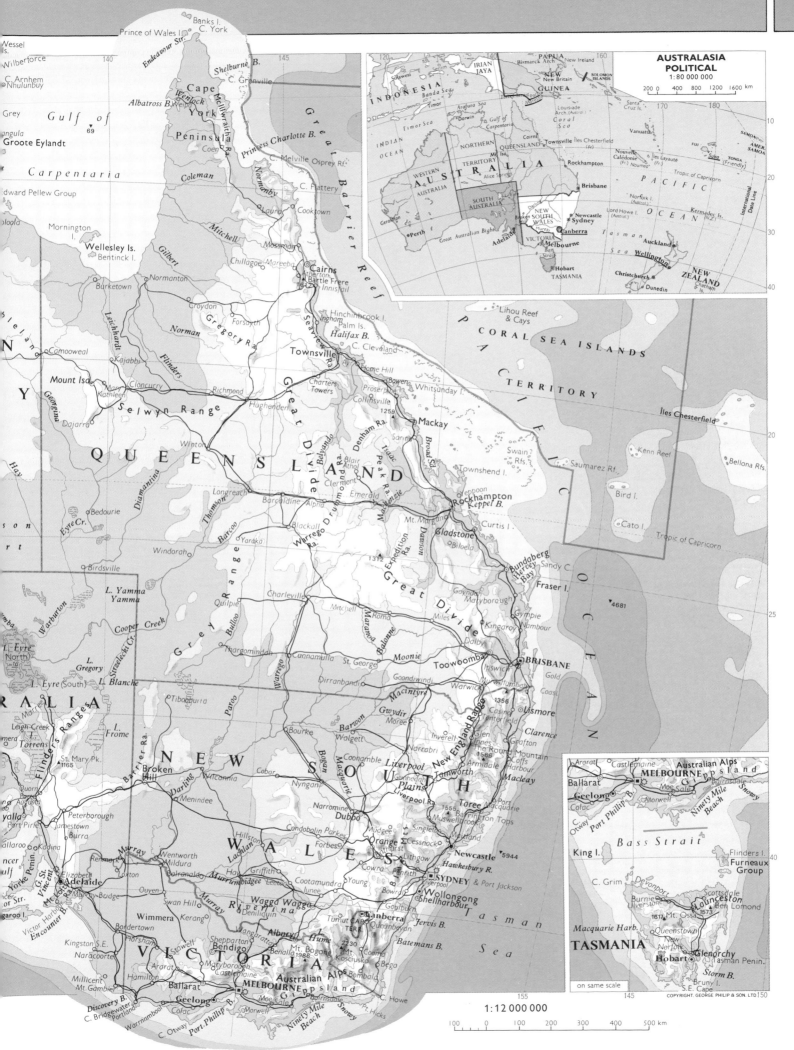

**AUSTRALASIA
POLITICAL**
1:80 000 000
200 0 400 800 1200 1600 km

1:12 000 000
100 0 100 200 300 400 500 km

TASMANIA
on same scale
COPYRIGHT. GEORGE PHILIP & SON. LTD.

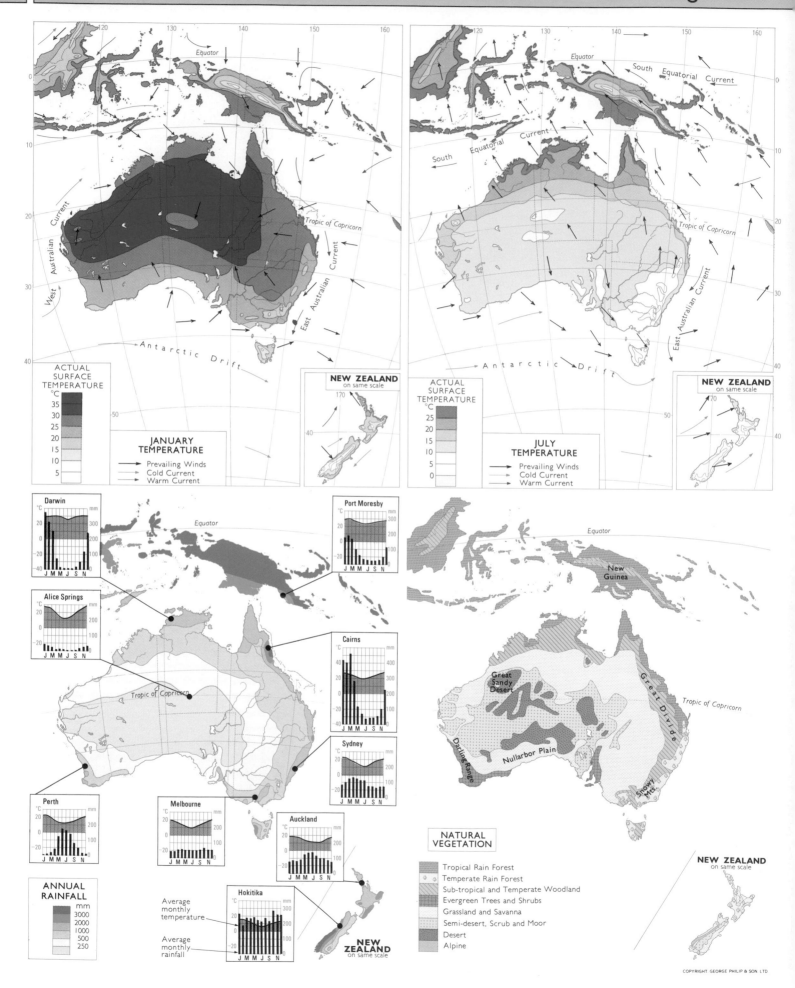

ACTUAL SURFACE TEMPERATURE °C
35
30
25
20
15
10
5

JANUARY TEMPERATURE
→ Prevailing Winds
→ Cold Current
→ Warm Current

ACTUAL SURFACE TEMPERATURE °C
25
20
15
10
5
0

JULY TEMPERATURE
→ Prevailing Winds
→ Cold Current
→ Warm Current

NEW ZEALAND on same scale

Darwin
Alice Springs
Port Moresby
Cairns
Sydney
Perth
Melbourne
Auckland
Hokitika

Average monthly temperature
Average monthly rainfall

ANNUAL RAINFALL mm
3000
2000
1000
500
250

NEW ZEALAND on same scale

New Guinea
Great Sandy Desert
Darling Range
Nullarbor Plain
Great Divide
Snowy Mts.
Tropic of Capricorn
Equator

NATURAL VEGETATION
Tropical Rain Forest
Temperate Rain Forest
Sub-tropical and Temperate Woodland
Evergreen Trees and Shrubs
Grassland and Savanna
Semi-desert, Scrub and Moor
Desert
Alpine

NEW ZEALAND on same scale

COPYRIGHT GEORGE PHILIP & SON. LTD

1:60 000 000

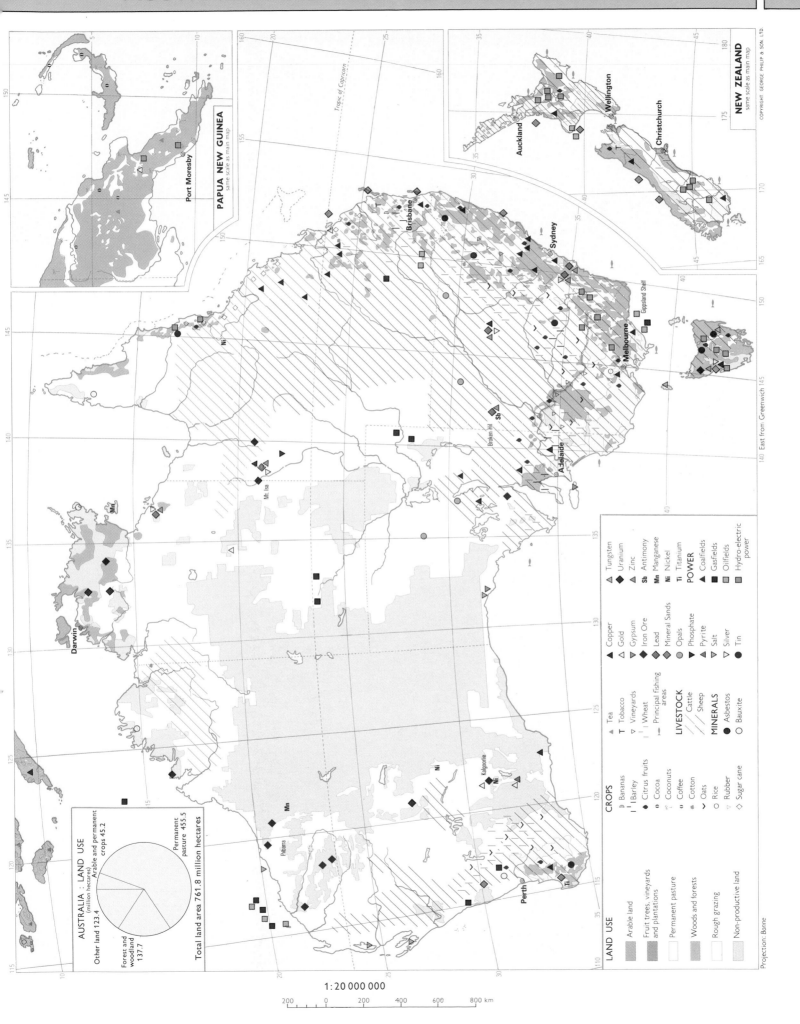

PAPUA NEW GUINEA
same scale as main map

Port Moresby

NEW ZEALAND
same scale as main map

Auckland
Wellington
Christchurch

COPYRIGHT GEORGE PHILIP & SON LTD.

Tropic of Capricorn

Brisbane
Sydney
Melbourne
Gippsland Shelf
Broken Hill
Adelaide
Sb
Ni
Mt. Isa
Mn
Darwin
Pilbara
Perth
Kalgoorlie
Ni
Ni
Mn
Ti

140 East from Greenwich 145

CROPS
- ⊅ Bananas
- I Barley
- ◆ Citrus fruits
- ○ Cocoa
- ◆ Coconuts
- ○ Coffee
- ⚭ Cotton
- 〉 Oats
- ○ Rice
- ⊳ Rubber
- ◇ Sugar cane
- ◄ Tea
- T Tobacco
- ▽ Vineyards
- I Wheat
- - - Principal fishing areas

LIVESTOCK
- ╱ Cattle
- ╱ Sheep

MINERALS
- ● Asbestos
- ○ Bauxite
- ▲ Copper
- △ Gold
- ◆ Gypsum
- ◆ Iron Ore
- ◆ Lead
- ◆ Mineral Sands
- ○ Opals
- ▼ Phosphate
- ▲ Pyrite
- ▽ Salt
- ▽ Silver
- ● Tin
- △ Tungsten
- ◆ Uranium
- ▲ Zinc
- **Sb** Antimony
- **Mn** Manganese
- **Ni** Nickel
- **Ti** Titanium

POWER
- ▲ Coalfields
- ■ Gasfields
- ■ Oilfields
- ■ Hydro-electric power

LAND USE
- Arable land
- Fruit trees, vineyards and plantations
- Permanent pasture
- Woods and forests
- Rough grazing
- Non-productive land

AUSTRALIA : LAND USE
(million hectares)

Other land 123.4
Arable and permanent crops 45.2
Permanent pasture 455.5
Forest and woodland 137.7
Total land area 761.8 million hectares

Projection: *Bonne*

1 : 20 000 000

200 0 200 400 600 800 km

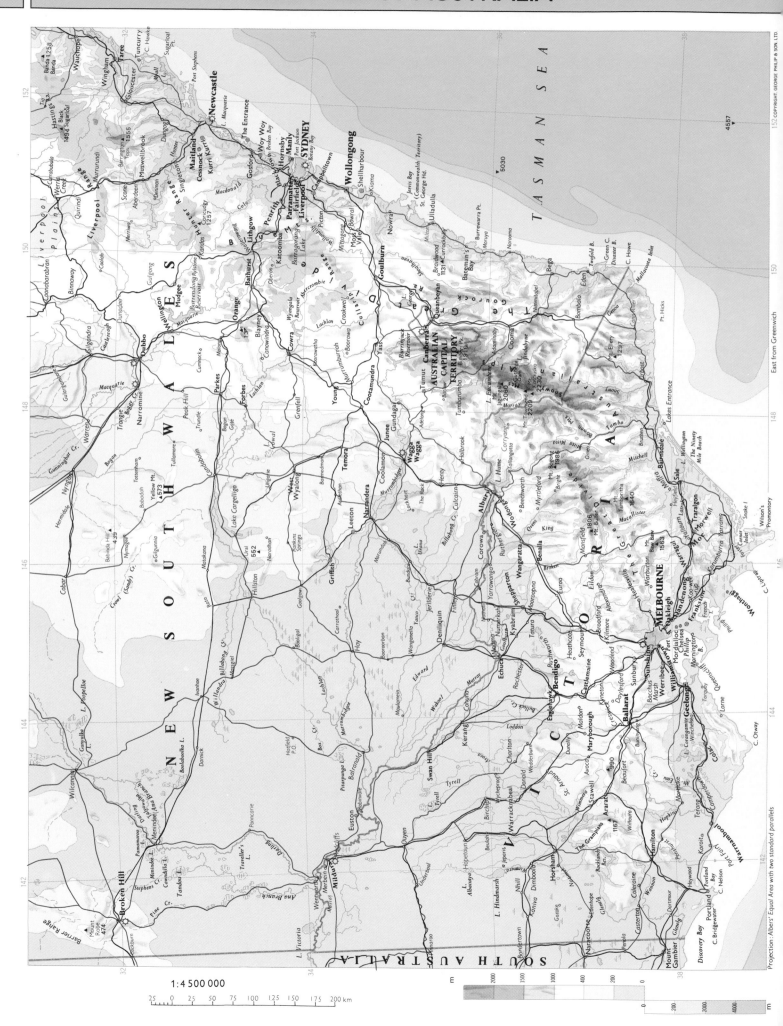

1 : 4 500 000

25 0 25 50 75 100 125 150 175 200 km

Projection: Albers' Equal Area with two standard parallels

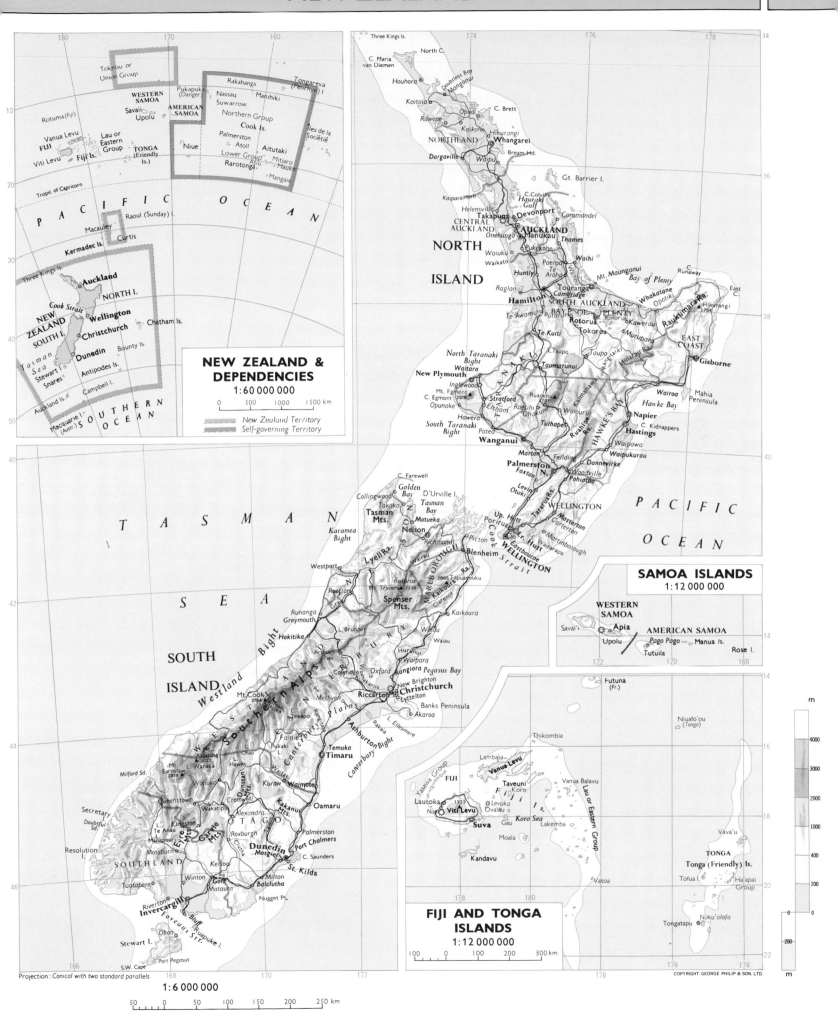

NEW ZEALAND & DEPENDENCIES

1:60 000 000

0   500   1000   1500 km

New Zealand Territory
Self-governing Territory

SAMOA ISLANDS

1:12 000 000

FIJI AND TONGA ISLANDS

1:12 000 000

100   0   100   200   300 km

Projection: Conical with two standard parallels

COPYRIGHT. GEORGE PHILIP & SON, LTD.

1:6 000 000

50   0   50   100   150   200   250 km

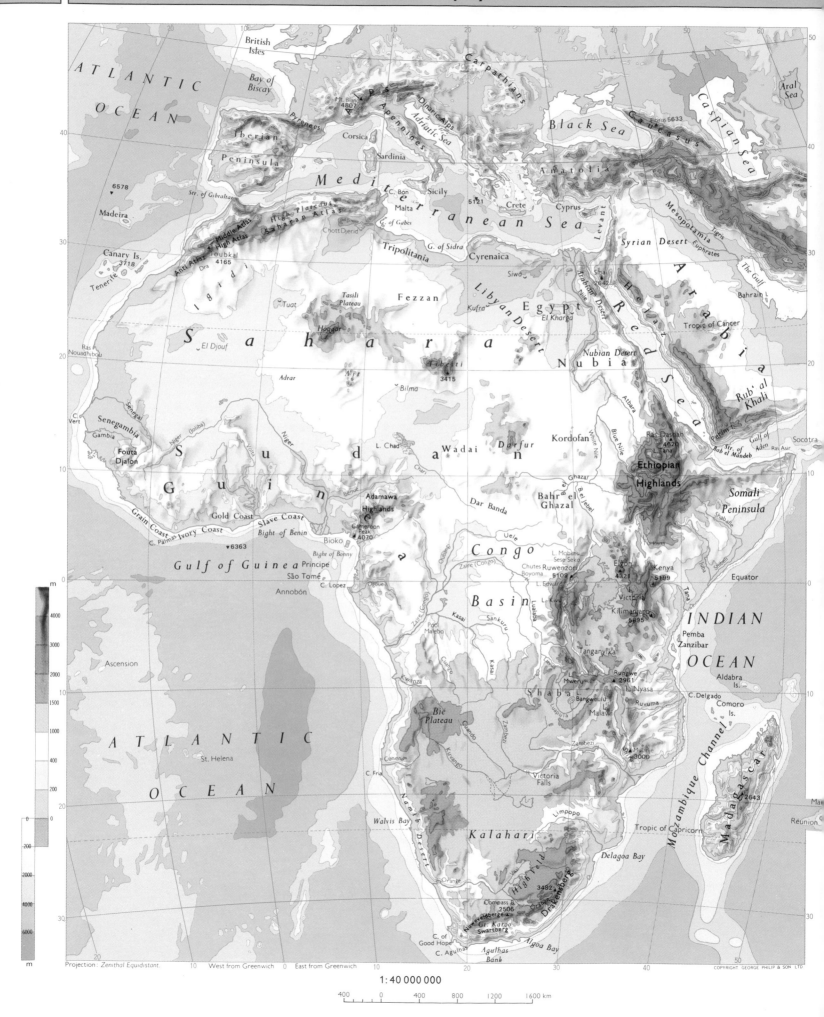

ATLANTIC OCEAN

British Isles

Bay of Biscay

Alps
Mt. Blanc 4807
Pyrenees
Iberian Peninsula
Corsica
Sardinia
Apennines
Adriatic Sea
Dinaric Alps
Carpathians
Black Sea
Caucasus
Elbrus 5633
Aral Sea
Caspian Sea

Madeira
6578

Str. of Gibraltar
C. Bon
Sicily
Malta
Crete
Cyprus
Anatolia
5121

Mediterranean Sea

Levant
Mesopotamia
Tigris
Euphrates
Syrian Desert

Canary Is.
Tenerife 3718
Ras Nouadhibou

Middle Atlas
High Plateaus
Saharan Atlas
High Atlas
Toubkal 4165
Anti Atlas
Dra

G. of Gabes
Chott Djerid
Tripolitania
G. of Sidra
Cyrenaica

Arabia
The Gulf
Bahrain
Tropic of Cancer

Igidi
Tuat
Tasili Plateau
Fezzan

Libyan Desert
Siwa
Kufra
El Kharga
Egypt
Arabian Desert
Nile

Sahara
Hoggar

Adrar
Air
Bilma

Tibesti
3415

Nubian Desert
Nubia

Red Sea
Atbara
Shan 26 42

Hejaz
Perim
Str. of Bab el Mandeb
Gulf of Aden
Socotra
Ras Asir

Rub' al Khali

El Djouf

C. Vert
Senegal
Senegambia
Gambia
Fouta Djalon

Niger (Joliba)
Volta
Niger

Sudan
L. Chad
Wadai
Chari

Darfur
Kordofan
White Nile
Blue Nile

Ras Dashan 4620
L. Tana
Ethiopian Highlands

Somali Peninsula
Shabelle

Guinea

Grain Coast
Gold Coast
Slave Coast
Ivory Coast
C. Palmas
Bight of Benin
Bioko
6363

Adamawa Highlands
Cameroon Peak 4070

Benue
Dar Banda
Bahr el Ghazal
Bahr el Ghazal
B. el Jebel

L. Moburu Sese Seko
L. Edward
L. Kivu

Elgon 4321
Ruwenzori 5109
Kenya 5199
Equator

INDIAN OCEAN

Gulf of Guinea
Principe
São Tomé
Annobón
C. Lopez
Ogoue

Congo Basin

Zaire (Congo)
Ubangi
Uele
Chutes Boyoma

Victoria
L.
Kilimanjaro 5895

Pemba
Zanzibar

Ascension

Zaire (Congo)
Kasai
Lualaba
Sankuru
Kasai

L. Tanganyika
Lomami

Rungwe 2961
L. Nyasa
Aldabra Is.
C. Delgado
Comoro Is.

ATLANTIC OCEAN
St. Helena

Kwanza
Cuango
Culozo

Mweru
L. Bangweulu
Luapula
Malawi
Ruvuma

Bié Plateau

Cuando
Cubango
Conene
C. Fria

Shaba
Luangwa
Zambezi

Zambezi
Muchinje 3000
Victoria Falls

Mozambique Channel
Madagascar
2643
Ma
Réunion

Kalahari
Namib Desert
Walvis Bay
Limpopo

Tropic of Capricorn

Delagoa Bay

Orange
High Veld
Vaal
3482
Drakensberg

Compass B. 2506
Karoo
Gr. Karoo
Swartberg
Nieuwveld
C. of Good Hope
C. Agulhas
Algoa Bay
Agulhas Bank

m
4000
3000
2000
1500
1000
400
200
0
0
200
2000
4000
6000
m

Projection: Zenithal Equidistant.   West from Greenwich   East from Greenwich   COPYRIGHT GEORGE PHILIP & SON LTD

1:40 000 000

400   0   400   800   1200   1600 km

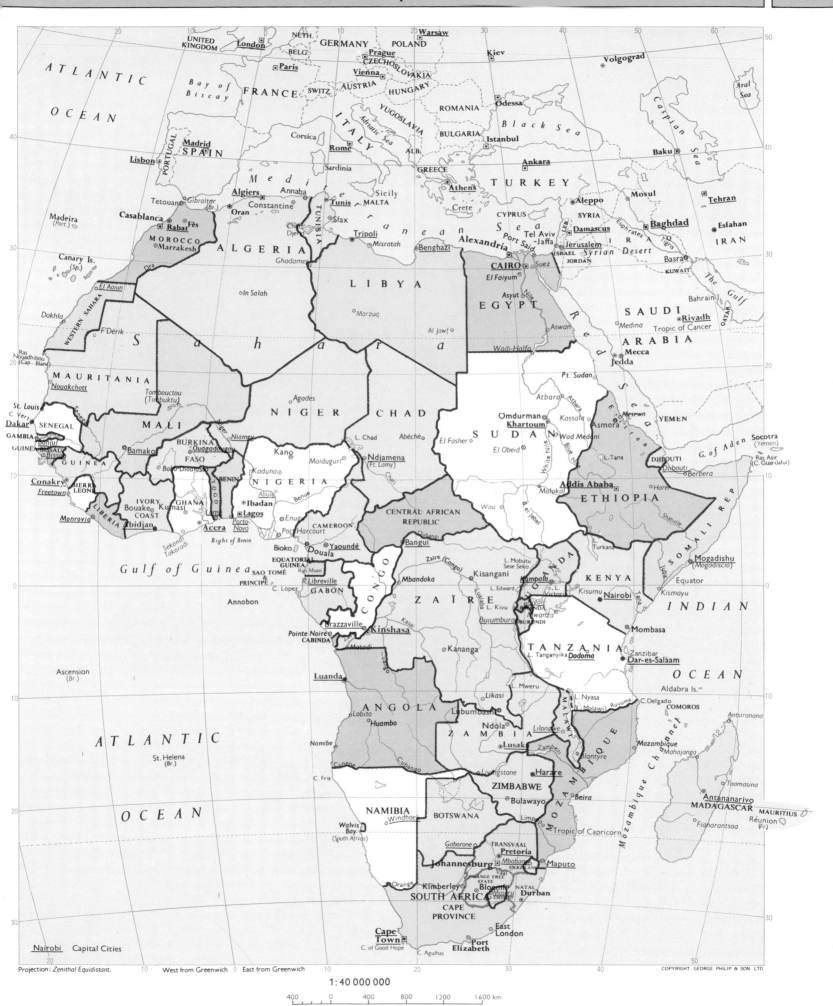

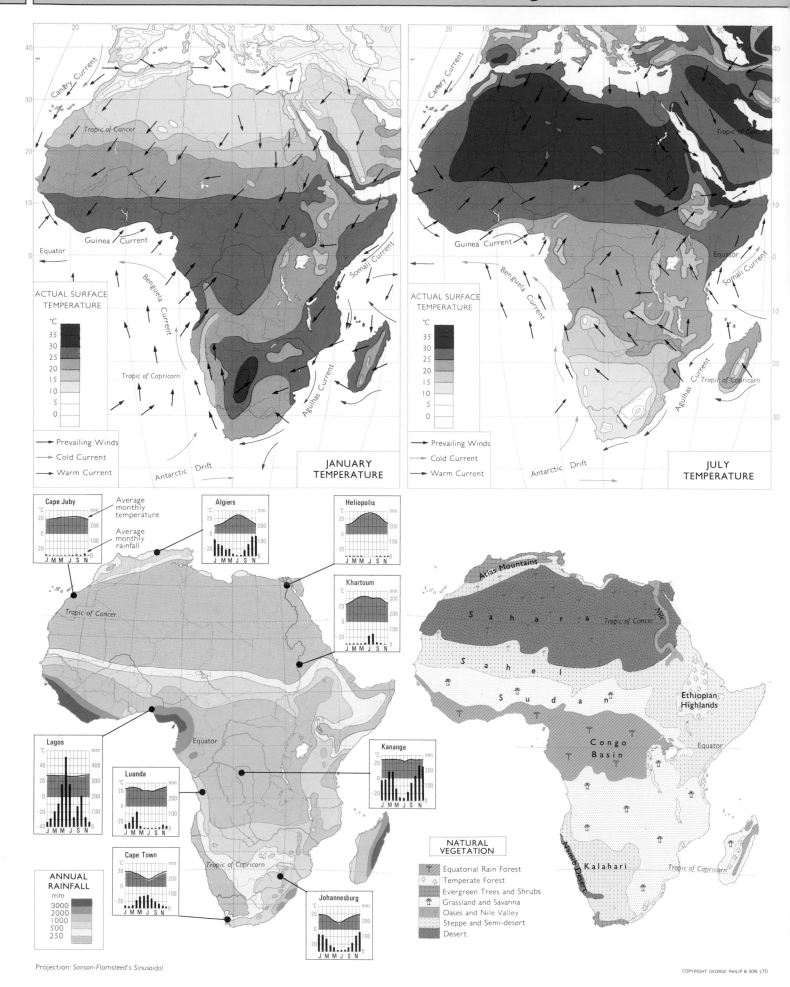

ACTUAL SURFACE TEMPERATURE

°C
35
30
25
20
15
10
5
0

→ Prevailing Winds
→ Cold Current
→ Warm Current

Canary Current
Tropic of Cancer
Guinea Current
Equator
Benguela Current
Somali Current
Tropic of Capricorn
Agulhas Current
Antarctic Drift

JANUARY TEMPERATURE

ACTUAL SURFACE TEMPERATURE

°C
35
30
25
20
15
10
5
0

→ Prevailing Winds
→ Cold Current
→ Warm Current

Canary Current
Tropic of Cancer
Guinea Current
Benguela Current
Equator
Somali Current
Tropic of Capricorn
Agulhas Current
Antarctic Drift

JULY TEMPERATURE

Cape Juby
Average monthly temperature
Average monthly rainfall

Algiers

Heliopolis

Khartoum

Tropic of Cancer

Lagos

Equator

Luanda

Kananga

Cape Town

Tropic of Capricorn

Johannesburg

ANNUAL RAINFALL

mm
3000
2000
1000
500
250

Atlas Mountains

S a h a r a
Tropic of Cancer
Nile

S a h e l

S u d a n

Ethiopian Highlands

Congo Basin

Equator

Namib Desert

K a l a h a r i
Tropic of Capricorn

NATURAL VEGETATION

Equatorial Rain Forest
Temperate Forest
Evergreen Trees and Shrubs
Grassland and Savanna
Oases and Nile Valley
Steppe and Semi-desert
Desert

Projection: *Sanson-Flamsteed's Sinusoidal*

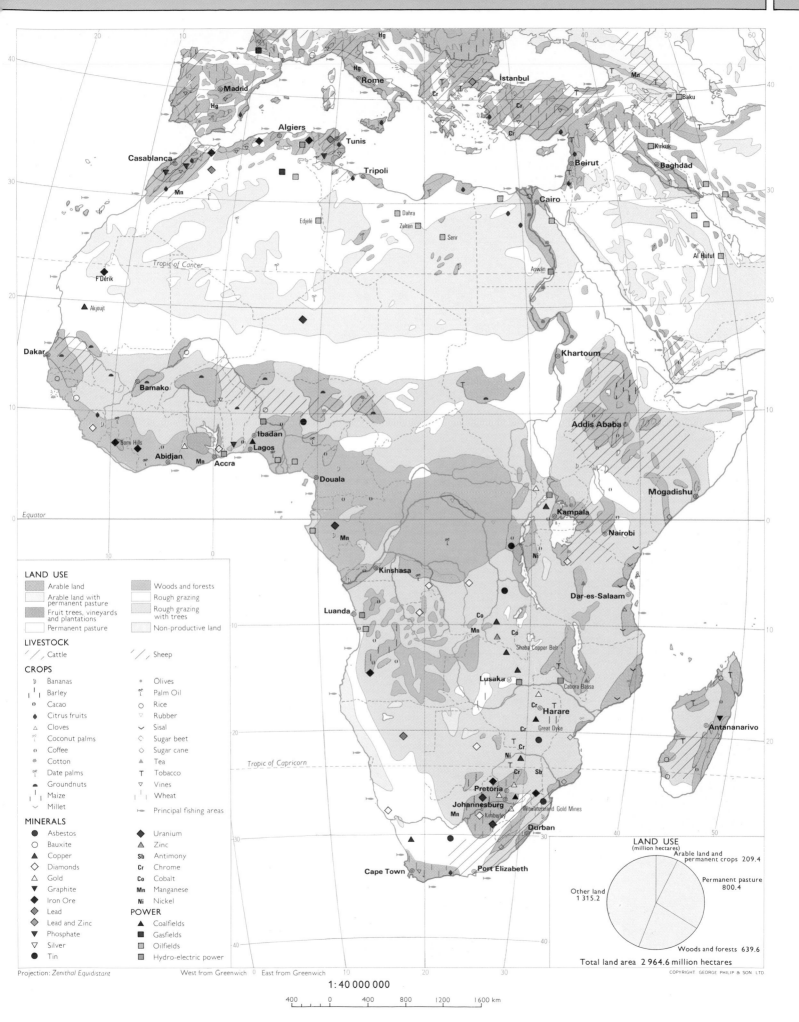

LAND USE

- Arable land
- Arable land with permanent pasture
- Fruit trees, vineyards and plantations
- Permanent pasture
- Woods and forests
- Rough grazing
- Rough grazing with trees
- Non-productive land

LIVESTOCK

- / / Cattle
- / / Sheep

CROPS

Ɗ Bananas	• Olives
Barley	↑ Palm Oil
ᴑ Cacao	○ Rice
♦ Citrus fruits	▽ Rubber
△ Cloves	◇ Sisal
⋏ Coconut palms	◇ Sugar beet
ᴑ Coffee	◇ Sugar cane
❀ Cotton	▲ Tea
↑ Date palms	T Tobacco
⚲ Groundnuts	▽ Vines
Maize	Wheat
ᴗ Millet	↦ Principal fishing areas

MINERALS

● Asbestos	◆ Uranium
○ Bauxite	△ Zinc
▲ Copper	Sb Antimony
◇ Diamonds	Cr Chrome
△ Gold	Co Cobalt
▼ Graphite	Mn Manganese
◆ Iron Ore	Ni Nickel
◈ Lead	
◈ Lead and Zinc	**POWER**
▽ Silver	▲ Coalfields
● Tin	■ Gasfields
	■ Oilfields
	■ Hydro-electric power

LAND USE
(million hectares)

- Arable land and permanent crops 209.4
- Permanent pasture 800.4
- Other land 1 315.2
- Woods and forests 639.6

Total land area 2 964.6 million hectares

Projection: *Zenithal Equidistant*

West from Greenwich   East from Greenwich

COPYRIGHT GEORGE PHILIP & SON LTD

1 : 40 000 000

400   0   400   800   1200   1 600 km

AFRICA: *statistics*

	Population								Land			Agriculture		
	Total	Density	Birth Rate	Death Rate	Life Expectancy	Growth 1965-80	Growth 1980-88	Urban	Area	Arable	Forest	Agricultural Population	Index of Production	Food Intake
	th.	persons per km²	per th. popn.	per th. popn.	yrs.	av. % per annum	av. % per annum	%	th. km²	th. km²	th. km²	% of total popn.	1979-81 = 100	calories per day
Algeria	23805	10	40	9	63	3.1	3.1	44	2382	75	47	25	121	2715
Angola	9421	8	47	20	45	2.8	2.5	25	1247	36	531	71	104	1969
Benin	4454	40	51	19	51	2.7	3.2	39	111	18	36	64	143	2184
Botswana	1164	2	47	12	68	3.5	3.3	21	585	14	10	65	100	2201
Burkina Faso	8546	31	47	19	47	2	2.6	8	274	31	68	85	148	2139
Burundi	5149	198	46	17	49	1.9	2.9	7	26	13	0.7	92	128	2343
Cameroon	11213	24	42	16	57	2.7	3.2	46	469	70	249	64	118	2028
Central Africa	2794	4	44	20	48	1.8	2.5	45	623	20	358	66	101	1949
Chad	5399	4	44	20	46	2	2.4	30	1259	32	130	77	127	1717
Congo	2100	6	44	17	59	2.7	3.4	41	342	7	212	60	116	2619
Egypt	51447	52	41	9	61	2.4	2.7	48	995	26	0.03	42	148	3342
Ethiopia	46144	42	44	24	48	2.7	2.5	12	1101	139	451	76	108	1749
Gabon	1077	4	39	16	53	3.5	3.9	43	258	5	200	70	112	2521
Gambia	822	82	47	21	44	2.6	3.3	21	10	2	2	82	131	2251
Ghana	14040	61	44	13	54	2.2	3.5	32	230	29	83	52	142	1759
Guinea	6641	27	47	22	42	1.9	2.4	24	246	16	100	76	109	1777
Guinea-Bissau	940	34	41	20	40	1.4	1.9	27	28	3	11	80	155	2505
Ivory Coast	11587	36	51	14	53	4.2	4.2	44	318	36	64	59	131	2562
Kenya	23021	40	54	12	56	3.6	4.2	22	569	24	37	78	125	2060
Lesotho	1673	56	41	12	56	2.3	2.7	19	30	3	0	82	108	2303
Liberia	2401	25	45	13	55	3	3.3	42	96	4	21	71	120	2381
Libya	4249	2	38	9	61	4.6	4.3	67	1760	22	7	13	126	3601
Madagascar	11259	19	46	14	54	2.5	3.3	23	582	31	147	78	117	2440
Malawi	8155	87	49	25	46	2.9	3.8	13	94	24	43	78	108	2310
Mali	7989	7	47	20	47	2.1	2.4	19	1220		85	82	135	2074
Mauritania	1907	2	46	19	46	2.3	2.6	38	1030	2	150	66	112	2322
Morocco	23920	54	35	10	61	2.5	2.7	47	446	85	52	39	150	2915
Mozambique	14967	19	45	19	48	2.5	2.7	23	784	31	149	83	103	1595
Namibia	1262	2	44	12	57		3.2	51	823	7	184	37	126	2197
Niger	6998	6	51	21	45	2.7	3	18	1267	35	25	89	124	2432
Nigeria	110131	121	50	16	52	2.5	3.4	33	911	313	143	66	126	2146
Rwanda	6657	266	51	17	49	3.3	3.3	7	25	11	5	92	97	1830
Senegal	7154	37	46	19	48	2.5	2.9	37	192	52	59	79	127	2350
Sierra Leone	3938	55	48	23	42	2	2.4	26	72	18	21	65	108	1855
Somalia	5882	9	51	20	47	2.7	2.9	36	627	9	88	72	131	2135
South Africa	33938	28	32	10	61	2.4	2.3	57	1221	132	45	15	104	2924
Sudan	23776	10	45	16	50	3	3.1	21	2376	125	468	64	128	2208
Swaziland	737	43	47	13	56		3.4	26	17	2	1	69	127	2553
Tanzania	24739	28	51	14	53	3.3	3.5	29	886	52	424	82	116	2192
Togo	3362	62	45	14	53	3	3.4	24	54	14	14	71	111	2207
Tunisia	7796	50	28	7	66	2.1	2.5	54	155	47	6	27	110	2994
Uganda	16195	81	50	15	51	2.9	3.2	10	200	67	57	82	108	2344
Zaire	33615	15	46	14	53	2.8	3.1	38	2268	67	1753	68	120	2164
Zambia	7486	10	51	14	54	3.1	3.6	53	741	52	292	70	126	2137
Zimbabwe	9257	24	42	10	63	3.1	3.6	26	387	28	199	70	123	2132

For explanations and metric/imperial conversion note see the statistics tables for Europe, Asia or the Americas.

Trade		Education		Health	Energy	Consumer Price Index	G.N.P.		G.D.P.		Loans & Debt		
Imports	Exports	Primary	Secondary					Growth per capita	Part formed by Agric.	Part formed by Indust.			
US$ per capita	US$ per capita	% of age group	% of age group	Popn. per doctor	Consumption in kg of oil equiv. per capita	1980 = 100	US$ per capita	% per year 1965-88	%	%	end 1987 US$ millions	as % of G.N.P.	
295	343	95	54	2327	1003	153	2680	3.2	12	42	18574	34	Algeria
72	195	93	13	17784	203			−4.8	10	39			Angola
94	38	65	16	15937	46		310	0.2	46	14	907	51	Benin
		100	31	6910	429	189	1050	8.9	3	57	518		Botswana
63	24	35	6	57183	18	139	190	1.6	38	25	825	44	Burkina Faso
40	16	59	4	21120	20	166	250	1.6	59	14	745	68	Burundi
193	153	100	23	13990	144	203	970	3.8	24	31	3002	23	Cameroon
67	47	66	13	23067	30	140	330	−0.3	41	13	573	51	Central Africa
30	26	43	6	38358	18	160	150	−2	43	18	280	35	Chad
271	421	100	52	8138	223	178	870	4.2	12	33	694	171	Congo
164	78	87	66	786	588	118	680	3.5	21	25	39338	104	Egypt
25	9	36	12	77356	21	127	130	0.1	42	18	2526	46	Ethiopia
776	1193	100	27	2793	1121	168	2700	1.1	11	14	1893	55	Gabon
168	140	75	20	11688	68	331			28	7	283	99	Gambia
60	75	63	35	14894	129	1583	390	−1.6	51	16	2390	46	Ghana
56	70	29	9	57390	59		350		40	22	1678	75	Guinea
78	26	60	11	7262	37						351	271	Guinea-Bissau
187	257	78	20	15234	172	154	740	1	36	25	12632	127	Ivory Coast
76	42	94	20	10101	99	233	330	1.9	31	19	5178	61	Kenya
		100	22	18614	10	287	370	4.7	21	28	373	101	Lesotho
87	160	66	20	9240	169	129	450	−1.6	37	28	1618		Liberia
1148	2524	100	87	694	2674		5460	−2.3	2	65			Libya
34	28	100	36	10002	39	416	210	−1.8	43	16	3235	172	Madagascar
34	32	64	4	11564	40	337	160	1.4	37	18	1228	85	Malawi
56	27	22	7	23487	24	230	210	1.6	54	12	1924	99	Mali
249	224	46	15	12113	113	480	440	−0.4	37	22	1931	193	Mauritania
177	117	79	34	4749	242	179	610	1.8	19	31	19500	103	Morocco
32	6	82	7	37949	86		170		50	12			Mozambique
		100	45										Namibia
60	52	29	6	38775	42	130	260	−2.2	34	24	1561	65	Niger
71	67	92	29	7978	133	274	370	1.1	30	43	29721	98	Nigeria
53	18	67	3	34681	42	145	300	1.6	37	23	565	26	Rwanda
164	90	55	13	13445	155	178	520	−0.6	22	27	3290	66	Senegal
34	30	58	17	13626	77	3952	300	0.2	45	19	659		Sierra Leone
77	16	20	12	16089	81	1113	290	0.3	65	9	1733	173	Somalia
431	591	100	39	1906	2465	299	1890	0.6	6	44			South Africa
29	20	50	20	10108	58	598	330	−0.5	37	15	8468	96	Sudan
		100	43	18848	291	253	790		21	20			Swaziland
47	14	69	3	26552	35	643	180	−0.4	61	8	4316	151	Tanzania
124	88	100	21	8724	52	144	290	0	29	18	1042	85	Togo
388	276	100	39	2154	496	191	1180	3.6	18	32	6012	60	Tunisia
29	20	58	8	21903	26	11644	260	−2.7	76	5	1256	23	Uganda
34	47	76	22	13041	73	1714	150	−2.4	32	33	7211	111	Zaire
100	116	100	19	7102	380	846	250	−2.1	12	36	4330	144	Zambia
114	147	100	46	7188	512	255	580	0.9	11	43	2537	40	Zimbabwe

Cape Verde, Land 4.0/Popn. 359; Comoros 2.2/434; Djibouti 22/484; Eq. Guinea 28/300; Mauritius 1.9/1056; Reunion 2.5/575; St. Helena 0.3/6; Sao Tome 0.9/115; Seychelles 0.3/67; Western Sahara 266/180.

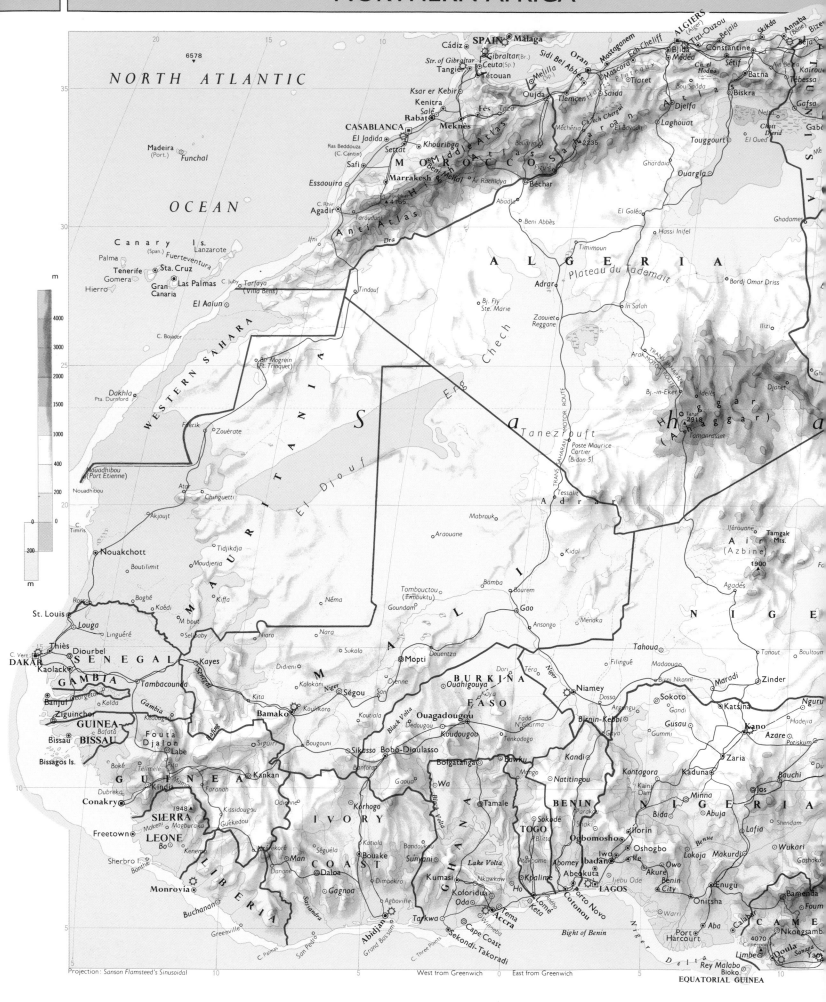

NORTH ATLANTIC

OCEAN

SPAIN
Málaga
Cádiz
Gibraltar (Br.)
Str. of Gibraltar
Ceuta (Sp.)
Tangier
Tétouan
Ksar er Kebir
Kenitra
Salé
Rabat
Meknès
CASABLANCA
El Jadida
Ras Beddouza
(C. Cantin)
Settat
Khouribga
Safi
MOROCCO
Marrakesh
Essaouira
Beni Mellal
Ar Rachidya
C. Rhir
Agadir
Taroudant
Dj. Toubkal
4165
Anti Atlas
Ifni
Dra
Abadla

ALGIERS (Alger)
Tizi-Ouzou
Bejaia
Skikda
Annaba (Bône)
Blida
Médéa
Constantine
Sétif
Mostaganem
Oran
Sidi Bel Abbès
Mascara
Tlemcen
Oujda
Fès
Taza
Saïda
Mécheria
El Bayadh
Chech Chergui
Hauts Plateaux
Ch. el Hodna
Batna
Ain Beïda
Tébessa
Kairou
Bou Saâda
Biskra
Djelfa
Laghouat
TUNISIA
Gafsa
Gabès
Né
Chott Djerid
El Oued
Touggourt
Béchar
4235
Ghardaïa
Ouargla
Ghadamès
El Goléa
Beni Abbès
Hassi Inifel
Timimoun

ALGERIA
Plateau du Tademaït
Adrar
Bordj Omar Driss
In Salah
Zaouiet Reggane
Bj. Fly Ste. Marie
Chech
Ilizi
Arak
TRANS-SAHARAN MOTOR ROUTE
Bj.-in-Eker
Idélès
Djanet
Hoggar
(Ahaggar)
Tahat
2918
Tamanrasset

Madeira (Port.)
Funchal

Canary Is.
Lanzarote
(Span.)
Fuerteventura
Palma
Tenerife
Sta. Cruz
Gomera
Gran Canaria
Hierro
Las Palmas
C. Juby
Tarfaya (Villa Bens)
El Aaiun
C. Bojador

WESTERN SAHARA
Dakhla
Pta. Durnford
Tindouf
Bir Mogreïn (Ft. Trinquet)
Fderik
Zouérate

MAURITANIA
Nouadhibou (Port Etienne)
Nouadhibou
C. Timris
Atar
Chinguetti
Akjoujt
Nouakchott
Boutilimit
Tidjikdja
Moudjeria
M bout

El Djouf
El Mreïti
Tanezrouft
Poste Maurice Cortier (Bidon 5)
Tessalit
Adrar

MALI
Mabrouk
Araouane
Kidal
Iférouane
Tamgak Mts.
Aïr (Azbine)
1900
Agadès
NIGER
Tombouctou (Timbuktu)
Bourem
Bamba
Goundam
Gao
Ansongo
Ménaka
Tahoua
Tanout
Boultoum

St. Louis
Louga
Linguère
Thiès
C. Vert
DAKAR
Kaolack
SENEGAL
Diourbel
Rosso
Boghé
Kaédi
M bout
Selibaby
Kiffa
Nara
Niaro
Sokolo
Douentza
Mopti
Filingué
Madaoua
Birni Nkonni
Maradi
Zinder
Nguru
GAMBIA
Banjul
Georgetown
Kolda
Tambacounda
Kayes
Kita
Didieni
Kolokani
Niger
Ségou
San
Djenné
Ouahigouya
Dori
Téra
Niamey
Dosso
Gaya
Birni Nkonni
Gandi
Gusau
Sokoto
Katsina
Hadejia
Azare
Kano
Ziguinchor
GUINEA BISSAU
Bissau
Bafatá
Bissagos Is.
Fouta Djalon
Labé
Gambia
Kédougou
Siguiri
Bamako
Koulikoro
Bougouni
Koutiala
Sikasso
BURKINA FASO
Ouagadougou
Dédougou
Koudougou
Fada N'Gourma
Tenkodogo
Argungu
Kainji Dam
Kontagora
Kaduna
Zaria
Kano
Minna
Bida
Abuja
Bauchi
Jos
Boké
Télimélé
Kindia
GUINEA
Kankan
Faranah
Bobo-Dioulasso
Banfora
Bolgatanga
Bawku
Mango
Natitingou
NIGERIA
Conakry
Dubreka
Kissidougou
Guéckédou
Odienné
Korhogo
Wa
Tamale
Sokodé
Ilorin
Oshogbo
Owo
Benin City
Lafia
Wukari
Shendam
SIERRA LEONE
1948
Makeni
Magburaka
Kenema
Bo
Man
Danané
IVORY COAST
Séguéla
Katiola
Bouake
Bondoukou
Sunyani
Kumasi
GHANA
Black Volta
Atakpame
BENIN
Parakou
Shaki
Iwo
Ife
Akure
Enugu
Aba
Freetown
Sherbro I.
Bontse
Mékoré
Gagnoa
Daloa
Dimbokro
Lake Volta
Nkawkaw
Ho
Kpalimé
TOGO
Abomey
Ibadan
Abeokuta
Ijebu Ode
Owo
Onitsha
Calabar
CAME
Bamenda
LIBERIA
Monrovia
Buchanan
Greenville
C. Palmas
San Pedro
Sassandra
Gagnoa
Agboville
Tarkwa
Koforidua
Oda
Accra
Tema
Winneba
Cape Coast
Sekondi-Takoradi
C. Three Points
Keta
Lomé
Cotonou
Porto Novo
LAGOS
Ikeja
Bight of Benin
Warri
Port Harcourt
Niger Delta
Rey Malabo
Bioko
Limbe
Douala
Nkongsamb
4070
Yao
EQUATORIAL GUINEA

m
4000
3000
2000
1500
1000
400
200
0
0
200
m

6578

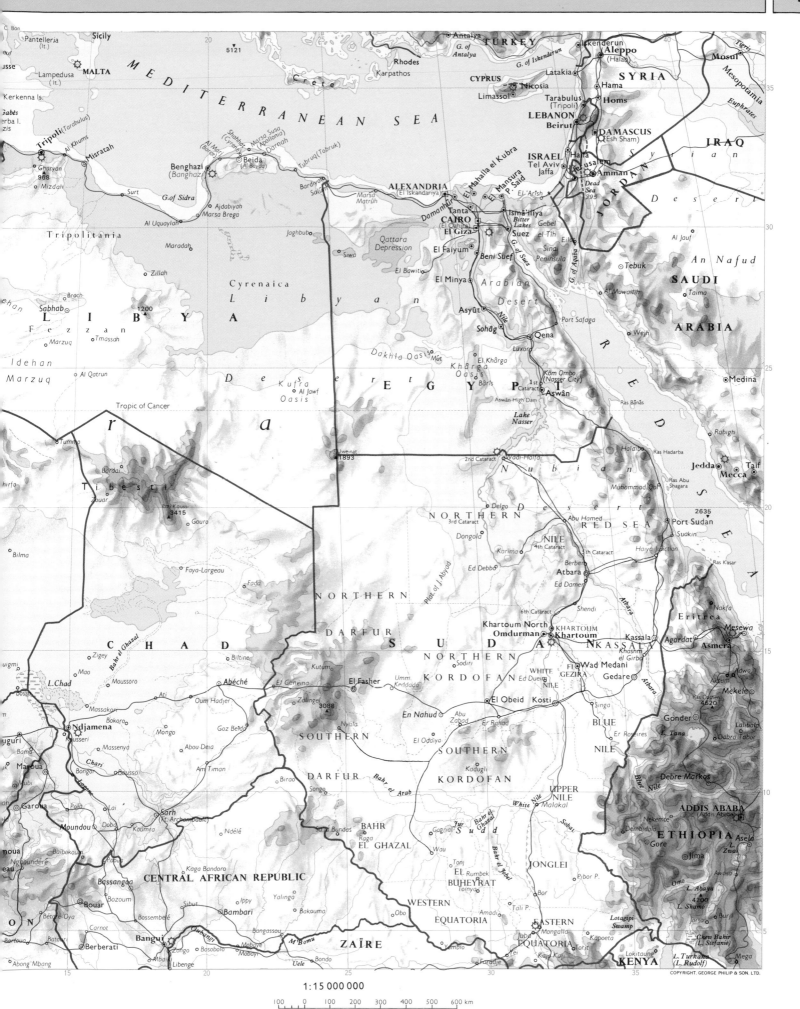

MEDITERRANEAN SEA

C. Bon
Pantelleria (It.)
Sicily
Lampedusa (It.)
MALTA
Kerkenna Is.
Gabès
erba I.
zis
Tripoli (Tarabulus)
Al Khums
Misratah
Gharyan
968
Mizdah
Surt
G. of Sidra
Ajdabiyah
Marsa Brega
Al Uquaylah
Tripolitania
Maradah
Zillah
Sabhah
Brach
1200
L I B Y A
Fezzan
Marzuq
Tmassah
Idehan
Marzuq
Al Qatrun

TURKEY
Antalya
G. of Antalya
Rhodes
Crete
Karpathos
CYPRUS
Nicosia
Limassol
Iskenderun
Aleppo (Halab)
Latakia
G. of Iskenderun
Mosul
SYRIA
Hama
Homs
Tarabulus (Tripoli)
LEBANON
Beirut
DAMASCUS (Esh Sham)
IRAQ
Mesopotamia
Euphrates
Tigris
ISRAEL
Tel Aviv
Jaffa
Haifa
Jerusalem
Amman
JORDAN
Dead Sea -395
Desert
An Nafud
SAUDI
ARABIA
Al Jauf
Tebuk
Al Muwailih
Taima
Medina
Rabigh
Jedda
Mecca
Taif

5121
20
Shahhat (Cyrene)
Marsa Susa (Apollonia)
Al Marj (Barke)
Benghazi (Banghazi)
Beida (Al Bayda)
Darnah
Tubruq (Tobruk)
Bardiyah
Salum
Marsa Matruh
ALEXANDRIA (El Iskandariya)
El Mahalla el Kubra
El Mansura
P. Said
El 'Arish
Damanhur
Tanta
CAIRO (El Qahira)
El Giza
Ismâ'iliya
Bitter Lakes
Suez
Gebel el Tih
El Faiyum
Beni Suef
Sinai Peninsula
Eilat
G. of Suez
G. of Aqaba
Jaghbub
Siwa
El Bawiti
El Minya
Arabian
Asyut
Sohâg
Qena
Desert
Port Safaga
Wejh
Nile
Luxor
Dakhla Oasis
Mut
El Khârga
Kharga Oasis
Baris
Kôm Ombo (Nasser City)
Aswân
1st Cataract
Aswân High Dam
E G Y P T
Lake Nasser
RED
Ras Bânas
Halaib
Ras Hadarba
SEA

Cyrenaica
Libyan
Desert
Tropic of Cancer
Tummo
Bordai
Tibesti
Emi Koussi 3415
Gouro
Fada
Faya-Largeau
Bilma
Zouar
Uweinat 1893
2nd Cataract
Wadi Halfa
Nubian
Desert
2635
Muhammad Qol
Ras Abu Shagara
Port Sudan
Suakin
NORTHERN
Delgo
3rd Cataract
Abu Hamed
RED SEA
Dongola
Karima
4th Cataract
5th Cataract
NILE
Haiya Junction
Ras Kasar

a
r
Kufra Oasis
Al Jawf
Ed Debba
Plat. of J. Abyad
Berber
Ed Damer
Atbara
Atbara
Eritrea
Nakfa
ghirfa
NORTHERN
6th Cataract
Shendi
Mesewa
Agordat
Asmera
Adwa

CHAD
Zigey
Mao
Moussoro
Bahr el Ghazal
Ati
DARFUR
Kutum
S U D A N
Khartoum North
Omdurman
KHARTOUM
Khartoum
Kassala
KASSALA
Khashm el Girba
Adwa
Aksum
Mekele
uigmi
L. Chad
Bol
Biltine
Abéché
El Geneina
El Fasher
NORTHERN
Sodiri
Umm Keddada
KORDOFAN
Ed Dueim
WHITE GEZIRA
NILE
Wad Medani
Gedare
4620
Ras Dashan
L'goua
Massakori
Bokoro
Mongo
Zalingei
3088
Nyala
En Nahud
Abu Zabad
El Obeid
Er Rahad
Kosti
Singa
BLUE
Gonder
L. Tana
Lalibela
Dabra Tabor
Ndjamena
Kousseri
Moussoro
Massenya
Oum Hadjer
Goz Beïda
SOUTHERN
El Odaiya
Kadugli
NILE
Er Roseires
Debre Markos
Maroua
Chari
Bongor
Bousso
Am Timan
DARFUR
Birao
Songo
Bahr el Arab
KORDOFAN
SOUTHERN
Jur
Bahr el Ghazal
Nile
Malakal
White
UPPER
NILE
Nekemte
Dembidolo
ADDIS ABABA (Addis Abeba)
Garoua
Pala
Lai
Doba
Kaumra
Sarh (Ft. Archambault)
Ndélé
Sara Bundas
BAHR
Raga
EL GHAZAL
Wau
Tonj
Rumbek
Pibor P.
Sobat
Gore
ETHIOPIA
Asela
Jima
L. Zwai
noua
Nghoundere
Baibokoum
Moundou
Bozoum
Bouar
Sibut
Ippy
Yalinga
Bakouma
Obo
CENTRAL AFRICAN REPUBLIC
BUHEYRAT
Toinya
Bor
WESTERN
Amadi
Omo
L. Abaya 4200
eau
Bétaré-Oya
Carnot
Bossangoa
Bossembélé
Bambari
Bangassou
Yalinga
Tali P.
EQUATORIA
EASTERN
Mongalla
Kapoeta
Lotagipi Swamp
L. Shamo
Jarso
Buri
ON
noua
Abong Mbang
Bouar
Batouri
Bangui
Mbaiki
Zongo
Mobaye
M'Bomu
Uele
Bondo
Yambio
Juba
Torit
EQUATORIA
Faraje
Kaji Kaji
Lokitaung
KENYA
L. Turkana (L. Rudolf)
Mega
Chew Bahir (L. Stefanie)
Berbérati
ZAÏRE

COPYRIGHT. GEORGE. PHILIP & SON. LTD.

1:15 000 000

100   0   100   200   300   400   500   600 km

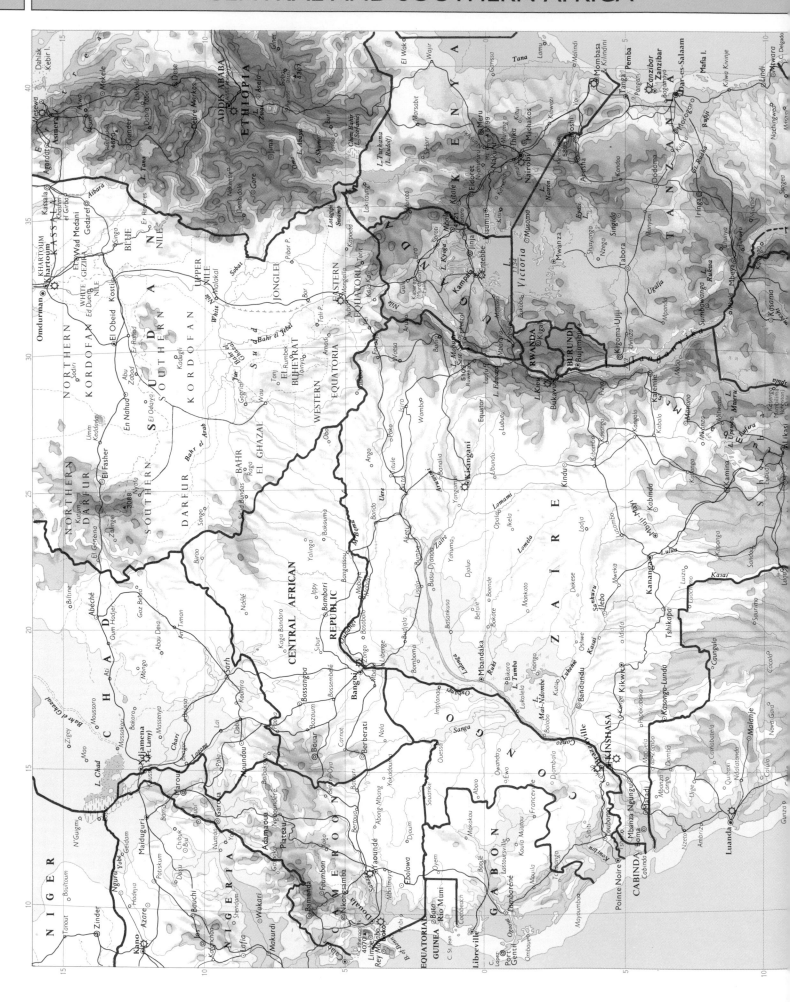

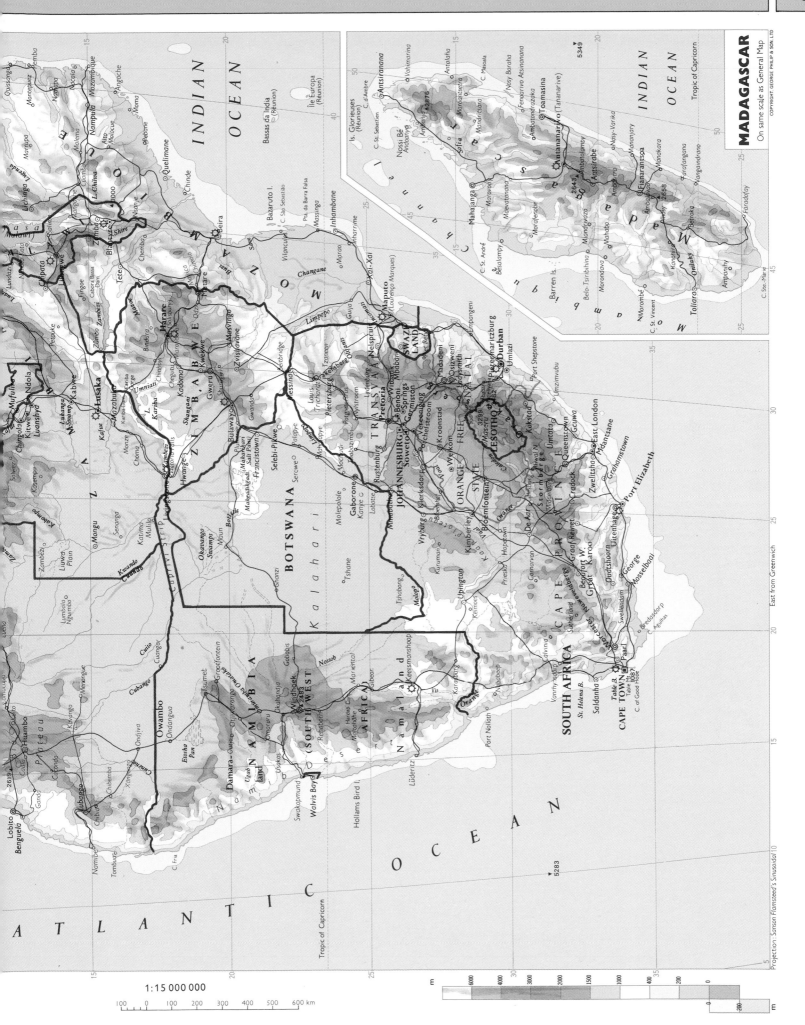

MADAGASCAR
On same scale as General Map

COPYRIGHT GEORGE PHILIP & SON LTD

INDIAN OCEAN

Tropic of Capricorn

Is. Glorieuses (Réunion)
Nossi Bé
Nosy Boraha

INDIAN OCEAN

Antsiranana
5349
Vohimarina
Antalaha
C. d'Ambre
C. Masoala
C. St. Sébastien
Andoany
Ambilobe
2876
Befandriana
Fenoarivo Atsinanana
Andapa
Bealanana
Maroantsetra
Sofia
Mandritsara
Mahajanga
Marovoay
Mananara
Ambatondrazaka
Toamasina (Tamatave)
Maevatanana
Antananarivo (Tananarive)
2643
Miandrivazo
Moramanga
Morafenobe
Ambatolampy
Antsirabe
Maintirano
Nosy-Varika
Belo-Tsiribihina
Morondava
Mananjary
Miandivazo
Manakara
C. St. André
Besalampy
2658
Ambalavao
Fianarantsoa
Farafangana
Barren Is.
Manandrano
Manja
Manombo
Vangaindrano
Belo-Tsiribihina
Morombe
Ankazoabo
N'Moromba
Toliarao (Tuléar)
Onilahy
Betroka
Ampanihy
C. St. Vincent
Faradofay
C. Ste. Marie

INDIAN OCEAN

Pemba
Mocímboa
Montepuez
Nampula
Ancuabe
Nacala
Angoche
Matuba
Moma
Quelimane
Chinde

Lichinga
L. Chirwa
Pebane

ATLANTIC OCEAN

Lobito
Benguela
2619
Namibe (Moçâmedes)
C. Fria
Tombua

NAMIBIA (SOUTH WEST AFRICA)
Walvis Bay
Swakopmund
Windhoek
2483
Hollams Bird I.
Lüderitz

BOTSWANA
Kalahari
Okavango Swamps

ZIMBABWE
Harare (Salisbury)
Bulawayo

SOUTH AFRICA
JOHANNESBURG
Soweto
Pretoria
TRANSVAAL
ORANGE FREE STATE
Bloemfontein
LESOTHO
3295
Maseru
CAPE PROVINCE
Kimberley
Durban
Port Elizabeth
East London
CAPE TOWN
Table Mt. 1087
C. of Good Hope
C. Agulhas

Tropic of Capricorn

Projection: Sanson Flamsteed's Sinusoidal 10

East from Greenwich

1:15 000 000

100   0   100   200   300   400   500   600 km

m 6000 4000 3000 2000 1500 1000 400 200 0

200 m

NORTH AMERICA: *physical*

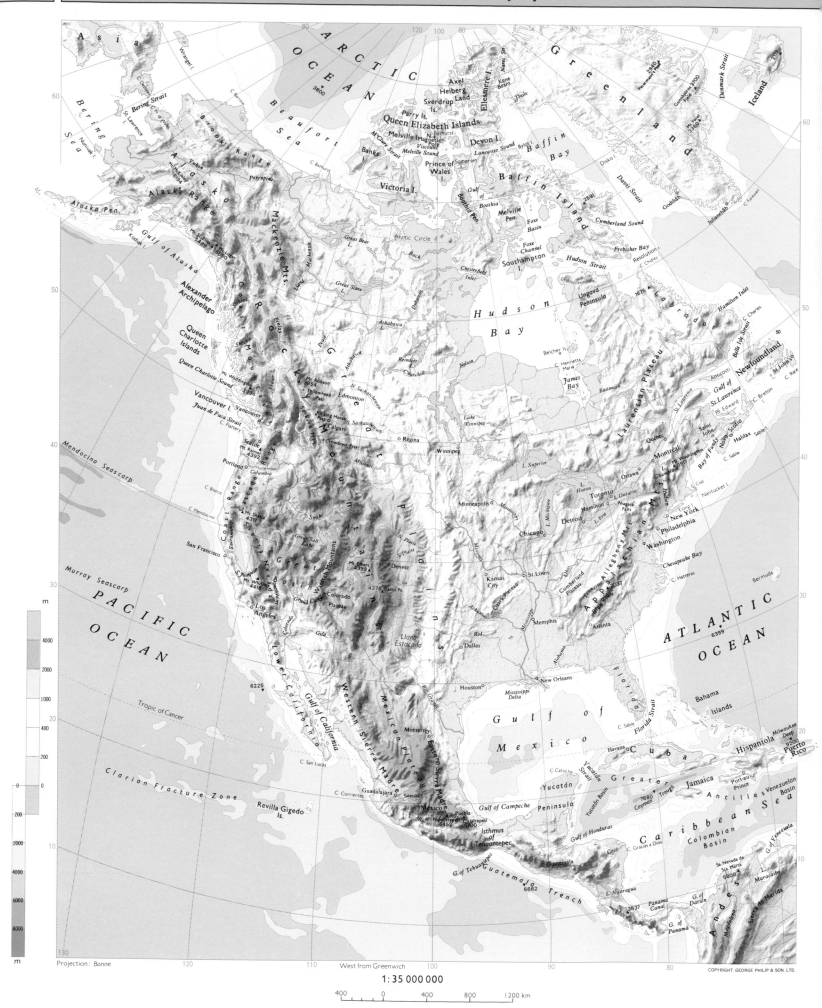

Projection: Bonne

West from Greenwich

COPYRIGHT. GEORGE PHILIP & SON, LTD.

1 : 35 000 000

400   0   400   800   1200 km

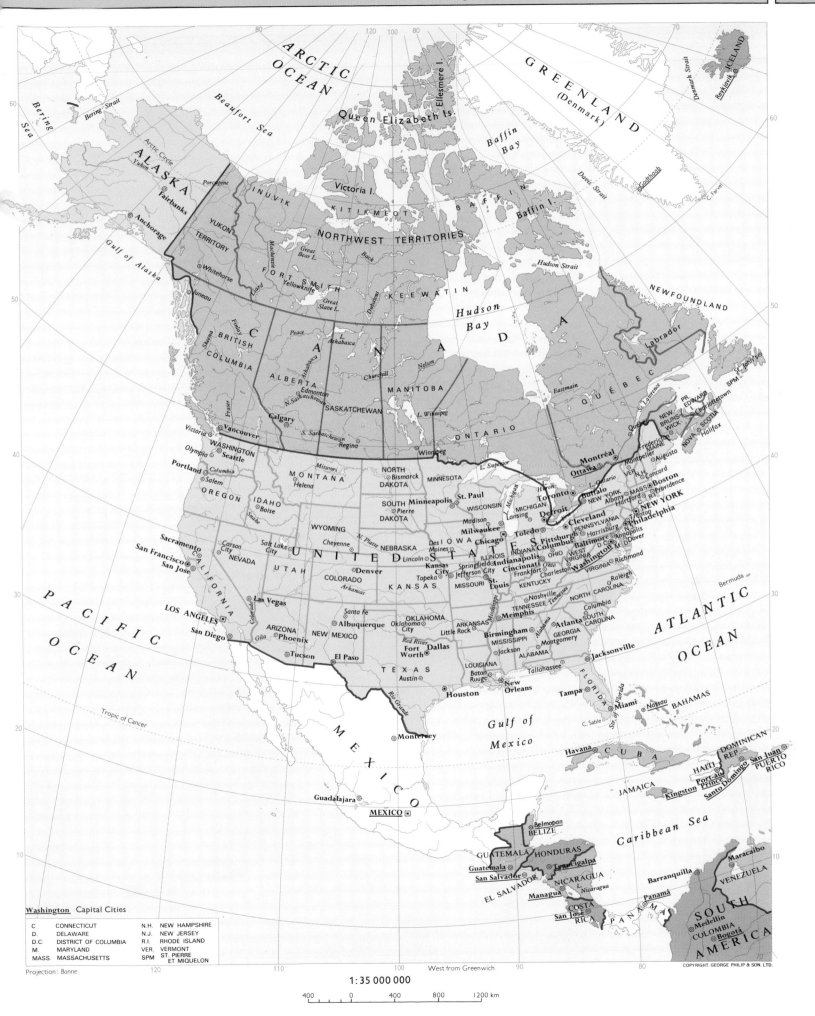

ARCTIC OCEAN

GREENLAND (Denmark)

Denmark Strait

ICELAND

Reykjavik

Bering Sea

Bering Strait

Beaufort Sea

Queen Elizabeth Is.

Ellesmere I.

Baffin Bay

Arctic Circle

ALASKA

Yukon

Fairbanks

Anchorage

Gulf of Alaska

Porcupine

INUVIK

Victoria I.

KITIKMEOT

BAFFIN

Baffin I.

Davis Strait

C. Farvel

Godthåb

YUKON TERRITORY

Whitehorse

Juneau

Liard

FORT SMITH

Yellowknife

Great Bear L.

Mackenzie

Great Slave L.

Dubawnt

Back

KEEWATIN

Hudson Strait

NEWFOUNDLAND

Skeena

Finlay

BRITISH COLUMBIA

C A N A D A

Peace

Athabasca

L. Athabasca

Churchill

Nelson

Hudson Bay

Labrador

QUÉBEC

St. John's

SPM

Fraser

ALBERTA

Edmonton

N. Saskatchewan

SASKATCHEWAN

S. Saskatchewan

MANITOBA

L. Winnipeg

Eastmain

St. Lawrence

Québec

PR. EDWARD I.

Charlottetown

NEW BRUNS- WICK

NOVA SCOTIA

Halifax

Fredericton

MAINE

Victoria

Vancouver

Calgary

Regina

ONTARIO

Winnipeg

L. Superior

Ottawa

Montréal

Montpelier

VER.

N.H.

Concord

Augusta

Olympia

WASHINGTON

Seattle

Portland

Columbia

Salem

OREGON

MONTANA

Helena

Missouri

IDAHO

Boise

Snake

NORTH DAKOTA

Bismarck

SOUTH DAKOTA

Pierre

MINNESOTA

St. Paul

Minneapolis

Madison

WISCONSIN

Michigan

MICHIGAN

Lansing

Huron

L. Ontario

Toronto

Detroit

Cleveland

Buffalo

NEW YORK

Albany

Boston

MASS.

Providence

R.I.

Hartford

C.

NEW YORK

PENNSYLVANIA

Philadelphia

Harrisburg

Trenton

N.J.

Dover

D.

WYOMING

Cheyenne

N. Platte

NEBRASKA

Lincoln

Des Moines

IOWA

Chicago

ILLINOIS

Milwaukee

Toledo

OHIO

Columbus

Pittsburgh

Indianapolis

INDIANA

Cincinnati

Frankfort

WEST VIRGINIA

Charleston

Baltimore

Annapolis

M.

D.C. Washington

Richmond

VIRGINIA

Sacramento

San Francisco

San Jose

CALIFORNIA

Carson City

NEVADA

Salt Lake City

UTAH

Denver

COLORADO

Arkansas

KANSAS

Kansas City

Topeka

Jefferson City

St. Louis

MISSOURI

Springfield

KENTUCKY

Nashville

TENNESSEE

Tennessee

NORTH CAROLINA

Raleigh

Columbia

Bermuda

LOS ANGELES

Las Vegas

Colorado

Gila

San Diego

ARIZONA

Phoenix

Tucson

Santa Fe

NEW MEXICO

Albuquerque

OKLAHOMA

Oklahoma City

Little Rock

ARKANSAS

Memphis

Mississippi

Birmingham

Montgomery

ALABAMA

Atlanta

GEORGIA

SOUTH CAROLINA

Jacksonville

ATLANTIC OCEAN

El Paso

Rio Grande

Red River

Fort Worth

Dallas

TEXAS

Austin

Houston

LOUISIANA

Baton Rouge

New Orleans

Jackson

MISSISSIPPI

Tallahassee

FLORIDA

Tampa

Miami

Str. of Florida

C. Sable

BAHAMAS

Nassau

Tropic of Cancer

UNITED STATES

PACIFIC OCEAN

MEXICO

Monterrey

Gulf of Mexico

Havana

CUBA

HAITI

DOMINICAN REP.

San Juan

PUERTO RICO

Port-au-Prince

Santo Domingo

JAMAICA

Kingston

Caribbean Sea

Guadalajara

MEXICO

Belmopan

BELIZE

GUATEMALA

HONDURAS

Tegucigalpa

Guatemala

San Salvador

EL SALVADOR

NICARAGUA

Managua

L. Nicaragua

COSTA RICA

San José

PANAMA

Panamá

Barranquilla

Maracaibo

VENEZUELA

Medellín

COLOMBIA

Bogotá

SOUTH AMERICA

Washington Capital Cities

C	CONNECTICUT	N.H.	NEW HAMPSHIRE
D.	DELAWARE	N.J.	NEW JERSEY
D.C.	DISTRICT OF COLUMBIA	R.I.	RHODE ISLAND
M.	MARYLAND	VER.	VERMONT
MASS.	MASSACHUSETTS	SPM	ST. PIERRE ET MIQUELON

Projection: Bonne

West from Greenwich

COPYRIGHT. GEORGE PHILIP & SON. LTD.

1:35 000 000

400   0   400   800   1200 km

NORTH AMERICA: *climate and natural vegetation*

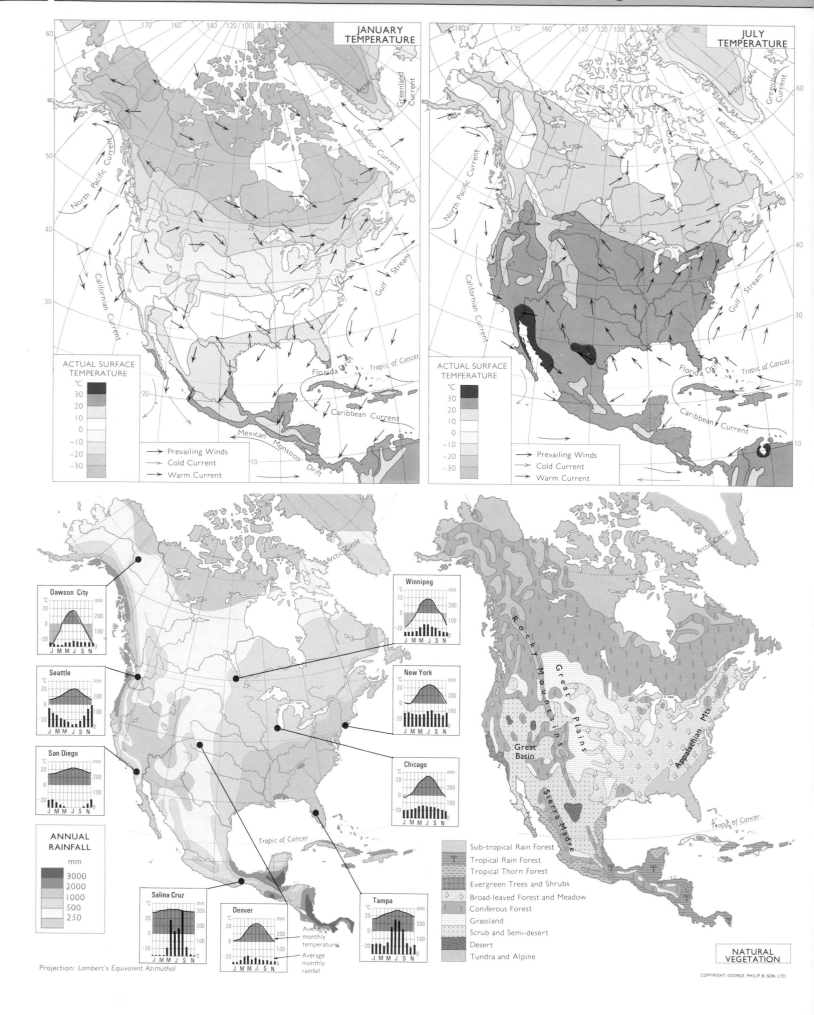

JANUARY TEMPERATURE

ACTUAL SURFACE TEMPERATURE
°C
30
20
10
0
-10
-20
-30

→ Prevailing Winds
→ Cold Current
→ Warm Current

JULY TEMPERATURE

ACTUAL SURFACE TEMPERATURE
°C
30
20
10
0
-10
-20
-30

→ Prevailing Winds
→ Cold Current
→ Warm Current

Dawson City
Seattle
San Diego
Winnipeg
New York
Chicago
Salina Cruz
Denver
Tampa

ANNUAL RAINFALL
mm
3000
2000
1000
500
250

Average monthly temperature
Average monthly rainfall

Projection: Lambert's Equivalent Azimuthal

NATURAL VEGETATION

Sub-tropical Rain Forest
Tropical Rain Forest
Tropical Thorn Forest
Evergreen Trees and Shrubs
Broad-leaved Forest and Meadow
Coniferous Forest
Grassland
Scrub and Semi-desert
Desert
Tundra and Alpine

COPYRIGHT. GEORGE PHILIP & SON. LTD.

LAND USE
- Arable land
- Arable land with grazing
- Market gardening, fruit trees, bushes and orchard land
- Permanent pasture
- Woods and forests
- Woods and forests with grazing land
- Rough grazing
- Non-productive land

LIVESTOCK
- Beef cattle
- Sheep
- Dairy cattle

CROPS
- ⋎ Bananas
- ● Citrus fruits
- ⌒ Coffee
- ● Cotton
- • Fruit
- ⚊ Groundnuts
- ⦀ Maize
- • Olives
- ○ Rice
- ⋎ Sisal
- • Soybeans
- ◇ Sugar cane
- T Tobacco
- ▼ Vegetables
- ⦀ Wheat
- → Principal fishing areas

MINERALS
- ● Asbestos
- ○ Bauxite
- ▲ Copper
- △ Gold
- ◆ Iron ore
- ◆ Lead
- ◆ Lead and Zinc
- ● Mica
- ▼ Phosphate
- ▽ Silver
- ◆ Uranium
- ▲ Zinc
- **Sb** Antimony
- **Co** Cobalt
- **Mg** Magnesium
- **Hg** Mercury
- **Mo** Molybdenum
- **Ni** Nickel
- **Ti** Titanium

POWER
- ▲ Coalfields
- ■ Gasfields
- ▣ Oilfields
- ▢ HEP

LAND USE (million hectares)
- Arable land and permanent crops 271.5
- Permanent pasture 346.7
- Woods and forests 718.3
- Other land 803.9

Total land area 2140.5 million hectares

Projection: Polyconic

1:32 000 000

400 0 400 800 1200 km

West from Greenwich

Map labels: Prudhoe Bay, Mayo, Mo, Pine Point, Schefferville, Wabush, Flin Flon, Edmonton, Ti, Vancouver, Mo, Timmins, Montréal, Seattle, Co, Ni, Shoshone, Mesabi, Toronto, Ti, Niagara, Detroit, New York, Chicago, Washington, Salt Lake City, Bingham, St. Louis, San Francisco, Hg, Mo, Los Angeles, Dallas, Hurricane Creek, San Diego, New Orleans, San Antonio, Mg, Houston, Monterrey, Havana, Sb, Veracruz, Guadalajara, Mexico, Chiapas Tabasco, Tropic of Cancer, Arctic Circle

	Population								Land			Agriculture		
	Total	Density	Birth Rate	Death Rate	Life Expectancy	Growth 1965-80	Growth 1980-88	Urban	Area	Arable	Forest	Agricultural Population	Index of Production	Food Intake
	th.	persons per km²	per th. popn.	per th. popn.	yrs.	av. % per annum	av. % per annum	%	th. km²	th. km²	th. km²	% of total popn.	1979-81 = 100	calories per day
Bahamas	242	24	18	6	70		2	75	10	0.1	3	7		2699
Barbados	254	633	15	9	75		0.3	44	0.4	0.3	0	8	75	3020
Canada	26104	3	14	7	77	1	1	76	9221	460	3540	4	100	3462
Costa Rica	2670	52	29	4	74	2.6	2.3	45	51	5	16	26	108	2803
Cuba	10394	92	18	7	75	1.5	0.9	75	111	33	33	21	110	3122
Dominican Rep.	6859	134	31	7	66	2.9	2.4	58	48	15	6	39	110	2477
El Salvador	5056	234	36	9	63	2.7	1.4	44	21	7	1	39	98	2160
Guadaloupe	338	185	19	7	74		0.5	48	2	0.4	0.7	11	120	2512
Guatemala	8688	76	39	6	62	2.8	2.9	33	108	19	40	53	120	2307
Haiti	6254	191	34	13	55	2	1.8	29	28	9	0.5	66	103	1902
Honduras	4837	40	40	8	64	3.2	3.6	42	112	18	18	57	114	2068
Jamaica	2429	216	22	5	74	1.5	1.4	51	11	3	2	28	110	2590
Martinique	330	298	19	6	74		0.2	75	1	0.2	0.3	9	127	2673
Mexico	83593	41	29	5	69	3.1	2.2	71	1923	247	441	32	112	3132
Nicaragua	3623	28	42	10	64	3.1	3.4	58	119	13	37	41	86	2495
Panama	2315	29	25	4	72	2.6	2.1	54	76	6	40	27	111	2446
Puerto Rico	3376	393	19	7	75		0.6	74	9	1	2	3	98	
Trinidad and Tobago	1241	236	27	7	70	1.3	1.6	67	5	1	2	8	81	3082
U.S.A.	245871	26	16	9	75	1	1	74	9167	1899	2652	3	92	3645
Argentina	31506	11	21	8	71	1.6	1.4	85	2737	358	595	11	108	3210
Bolivia	6917	6	47	5	53	2.5	2.7	50	1084	34	558	43	117	2143
Brazil	144369	16	29	6	65	2.4	2.2	75	8457	775	5579	26	132	2656
Chile	12760	16	22	6	72	1.8	1.7	85	749	56	87	14	124	2579
Colombia	30007	28	29	5	66	2.2	1.9	69	1039	53	512	30	120	2543
Ecuador	10154	35	35	5	65	3.1	2.8	55	277	27	118	33	116	2058
Guyana	1006	5	28	7	70			35	197	5	164	24	80	2359
Paraguay	4042	10	35	3	67	2.8	3.2	46	397	22	156	47	150	2853
Peru	20681	16	35	9	62	2.8	2.2	69	1280	37	692	36	126	2246
Surinam	429	2	28	7	67		2.6	48	161	0.7	149	17	112	2524
Uruguay	3004	17	18	10	71	0.4	0.5	85	174	14	7	14	108	2648
Venezuela	18759	20	28	4	70	3.5	2.8	83	882	39	311	12	114	2494

Population. This is the United Nation's estimate for the mid-year 1988 (thousands)

Population Density. This is the quoted population total divided by the quoted land area (persons per square kilometre).

Birth Rates and Death Rates. These are the registered or United Nation's estimated rates per thousand population.

Life Expectancy. This figure indicates the number of years that a child born today can expect to live if the levels of death of today last throughout its life. The figure is the average of that for men and women. The figure for women is usually higher than that for men (U.K. Male 75, female 78 years).

Population Growth. This shows the average annual percentage change in population for two periods, 1965–1980 and 1980–1988.

Urbanization. This is the percentage of the total population living in urban areas. The definition of urban is that of the individual nation and usually includes quite small towns.

Land Area. This is the total area of the country minus the area covered by major lakes and rivers (thousand square kilometres).

Arable Land and Permanent Crops. This excludes fallow land but includes temporary pasture (thousand square kilometres).

Forest and Woodland. This includes natural and planted woodland and land recently cleared of timber which will be replanted (thousand square kilometres).

Agricultural Population. This is the percentage of the economically active population working in agriculture. It also includes those people working in forestry, hunting and fishing.

Index of Agricultural Production. The base period for this index is 1979–1981 and it shows the level of production in each country in 1988 in comparison with that of the earlier period. Only edible crops and meat are included.

Food Intake. The figures are the average intake per person in calories per day for the year 1986.

Trade		Education		Health	Energy	Consumer Price Index	G.N.P.		G.D.P.		Loans & Debt		
Imports	Exports	Primary	Secondary					Growth per capita	Part formed by Agric.	Part formed by Indust.			
US$ per capita	US$ per capita	% of age group	% of age group	Popn. per doctor	Consumption in kg of oil equiv. per capita	1980 = 100	US$ per capita	% per year 1965-88	%	%	end 1987 US$ millions	as % of G.N.P.	
6673	6814	99	99	1050	2390	148	10570	−0.5	4	12	189	7	Bahamas
2752	2657	100	94	1300	1410	159	5990	2.3	6	13			Barbados
3547	3558	100	100	510	9690	162	15160	2.7	3	35	2340	0.5	Canada
516	433	100	42	960	470	703	1610	1.5	18	29	4100	67	Costa Rica
732	520	100	89	720	1420		1400		4	43			Cuba
260	104	100	47	1760	450	269	730	2.3	17	30	2609	53	Dominican Rep.
193	125	70	24	2830	170	391	860	−0.4	14	22	1762	39	El Salvador
4902	781	100	34	1020	930	174	4330	4.7	7	7			Guadaloupe
170	125	76	20	2180	190	202	950	1.2	25	16	2187	30	Guatemala
60	42	78	18	7180	50	141	360	0.5	32	17	713	29	Haiti
185	171	100	36	1510	200	148	810	0.7	22	24	2410	53	Honduras
497	267	100	58	2060	1090	284	940	−1.5	6	41	3322	99	Jamaica
6455	1130	100	47	900	950	183	4270	3.3	6	5			Martinique
152	250	100	55	1240	1600	9907	1830	2.5	9	34	90938	49	Mexico
255	83	98	42	1500	310		830	−2.5	21	34	5343	198	Nicaragua
539	154	100	59	980	640	119	2240	2.4	9	18	3722	68	Panama
		100	78	800	2210	124	5540	0.8	2	41			Puerto Rico
982	1178	95	76	960	7590	233	4210	1.3	4	39	1154	24	Trinidad and Tobago
1718	1027	100	100	470	9490	144	18350	1.5	2	30	12170	0.25	U.S.A.
185	202	100	74	370	1740	2.6 mill	2390	0.1	13	43	55709	63	Argentina
112	82	87	37	1540	340	9.1 mill	580	−0.5	24	24	4769	107	Bolivia
115	182	100	36	1080	760	53000	2020	4.1	11	38	100781	26	Brazil
315	399	100	70	1230	920	431	1310	0.2	6	31	15448	70	Chile
141	167	100	56	1190	780	526	1240	2.7	19	35	15851	41	Colombia
222	199	100	55	830	660	731	1040	3.2	16	31	9438	85	Ecuador
219	209	90	55	9600	650	209	410	−0.2	20	15			Guyana
297	236	99	30	1460	250	334	990	3.4	27	26	2246	50	Paraguay
146	126	100	65	1040	520	85519	1470	0.2	11	33	11049	45	Peru
1879	1935	100	51	1725	1370	255	2450	3.4	9	21			Surinam
379	396	100	71	510	610	2978	2190	1.4	15	40	3090	41	Uruguay
465	563	100	46	700	3380	159	3230	−0.9	6	38	31326	53	Venezuela

Antigua & Barbuda, Land 0.4/Popn. 82; Belize 23/145; Bermuda 0.05/55; Br. Virgin Is. 0.2/13; Cayman Is. 0.3/24; Dominica 0.8/94; Greenland 342/54; Grenada 0.3/92; Montserrat 0.1/12; Netherlands Antilles 1/189; St. Christopher-Nevis 0.4/44; St. Lucia 0.6/147; St. Pierre & M. 0.2/6; St. Vincent 0.3/113; Turks & Caicos Is. 0.4/11; U.S. Virgin Is. 0.3/110. Falkland Is. 12/2; Fr. Guiana 89/91.

Trade. The trade figures are for the year 1988. The total trade figures have been divided by the population and are a measure of the country's external trade (U.S. $ per capita).

Education. The ages of primary school are taken to be 6–11 years and secondary school 12–17 years. The percentage of total school age group in this type of education is shown.

Energy. All forms of energy have been converted to their equivalent in oil. Firewood and other traditional forms used in developing countries are not included and so the energy consumption in those countries is understated (kilograms of oil equivalent per capita).

Consumer Price Index. The base year is 1980 which is 100 and the level of consumer prices in 1987 or 1988 are shown in relation to the base year. It is a measure of inflation.

G.N.P. (Gross National Product) This figure is an estimate of the average production per person measured in U.S. dollars and for 1988. The G.N.P. measures the value of goods and services produced in a country, plus the balance, positive or negative, of income from abroad, for example investments, interest on capital, money returned from foreign labour, etc. The rate of change is the average annual percentage change during the period 1965–1988 in the G.N.P. The G.D.P. (Gross Domestic Product) is the G.N.P. minus the foreign balances. The adjoining two columns show the percentage contribution to the G.D.P. made by the agricultural and mining and manufacturing sectors.

Loans and Debts. This figure in millions of U.S. dollars shows the external public debt ar the end of 1988. This is then shown as a percentage of the annual G.N.P. The figures in red show official development assistance made by the developed countries and also as a percentage of the donor country's G.N.P.

To convert from square kilometres (km²) to square miles multiply by 0.39
To convert from kilograms to pounds multiply by 2.2

CANADA

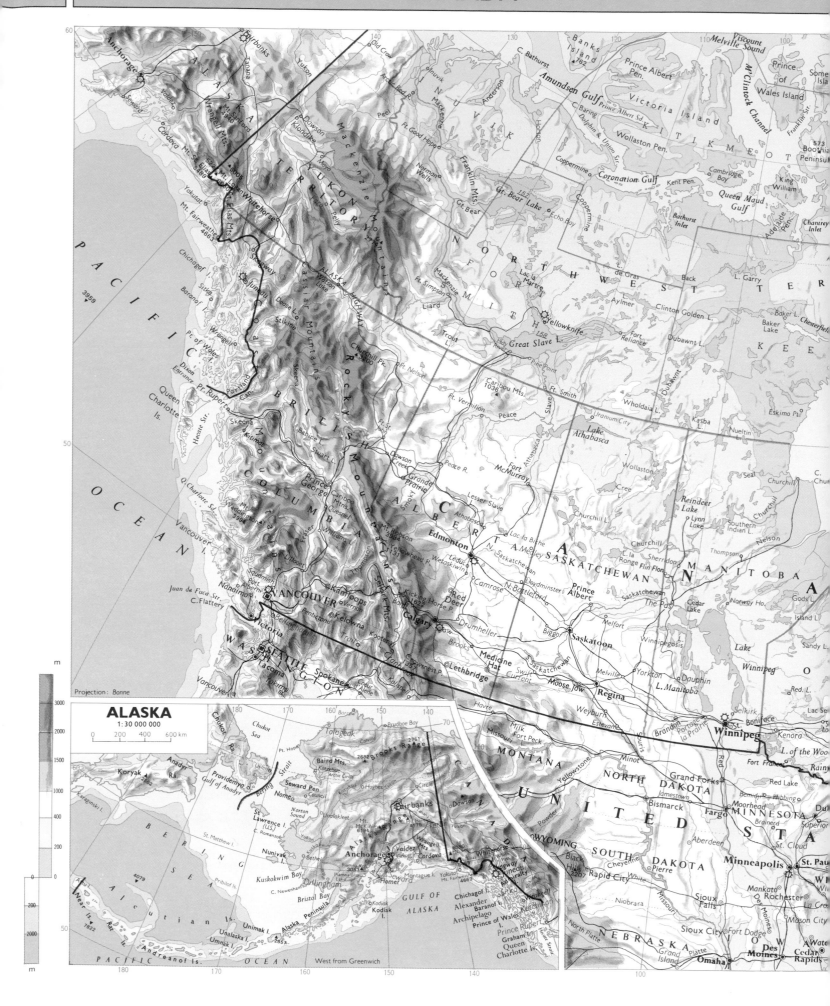

ALASKA
1 : 30 000 000
0   200   400   600 km

Projection: Bonne

Devon Island
Lancaster Sound
Baffin Bay
GREENLAND
ATLANTIC

Brodeur
Peninsula
2136
Bylot
Pond Inlet
Svartenhuk Peninsula
Angmagssalik
60

C. Hewett
Disko I.
Sondre Stromfjord
King Frederik VI Coast

Melville
Peninsula
Committee B.
Fury & Hecla Str.
Home B.
C. Dyer
Godthåb
Frederikshaab
50

Foxe
Prince
Charles
2591
Cumberland
Peninsula
Frederikshaab
Juilanehaab
Sydproven

Wager B.
C. Dorchester
Foxe
Basin
Nettilling L.
Cumberland Sd.
C. Mercy
C. Farewell

Southampton I.
Foxe
Penin.
Amadjuak
L.
Frobisher
Bay
3809

Roes Welcome Sd.
Channel
Coats I.
Frobisher Bay
Resolution I.

field Inlet
Mansel
I.
Hudson Strait
C. Chidley

Hudson
Ivujivik
Maricourt
(Wakeham Bay)
Koartac
Akpatok
I.

Bay
Ungava
Payne (Payne Bay)
Bella
Ungava Bay
Port Nouveau-Quebec
(George R.)

257
Ottawa
Is.
Payne L.
Peninsula
Leaf
George
Nain
NEW

King George Is.
Kuujjuaq
L. Minto
Hopedale
C. Harrison
Indian Harbour
50

Belcher
Is.
Clearwater
Lac Bienville
Schefferville
Petitsikapau
Michikamau
Rigolet
Cartwright
Battle Harb.

C. Henrietta
Maria
A
Paste de
la Baleine
(Great Whale River)
LABRADOR
Happy Valley
Goose Bay

Big
Trout L.
D
Ft. George
QUEBEC
Labrador City
1128
Kaniapiskau
Churchill

Severn
Winisk
James Bay
Akimiski
I.
Gagnon
Natashquan
NEWFOUNDLAND
Gander
Bonavista

Attawapiskat
Eastmain
Mingan
Anticosti I.
Corner Brook
Grand Falls
Carbonear
St. John's

Albany
Moosonee
Fort Rupert
(Rupert House)
Rupert R.
Mistassini
Sept Iles
Port Cartier
Kay's Channel
Port aux Basques
C. Race

St. Joseph
Missinaibi
Harricanaw
Chibougamau
Baie Comeau
R. St. Lawrence
Gaspé
C. Gaspé
St. Lawrence
Gulf of
St. Lawrence
Cabot Str.
Cape Breton
ST. PIERRE
& MIQUELON (Fr.)

ONTARIO
Geraldton
Nipigon
Hearst
Oba
Mattagami
Gouin
Reservoir
Matane
Rimouski
Campbellton
Bathurst
Chatham
PR. EDWARD I.
Summerside
Charlottetown
Sydney
Glace Bay

Thunder Bay
Lake Superior
Timmins
Kirkland Lake
Rouyn
Val d'Or
La Tuque
St. John
Saguenay
Rivière
du Loup
NEW
BRUNSWICK
Moncton
Northumberland Str.
Amherst
New Glasgow
Truro
Sable I.
(Nova Scotia)

Marquette
Sault Ste.
Marie
Sudbury
North Bay
Cabonga
Reservoir
Shawinigan
Trois Rivieres
Jonquiere
Chicoutimi
Quebec
1190
Thetford Mines
Fredericton
Saint John
Dartmouth
Halifax
6309

Escanaba
Green Bay
Georgian
Bay
Orillia
Sault Ste. Marie
Ottawa
Hull
Cornwall
MONTREAL
St. Hyacinthe
Sherbrooke
MAINE
Bangor
Kentville
NOVA
SCOTIA
Bridgewater
C. Sable
40

WISCONSIN
Wausau
Appleton
Traverse
City
Lake
Huron
Owen Sound
Oshawa
L. Ontario
Peterboro
Kingston
Burlington
L. Champlain
1917
VERMONT
Portland
Lewiston
B. of Fundy
Yarmouth

Saginaw
Grand
Rapids
London
Sarnia
TORONTO
Hamilton
Niagara
Falls
Rochester
Syracuse
NEW
YORK
Albany
Springfield
NEW
HAMPSHIRE
Concord
Manchester
BOSTON
MASS.
C. Cod

MILWAUKEE
Kitchener
L. Erie
Buffalo
Binghamton
Scranton
CONN.
Providence
New Haven

CHICAGO
Gary
DETROIT
Windsor
Toledo
CLEVELAND
Akron
OHIO
PENNSYLVANIA
Allentown
Newark
NEW YORK
NEW JERSEY
INDIANA

West from Greenwich
COPYRIGHT. GEORGE PHILIP & SON. LTD

1:15 000 000

100   0   100   200   300   400   500   600 km

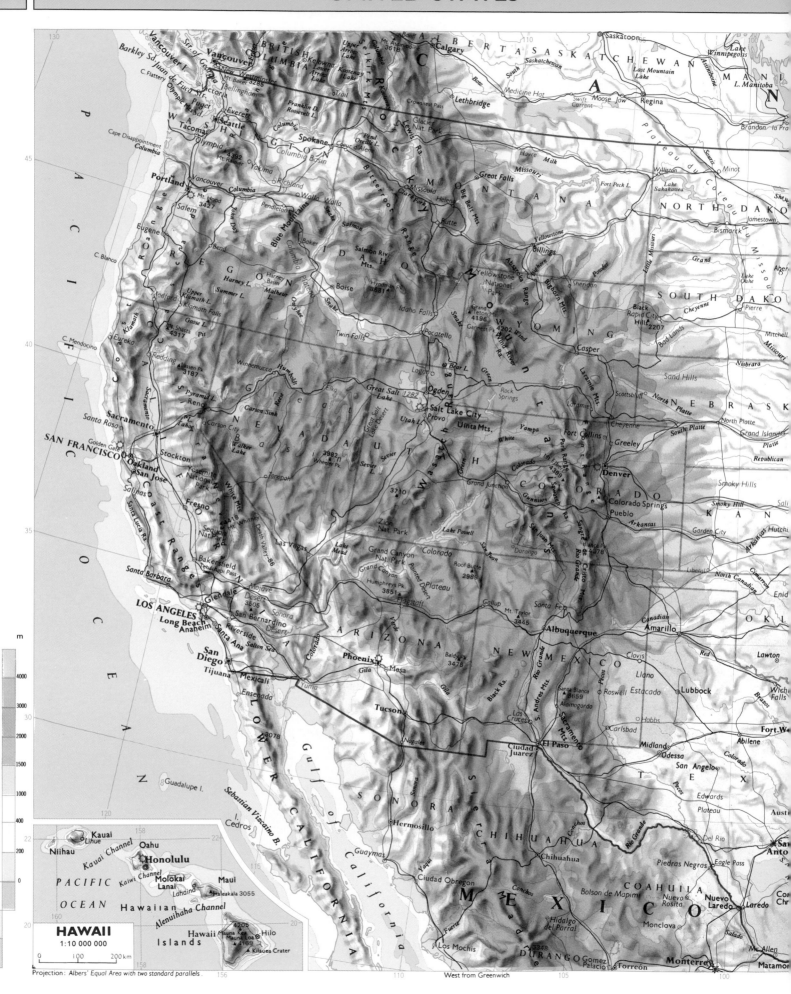

HAWAII
1:10 000 000

0   100   200km

Projection : Albers' Equal Area with two standard parallels .

West from Greenwich

1:12 000 000

100   0   100   200   300   400   500 km

COPYRIGHT. GEORGE PHILIP & SON. LTD.

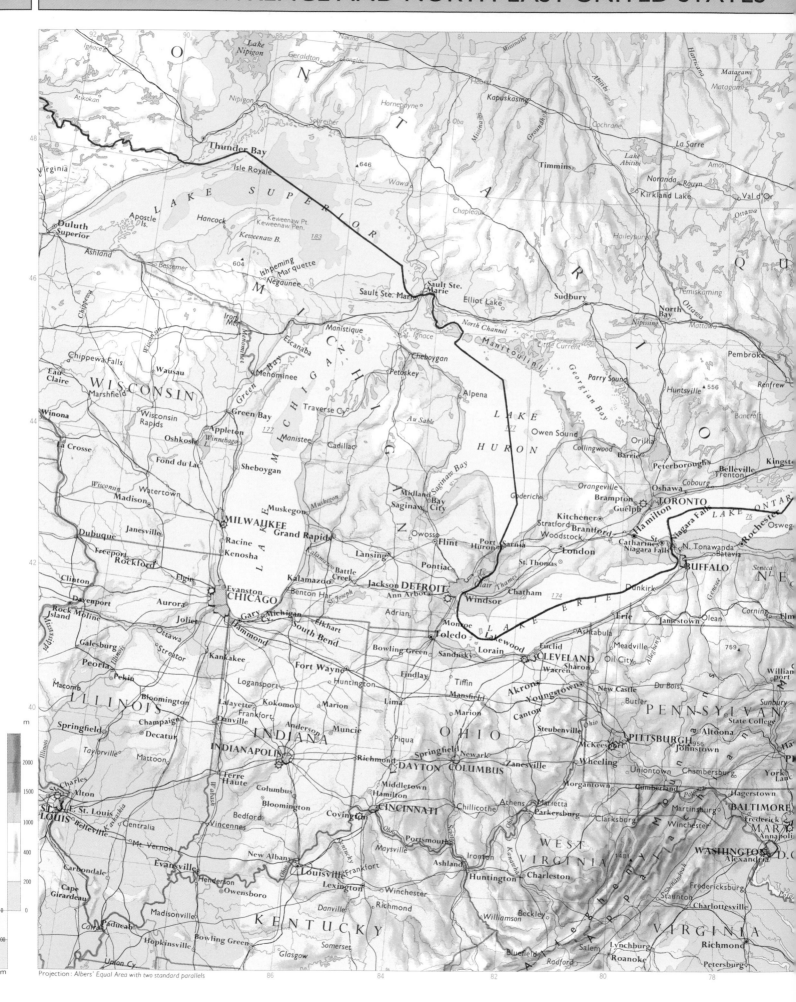

O N T A R I O

Lake Nipigon
Nakina
Geraldton
Longlac
Hearst
Kapuskasing
Cochrane
Matagami L.
Matagami

Atikokan
Nipigon
Hornepayne
Oba
Missinaibi
Groundhog
La Sarre
Amos
Noranda
Rouyn
Val d'Or

Virginia
Thunder Bay
Isle Royale
646
Wawa
Timmins
Lake Abitibi
Kirkland Lake

LAKE SUPERIOR
Schreiber
Chapleau
Haileybury
Ottawa

Duluth
Superior
Apostle Is.
Hancock
Keweenaw Pt.
Keweenaw Pen.
183
Keweenaw B.
Temiskaming
North Bay
Nipissing
Mattawa

Ashland
Bessemer
604
Ishpeming
Marquette
Negaunee
Sault Ste. Marie
Sault Ste. Marie
Elliot Lake
Sudbury
Pembroke

Chippewa Falls
Iron Mtn.
Manistique
St. Ignace
North Channel
Manitoulin I.
Little Current
556
Renfrew

Eau Claire
Wausau
Escanaba
Green Bay
Menominee
Cheboygan
Petoskey
Georgian Bay
Parry Sound
Huntsville
Bancroft

WISCONSIN
Marshfield
Green Bay
Menominee
Traverse Cy.
Alpena
LAKE HURON
Owen Sound
Collingwood
Orillia
Barrie

Wisconsin Rapids
Appleton
Oshkosh
Winnebago
Manistee
Cadillac
Au Sable
177
Goderich
Orangeville
Brampton
Guelph
TORONTO
Peterborough
Belleville
Trenton
Cobourg
Kingsto

Winona
La Crosse
Fond du Lac
Sheboygan
Midland
Bay City
Saginaw
Owosso
Port Huron
Sarnia
Kitchener
Stratford
Woodstock
Brantford
Hamilton
St. Catharines
Niagara Falls
Oshawa
LAKE ONTARIO
75
Oswego

Madison
Watertown
Muskegon
Muskegon
Flint
Lansing
Pontiac
London
St. Thomas
N. Tonawanda
Batavia
Rochester

Dubuque
Janesville
MILWAUKEE
Racine
Kenosha
Grand Rapids
Kalamazoo
Battle Creek
Jackson
Ann Arbor
DETROIT
Windsor
Chatham
174
BUFFALO
Seneca L.
N. L. E

Clinton
Freeport
Rockford
Elgin
Evanston
CHICAGO
Benton Har.
St. Joseph
Adrian
Monroe
St. Clair
Thames
LAKE ERIE
Dunkirk
Erie
Corning
Elm

Davenport
Rock Island
Moline
Aurora
Joliet
Gary
Michigan City
Elkhart
South Bend
Bowling Green
Sandusky
Toledo
Lakewood
Lorain
Euclid
CLEVELAND
Ashtabula
Meadville
Oil City
759
Jamestown
Olean
William port

Galesburg
Ottawa
Streator
Hammond
Kankakee
Fort Wayne
Huntington
Findlay
Tiffin
Mansfield
Akron
Warren
Sharon
New Castle
Du Bois

Macomb
Peoria
Pekin
Logansport
Kokomo
Marion
Lima
Marion
Canton
Youngstown
Butler
PENNSYLVAN
State College
Sunbury

ILLINOIS
Bloomington
Lafayette
Frankfort
Danville
Anderson
Muncie
Piqua
OHIO
Steubenville
Ohio
956
PITTSBURGH
Altoona
Johnstown

Springfield
Champaign
Decatur
INDIANAPOLIS
INDIANA
Richmond
Springfield
Newark
Zanesville
Wheeling
McKeesport
Uniontown
Chambersburg
York
Lanc

Taylorville
Mattoon
Terre Haute
Columbus
Bloomington
Bedford
Vincennes
DAYTON
COLUMBUS
Hamilton
Middletown
Chillicothe
Morgantown
Cumberland
Hagerstown
BALTIMORE

St. Charles
Alton
ST. LOUIS
St. Louis
Belleville
Centralia
Covington
CINCINNATI
Athens
Marietta
Parkersburg
Clarksburg
Martinsburg
Winchester
Frederick
MARY
Annapoli
WASHINGTON D.C.
Alexandria

Carbondale
Evansville
Henderson
New Albany
Louisville
Frankfort
Maysville
Portsmouth
Ironton
Ashland
Huntington
Charleston
WEST VIRGINIA
1491
Fredericksburg
Staunton
Charlottesville

Cape Girardeau
Madisonville
Owensboro
Lexington
Winchester
Richmond
Beckley
Williamson
VIRGINIA
Richmond
Petersburg

Paducah
Hopkinsville
Bowling Green
Danville
Glasgow
Somerset
Bluefield
Radford
Salem
Lynchburg
Roanoke

KENTUCKY

92 90 88 86 84 82 80 78

m
2000
1500
1000
400
200
0
200
m

Chibougamau
556 ▲ Chibougamau L.

Port Cartier

West Pt. A n t i c o s t i I.
Jupiter
Heath Pt.
▼ 572

Pipmuacan L.

Gouin
Res.

Cap Chat
1310
Shickshock Mts.
Matane
Gaspé Peninsula
Gaspé
C. Gaspé

GULF OF
ST. LAWRENCE

Dolbeau
St. Félicien
Lac
St. Jean
Roberval
Chicoutimi
Saguenay
Rimouski
Dalhousie
Chaleur Bay
Bathurst
Miramichi B.
North Pt.
Tignish
Magdalen
Is.
(Quebec)
C. North

Jonquière
Rivière du Loup
Campbellton
Newcastle
Chatham
PRINCE EDWARD
ISLAND
532 ▲
Cape Breton
Island

Q U E B E C
La Tuque
Baie St. Paul
Edmundston
819 ▲
N E W
B R U N S W I C K
Summerside
East Pt.
Charlottetown
Glace Bay
Sydney

Grand'Mère
Shawinigan
Quebec
Montmagny
Grand Falls
Chipman
Northumberland Str.
New Glasgow
Bras d'Or
L.

Trois Rivières
960 ▲
Lévis
St. John
Presque Isle
Houlton
Grand L.
Moncton
Springhill
Stellarton
Chedabucto B.

Victoriaville
Thetford Mines
Mt. Katahdin
1606
Fredericton
Sussex
Truro
Canso

Joliette
Drummondville
Moosehead
L.
Saint
John
N
O
V
A

Sorel
St.
Jérôme
St. Hyacinthe
Mégantic
M A I N E
Penobscot
St. Stephen
Bay of Fundy
Kentville
S
C
O
T
I
A
Dartmouth

MONTREAL
Sherbrooke
Magog
Bangor
Grand
Manan I.
Digby
Bridgewater
Halifax

gham
Ottawa
Ottawa
St. Jean
Valleyfield
Newport
Waterville
L. Rossignol

Cornwall
Plattsburgh
L.
Champlain
Burlington
Berlin
Augusta
Mt. Desert
Yarmouth
Shelburne

Ogdensburg
Montpelier
Barre
V E R M O N T
N E W   H A M P S H I R E
1917
Auburn
Lewiston
Rockland
L. Sable

Vatertown
1629
L.
George
Rutland
Laconia
Rochester
Portland
Biddeford

Rome
Glen Falls
Concord
Dover
Portsmouth

racuse
Utica
Schenectady
Troy
Keene
Manchester
Nashua
Lawrence
Lowell

Y O R K
Albany
Pittsfield
Bennington
Fitchburg
Salem
Massachusetts

Binghamton
Catskill
Mts.
1281
Worcester
Newton
BOSTON
Bay
MASS
Holyoke
Cambridge
Quincy
C. Cod

Springfield
Woonsocket
Pawtucket
Brockton
Cape
Cod B.

Poughkeepsie
Hartford
New Britain
Providence
Fall River
New Bedford
Nantucket
Sd.

Newburgh
Waterbury
Meriden
R.I.
Newport
Nantucket I.

Middletown
New
Haven
London
Block I.
Martha's Vineyard

Wilkes Barre
Bridgeport
Stamford
Long Island

Hazleton
Paterson
Yonkers

Bethlehem
Newark
NEW YORK
Allentown
Jersey City
Reading
Edison
Elizabeth

LPHIA
Trenton
ark
Camden
NEW
JERSEY
Wilmington
Vineland
A T L A N T I C
Dover
Atlantic City

DELAWARE
Cape May
O C E A N

bury

Cape Charles

64 COPYRIGHT. GEORGE PHILIP & SON. LTD.

1:6 000 000

50   0   50   100   150   200   250 km

San Diego • Yuma • Phoenix
Tijuana • Mexicali
Ensenada • Tucson
3078 ▲

Nogales • Ciudad Juárez • El Paso
Agua Prieta
UNITED STATES
Carlsbad
Wichita Falls
Fort Worth • Dallas
Abilene • Shreveport • Jackson • Birmingham • Montgomery

Hermosillo
Chihuahua
3200 ▲ Villa Ahumada
Delicias
San Angelo • Waco
Austin • Houston
Alexandria • Baton Rouge • Mobile • Pensacola
Beaumont • Lake Charles
New Orleans • C. San Blas

Empalme
Guaymas
Sta. Rosalía
Ciudad Obregón
Navojoa
Los Mochis
Guamúchil
2896 Piedras Negras • Eagle Pass
Nueva Rosita
Sabinas
Monclova • Falcon Res.
Nuevo Laredo
Laredo
San Antonio
Port Arthur • Galveston
Mississippi Delta

Culiacán
Torreón • Saltillo
3150 ▲ Hidalgo del Parral
Nazas
S. Pedro
Gómez Palacio
Concepción del Oro
Monterrey
Montemorelos
Reynosa
Matamoros
Rio Grande del Norte
Corpus Christi
Padre I.
Laguna de la Madre
GULF OF MEXICO

Mazatlán • Durango
Rosario
4054 ▲
Matehuala
Ciudad Victoria
Fresnillo
Zacatecas
Ciudad Mante
Tropic of Cancer
Yucatán

C. San Lucas
2406 ▲
3353 ▲
San Luis Potosí
Ciudad Madero
Tampico
Progreso
Mérida • Valladolid
I. de Cozumel

Tepic
R. Grande de Santiago
Aguascalientes
León
Irapuato
Querétaro
Pánuco
C. Rojo
Tuxpan
Peto

Guadalajara
Ameca
Zamora
Celaya
Pachuca
Campeche

Colima Vol.
3960 ▲
Morelia
MEXICO
Toluca
Jalapa Enríquez
Veracruz
Gulf of Campeche
YUCATAN
Laguna de Términos
Chetumal

Manzanillo
Cuernavaca
Iguala
Balsas
Puebla
Orizaba
Minatitlán
Coatzacoalcos
Ciudad del Carmen
Villahermosa

Acapulco
Chilpancingo
3703 Popocatépetl 5452
Mexcala
Oaxaca
3395 ▲
Tuxtla Gutiérrez
Usumacinta
Belmopan
Belize
Turneffe Is.
BELIZE

Ometepec
de
Juchitán
San Cristóbal
Pto. Barrios Gulf of Ho
3138 ▲
Salina Cruz
Tonalá
Chiapa
GUATEMALA
Tela
La Ceiba

G. of Tehuantepec
Tapachula
417 ▲ Zacapa
S. Pedro Sula
HONDURAS
Comayagua
Tegucigalpa

Quezaltenango
Sta. Ana
San Salvador
EL SALVADOR
S. Miguel
G. of Fonseca
Leon • Choluteca
NICARA
Managua
Gran

PACIFIC OCEAN
C. Corrientes
Nicoya Pen.
Nicoya
Puntar

PANAMA CANAL 1:1 000 000
0 10 20km
Colón • Coco Solo
Fort Sherman
Cristóbal
Margarita
Puerto Pilón
Gatún Locks
Gatún Dam
Gatun Lake
Zorra
El Limón
Madden L.
Madden Dam
Frijoles
Buenos Aires
Escobal
Colorado
Darién
Chagres
Gamboa
The Gaillard Cut
Balboa Hill 350
Culebra
Paraíso
Pedro Miguel
Les Cascadas
Pedro Miguel Locks
Miraflores Locks
Fort Clayton
Curundu
Corozal
Arraiján
Balboa
Fort Amador
Ancon
PANAMA
La Chorrera

m
4000
3000
2000
1500
400
200
0
200
2000
m

JAMAICA 1:5 000 000
0 50 km
Montego Bay
Falmouth
St. Ann's Bay
Galina Point
Annotto Bay
Port Antonio
Savanna la Mar
Mandeville
KINGSTON
2256
Morant Point
May Pen
Spanish Town
Morant Bay
Portland Point

TRINIDAD AND TOBAGO 1:5 000 000
0 50 km
Charlotteville
Tobago
Scarborough
Port of Spain
Arima 940
Sangre Grande
Gulf of Paria
San Fernando
Rio Claro
Princes Town
TRINIDAD
Point Fortin
Siparia
Serpent's Mouth

LEEWARD ISLANDS 1:5 000 000
0 50 km
The Valley
Anguilla (Br.)
Marigot
St. Martin (Fr.)
St. Maarten (Neth.)
St. Barthélemy (Fr.)
Saba (Neth.)
St. Eustatius (Neth.)
Codrington
Barbuda
St. Christopher (St. Kitts)
ST. CHRISTOPHER-NEVIS
Basseterre
ANTIGUA & BARBUDA
Charlestown
Nevis
St. John's
Antigua
Redonda
Montserrat
Plymouth
Guadeloupe Passage
GUADELOUPE (Fr.)
Grande Terre
Moule
Ste Rose
Basse Terre
Désirade (Fr.)
Basse Terre
Pointe-à-Pitre
I. des Saintes (Fr.)
Marie-Galante (Fr.)
Grand Bourg
Dominica Passage
Portsmouth
Morne Diablotin 1490
DOMINICA (Windward Is.)
Roseau

WINDWARD ISLANDS 1:5 000 000
0 50 km
Martinique Passage
Mt. Pelée 1397
Ste. Marie
St. Pierre
Fort de France
Le François
Lamentin
MARTINIQUE (Fr.)
Ste. Anne
St. Lucia Channel
Soufrière
ST. LUCIA
Castries
Vieux Fort
St. Vincent Passage
Soufrière
1178
Georgetown
ST. VINCENT
Kingstown
& Bequia
THE GRENADINES
Mustique
Canouan
Union
The Grenadines
Carriacou
Hillsborough
Ronde
St. George's
840
Grenville
Grenada
GRENADA
BARBADOS
Speightstown
Bridgetown

Projection: Bonne

ATLANTIC OCEAN

Tropic of Cancer

CARIBBEAN SEA

West from Greenwich

1:15 000 000

100 0 100 200 300 400 500 600 km

COPYRIGHT. GEORGE PHILIP & SON. LTD.

SOUTH AMERICA: *physical*

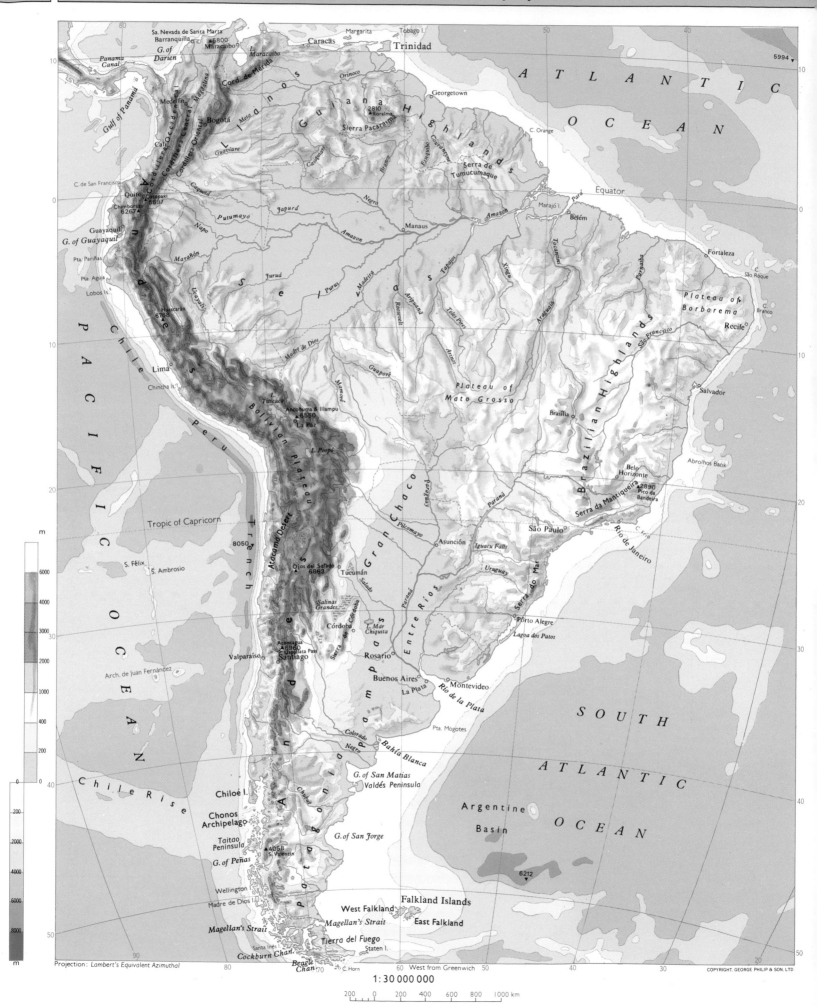

ATLANTIC OCEAN

PACIFIC OCEAN

SOUTH ATLANTIC OCEAN

Panama Canal
Gulf of Panama
Sa. Nevada de Santa Marta
Barranquilla
▲5800 Maracaibo
G. of Darien
L. Maracaibo
Cord. de Mérida
Caracas
Margarita
Tobago I.
Trinidad
5994▼

Medellin
Bogotá
Cali
Orinoco
Georgetown
Guiana Highlands
Sierra Pacaraima
▲2810 Roraima
Serra de Tumucumaque
C. Orange

C. de San Francisco
Quito
▲Cotopaxi 5897
Chimborazo 6267
Guayaquil
G. of Guayaquil
Napo
Putumayo
Japurá
Negro
Manaus
Amazon
Marajó I.
Pará
Belém
Equator

Pta. Pariñas
Pta. Aguja
Lobos Is.
Marañón
Ucayali
Juruá
Purus
Amazon
Madeira
Tapajós
Xingu
Araguaia
Tocantins
Parnaíba
Fortaleza
São Roque
C. Branco

Huascarán ▲6768
Lima
Chincha Is.
Madre de Dios
Guaporé
Roosevelt
Teles Pires
Arinos
São Francisco
Plateau of Borborema
Recife

L. Titicaca
Ancohuma & Illampu ▲6580
La Paz
Bolivian Plateau
L. Poopó
Mamoré
Guaporé
Plateau of Mato Grosso
Brasília
Abrolhos Bank
Salvador

Tropic of Capricorn
S. Félix
S. Ambrosio
Atacama Desert
▲8050
Ojos del Salado ▲6863
Tucumán
Salado
Gran Chaco
Pilcomayo
Paraguay
Paraná
Asunción
Iguaçu Falls
São Paulo
Serra da Mantiqueira
▲2890 Pico da Bandeira
Belo Horizonte
Rio de Janeiro
C. Frio
Serra do Mar

Chile Rise
Arch. de Juan Fernández
Valparaíso
Salinas Grandes
Córdoba
Sierra de Córdoba
L. Mar Chiquita
Aconcagua ▲6960
Uspallata Pass
Santiago
Rosario
Entre Ríos
Uruguay
Pôrto Alegre
Lagoa dos Patos

Buenos Aires
La Plata
Montevideo
Río de la Plata
Pta. Mogotes

Colorado
Negro
Bahía Blanca
G. of San Matias
Valdés Peninsula
Argentine Basin
6212

Chiloé I.
Chonos Archipelago
Taitao Peninsula
G. of Peñas
S. Valentin ▲4058
Wellington
Chubut
G. of San Jorge
Patagonia
Pampas

Madre de Dios I.
West Falkland
Falkland Islands
East Falkland
Magellan's Strait
Santa Inés I.
Tierra del Fuego
Staten I.
Cockburn Chan.
Beagle Chan.
C. Horn

m
6000
4000
3000
2000
1000
400
200
0
m
200
2000
4000
6000
8000

Projection: Lambert's Equivalent Azimuthal

West from Greenwich

1:30 000 000

200 0 200 400 600 800 1000 km

COPYRIGHT. GEORGE PHILIP & SON LTD

COSTA
RICA

Barranquilla
Cartagena · Ciénaga
Maracaibo · Cabimas
Barquisimeto
San José
PANAMA
G. of
Darién
Panamá
Monteria
G. of
Panamá

Medellín
Manizales
Pereira
Buenaventura · Ibagué
Cali
Popayan
Pasto

COLOMBIA

Punto Fijo
Port of Spain
TRINIDAD AND TOBAGO
Cumaná
Valencia · **Caracas**
Maturín

Cúcuta
San Cristóbal
Bucaramanga

VENEZUELA

Orinoco
Ciudad Guayana
Ciudad Bolívar

Georgetown

Paramaribo
GUYANA · **SURINAM** · Cayenne
FRENCH GUIANA
C. Orange

Bogotá

Branco

Macapá

**NORTH
ATLANTIC
OCEAN**

Equator

Quito
ECUADOR
Guayaquil
G. de Guayaquil
Cuenca
Iquitos
Piura

Putumayo

Benjamim
Constant

Japurá

Manaus

Ilha de
Marajó

Amazon
Santarem

Belém
(Pará)

São Luís

Equator

Chiclayo
Trujillo
Chimbote

Marañón
Ucayali

Juruá

Purus

Madeira

Pôrto Velho

Tapajós

Xingu

Tocantins

Bacabal

Teresina

Araguaia

Parnaíba

Fortaleza (Ceara)

C. de São Roque
Natal

Juazeiro do
Norte

João Pessoa
(Paraiba)
**Recife
(Pernambuco)**

PERU

Callao · **Lima**
Huancayo
Ica
Cuzco

Rio Branca

Madre de Dios

Guaporé

Mamoré

São Francisco

B R A Z I L

Maceió

Aracaju

Titicaca

BOLIVIA

Arequipa · **La Paz**
Cochabamba
Oruro
Sucre
Santa Cruz

Corumbá

Cuiabá

Brasília
Goiânia

Montes Claros

**Salvador
(Bahia)**

Arica

Iquique

Campo Grande

Paraguay

Uberaba
Ribeirão
Prêto

Belo
Horizonte

Gov. Valadares

Vitória

Tropic of Capricorn

Antofagasta

San Félix
(Chile)
San Ambrosio
(Chile)

PARAGUAY

Pilcomayo

Asunción

Paraná

Bauru

Londrina

Campos

Campinas · Niterói
**SÃO
PAULO** · Santos
RIO DE JANEIRO

Salta

San Miguel
de Tucumán

Resistencia
Corrientes

Posadas

Uruguay

Ponta Grossa
Curitiba

Florianópolis

C H I L E

Santiago
del Estero

Salado

ARGENTINA
Córdoba
San Juan
Santa Fe
Paraná
Rosario

URUGUAY

Pôrto
Alegre

Pelotas

Lagoa dos Patos

Viña del Mar
Valparaíso
Juan Fernández
(Chile)

Santiago

Mendoza
Mercedes

**BUENOS
AIRES**
La
Plata

Montevideo

Rio de la Plata

**SOUTH
ATLANTIC
OCEAN**

Talcahuano
Concepción

Talca

Mar del Plata

Bahía Blanca

Colorado

P A C I F I C   O C E A N

Valdivia

Negro

Viedma

Puerto Montt
San Carlos
de Bariloche

Chiloé

Chonos
Arch.

Península
Valdés
Trelew

Chubut

Golfo
Comodoro Rivadavia
San Jorge

I. Wellington

**FALKLAND ISLANDS
(ISLAS MALVINAS)
(U.K.)**
Stanley

Strait of Magellan
Río Gallegos
Punta
Arenas
Cape Horn
Tierra
del
Fuego

Projection: Lambert's Equivalent Azimuthal

West from Greenwich

BUENOS AIRES   Capital Cities

1:30 000 000

200   0   200   400   600   800   1000 km

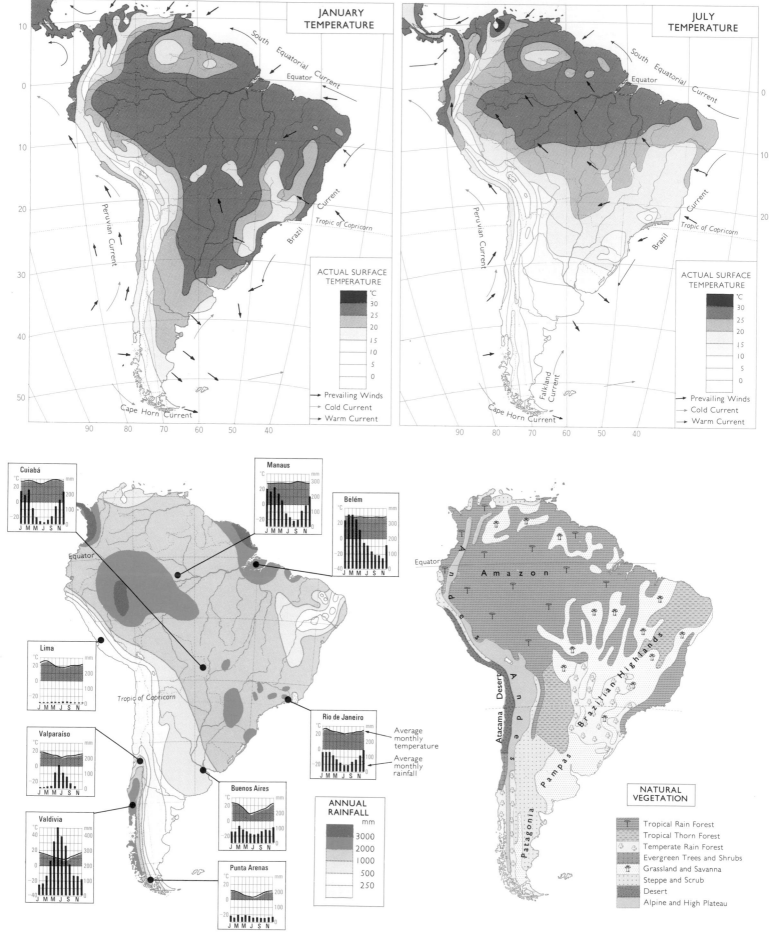

JANUARY TEMPERATURE

South Equatorial Current
Equator
Peruvian Current
Brazil Current
Tropic of Capricorn
Cape Horn Current

ACTUAL SURFACE TEMPERATURE
°C
30
25
20
15
10
5
0

→ Prevailing Winds
→ Cold Current
→ Warm Current

JULY TEMPERATURE

South Equatorial Current
Equator
Peruvian Current
Brazil Current
Tropic of Capricorn
Falkland Current
Cape Horn Current

ACTUAL SURFACE TEMPERATURE
°C
30
25
20
15
10
5
0

→ Prevailing Winds
→ Cold Current
→ Warm Current

Cuiabá
Manaus
Belém
Equator
Lima
Tropic of Capricorn
Valparaíso
Rio de Janeiro
Average monthly temperature
Average monthly rainfall
Buenos Aires
Valdivia
Punta Arenas

ANNUAL RAINFALL
mm
3000
2000
1000
500
250

Equator
Andes
Amazon
Atacama Desert
Brazilian Highlands
Pampas
Patagonia

NATURAL VEGETATION

Tropical Rain Forest
Tropical Thorn Forest
Temperate Rain Forest
Evergreen Trees and Shrubs
Grassland and Savanna
Steppe and Scrub
Desert
Alpine and High Plateau

Projection: Lambert's Equivalent Azimuthal

LAND USE
(million hectares)

Other land 283.5

Arable land and permanent crops 104.1

Permanent pasture 441.8

Woods and forests 924.3

Total land area 1 753.7 million hectares

Maracaibo
Caracas
Oficina
Cerro Bolivar
Moengo
Bogotá

Mn Serra do Navio
Equator

Quito

Cerro de Pasco
Lima
Marcona
Toquepala
La Paz
Colquri
Sb Potosi
Chuquicamata
Tropic of Capricorn

Ni
Brasilia

Mn Urucum
Itabira
Morro Velho
Mn
Rio de Janeiro
Itaipú
São Paulo

Asunción

El Romeral

Recife
Cr

Santiago
Mo
El Teniente
Buenos Aires **Montevideo**

Concepción

El Chocón

Comodoro Rivadavia

LAND USE
Arable land
Fruit trees, vineyards and plantations
Permanent pasture
Woods and forests
Rough grazing
Non-productive land

LIVESTOCK
/// Cattle
/// Sheep

CROPS
ⅅ Bananas	◇ Sugar cane
o Cacao	▲ Tea
◆ Citrus fruits	T Tobacco
o Coffee	▽ Vines
✤ Cotton	⑴ Wheat
⑴ Maize	
O Rice	⊱ Fisheries

MINERALS
O Bauxite	**Cr** Chrome
▲ Copper	**Mn** Manganese
◇ Diamonds	**Mo** Molybdenum
△ Gold	**Ni** Nickel
◆ Iron ore	**POWER**
◆ Lead and zinc	▲ Coalfields
◇ Saltpetre	◻ Oilfields
▽ Silver	◼ Gasfields
● Tin	◼ Hydro-electric power stations
Sb Antimony	

Projection: Lambert's Equivalent Azimuthal

West from Greenwich

COPYRIGHT GEORGE PHILIP & SON LTD

1:30 000 000

200 0   200 400 600 800 1000 km

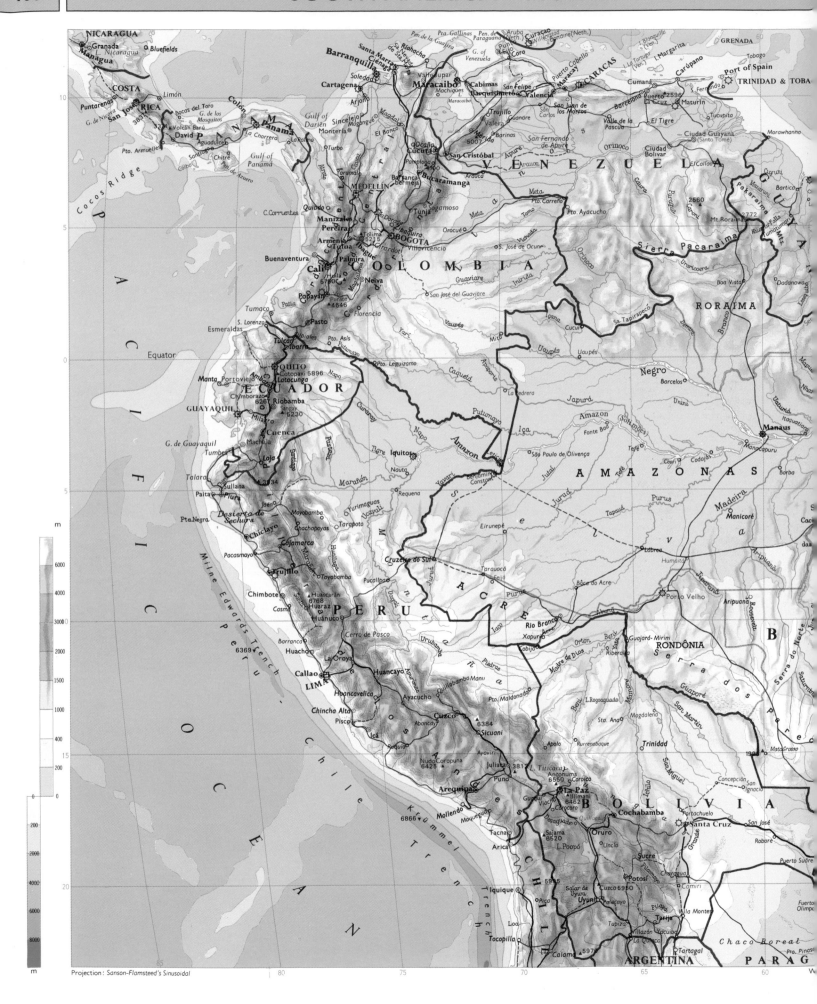

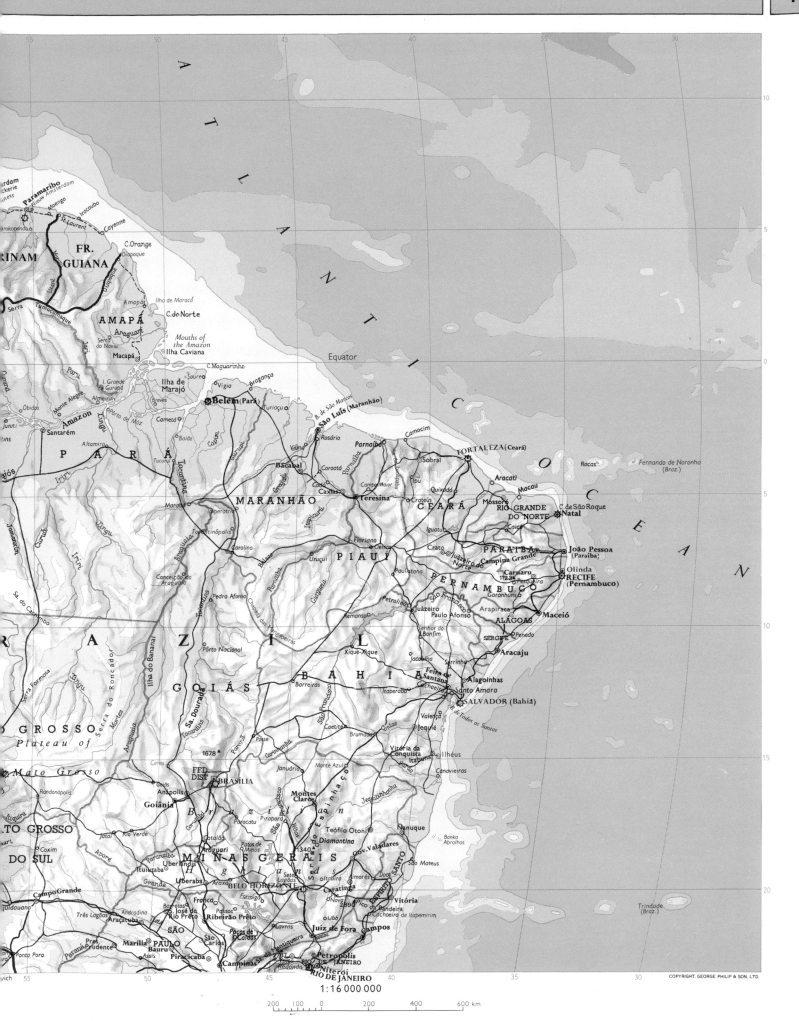

1:16 000 000

200 100 0 200 400 600 km

COPYRIGHT. GEORGE PHILIP & SON, LTD.

SOUTH AMERICA – SOUTH

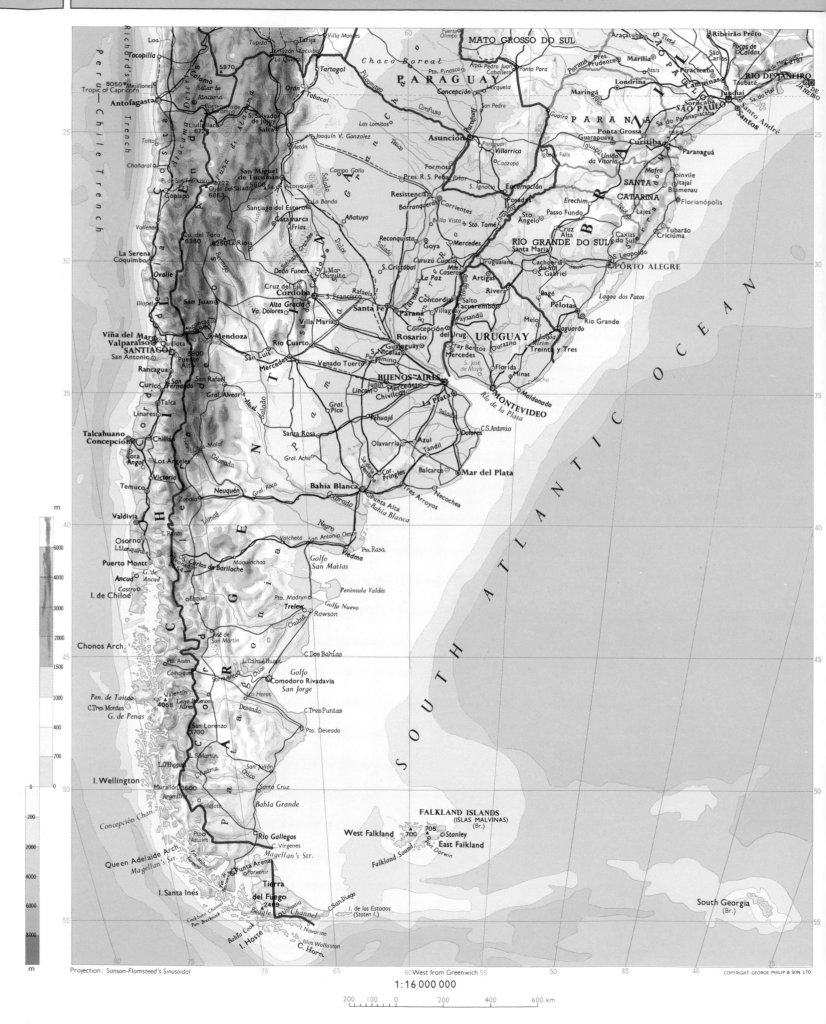

Peru-Chile Trench

Tocopilla
Mejillones
8050
Tropic of Capricorn
Antofagasta
5970
Calama
Salar de Atacama
Desierto de Atacama
Chañaral
Copiapó
6723 Llullaillaco
6883 Ojos del Salado
Tupiza
Tarija
Villa Montes
Tartagal
Oran
Tabacal
Metán
Joaquín V. Gonzalez
La Quiaca
Tacuaribo
Chaco Boreal
PARAGUAY
Pto. Pinasco
Apa. Pedro Juan Caballero
Ponta Porã
Concepción
Horqueta
San Pedro
Confuso
Campo Gallo
Las Lomitas
Pilar
Pres. R. S. Peña
Pres. Prudente
Marília
Assis
Londrina
Maringá
Araçatuba
Ribeirão Prêto
S. Tietê
Pocos de Caldas
RIO DE JANEIRO
Campinas
Taubaté
Sa. de Mantiqueira 2787
SÃO PAULO
Santo André
Santos

Talca
P. de San Francisco
Co. del Toro 6380
4250 La Rioja
San Miguel de Tucumán
5500 Sa. de Aconquija
Santiago del Estero
La Banda
Catamarca
Frias
Añatuya
Salado
Dulce
Reconquista
Resistencia
Barranqueras Corrientes
Bella Vista
Sto. Tomé
Goya
Mercedes
Curuzú Cuatiá
Formosa
S. Ignacio
Posadas
Encarnación
Iguaçu Falls
União da Vitoria
Ponta Grossa
Guarapuava
Curitiba
Paranaguá
Joinvile
Itajaí
Blumenau
Florianópolis
Mafra
SANTA CATARINA
PARANÁ
Asunción
Paraguarí
Villarrica
Caazapá
Cruz Alta
Passo Fundo
Lajes
Caxias do Sul
Criciúma
Tubarão
RIO GRANDE DO SUL
Santa Maria
Sto. Ângelo
Erechim
Cachoeira
PÔRTO ALEGRE
Vallenar
La Serena
Coquimbo
Ovalle
Illapel
San Juan
Dean Funes
L. Mar Chiquita
Cruz del Eje
Córdoba
Alta Gracia
Va. Dolores
S. Francisco
Rafaela
Santa Fe
Paraná
Concepción del Urug.
Santa María
S. Cristóbal
La Paz
Mte. Caseros
Uruguaiana
Artigas
Rivera
Bagé
Pelotas
Rio Grande
Lagoa dos Patos
S. Gabriel
S. Leopoldo
Viña del Mar
Valparaíso
SANTIAGO
Quillota
San Antonio
Puente del Inca 6800
Mendoza
Uspallata
Villa María
Río Cuarto
San Luis
Mercedes
Rosario
Guayeguay
S. Nicolás
Pergamino
Concordia
Salto
Paysandú
Tacuarembó
Villaguay
Melo
Jaguarão
Maldonado
MONTEVIDEO
URUGUAY
Durazno
Florida
Minas
Treinta y Tres
Fray Bentos
Mercedes
S. José de Mayo
Rancagua
San Fernando
Curicó
Talca
Linares
San Rafael
Gral. Alvear
Lincoln
Junín
Mercedes
Chivilcoy
BUENOS AIRES
La Plata
Río de la Plata
Gral. Pico
Pehuajó
Santa Rosa
Gral. Acha
Olavarría
Azul
Tandil
Dolores
C.S. Antonio
Talcahuano
Concepción
Chillán
Lota
Angol
Los Angeles
Victoria
Temuco
Valdivia
Osorno
L. Llanquihue
Puerto Montt
Ancud
G. de Ancud
Castro
I. de Chiloé
Chonos Arch.
Neuquén
Zapala
Gral. Roca
Bahía Blanca
Punta Alta
Bahía Blanca
Cor. Pringles
Tres Arroyos
Necochea
Balcarce
Mar del Plata
Colorada
Malal
Río Colorado
Valcheta
San Antonio Oeste
Viedma
Pta. Rasa
Golfo San Matías
Negro
Maquinchao
S. Carlos de Bariloche
Esquel
José de San Martín
Pto. Madryn
Península Valdés
Golfo Nuevo
Trelew
Rawson
Chubut
L. Colhué Huapi
L. Musters
C. Dos Bahías
Pto. Aisén
Coihaique
Sarmiento
Las Heras
Comodoro Rivadavia
San Jorge
Pen. de Taitao
C. Tres Montes
G. de Penas
San Valentín 4058
Lago Buenos Aires
Deseado
C. Tres Puntas
Pto. Deseado
I. Wellington
San Lorenzo 3700
L. S. Martín
L. O'Higgins
Murallón 3600
Argentino
L. Viedma
San Julián
San Martín
Santa Cruz
Bahía Grande
CHILE
ARGENTINA
PATAGONIA
Chubut

SOUTH ATLANTIC OCEAN

FALKLAND ISLANDS
(ISLAS MALVINAS)
(Br.)
West Falkland
700
705
Stanley
East Falkland
Falkland Sound
Port Darwin

Queen Adelaide Arch.
Puerto Natales
Río Gallegos
C. Vírgenes
Magellan's Str.
Punta Arenas
Porvenir
Tierra del Fuego 2469
I. Santa Inés
I. de los Estados (Staten I.)
San Diego
Ushuaia
Beagle Channel
I. Navarino
Islas Wollaston
I. Hoste
Bahía Cook
C. Horn

South Georgia
(Br.)

m
6000
4000
3000
2000
1500
1000
400
200
0
200
2000
4000
6000
8000
m

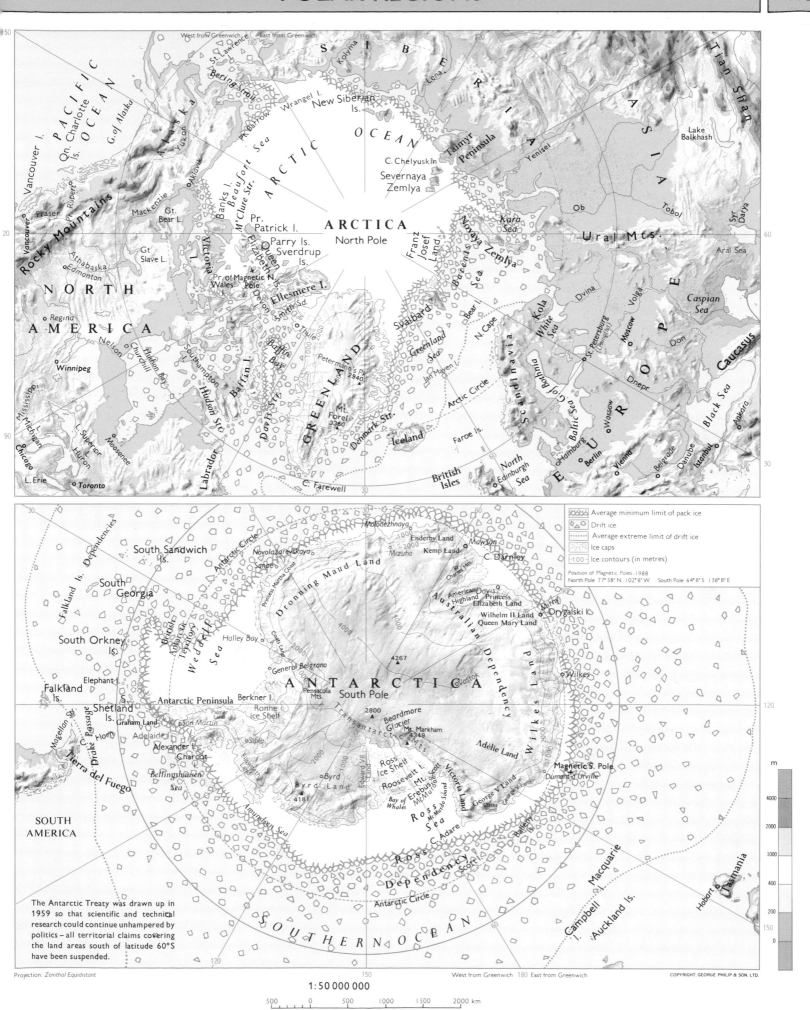

The Antarctic Treaty was drawn up in 1959 so that scientific and technical research could continue unhampered by politics – all territorial claims covering the land areas south of latitude 60°S have been suspended.

Average minimum limit of pack ice
Drift ice
Average extreme limit of drift ice
Ice caps
-100- Ice contours (in metres)

Position of Magnetic Poles.1988
North Pole 77°58′N 102°8′W   South Pole 64°8′S 138°8′E

Projection: Zenithal Equidistant

West from Greenwich 180 East from Greenwich

COPYRIGHT. GEORGE PHILIP & SON. LTD.

1:50 000 000

500   0   500   1000   1500   2000 km

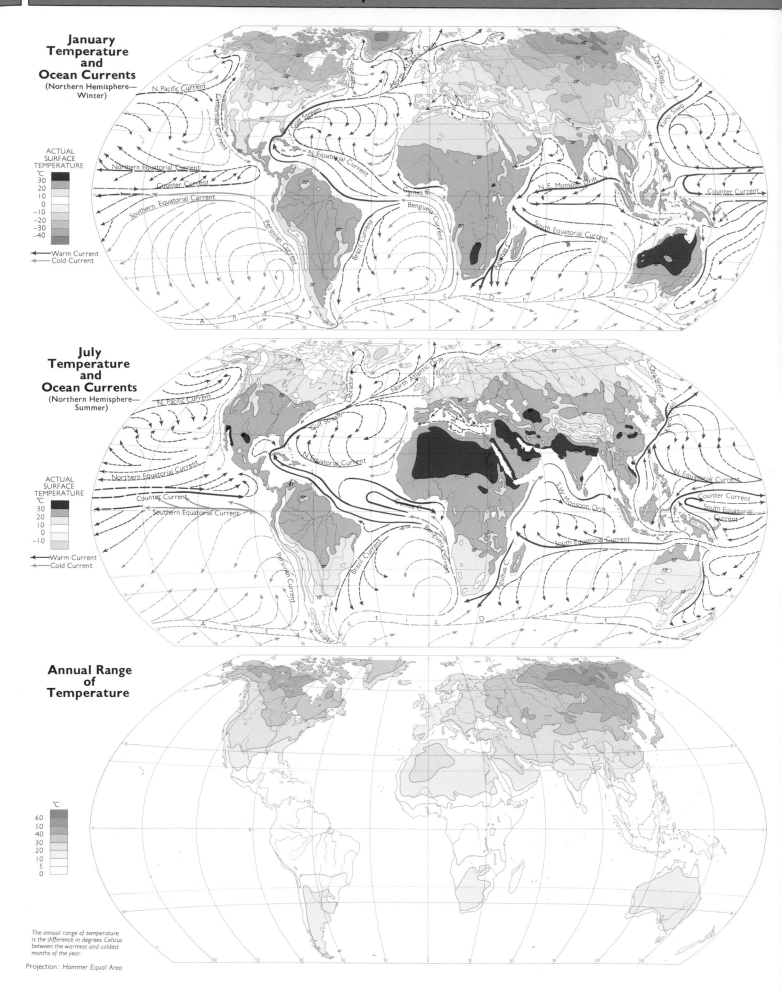

**January
Temperature
and
Ocean Currents**
(Northern Hemisphere—
Winter)

ACTUAL
SURFACE
TEMPERATURE
°C
30
20
10
0
-10
-20
-30
-40

Warm Current
Cold Current

N. Pacific Current
California Current
Gulf Stream
Labrador C.
North Atlantic Drift
Kuro Siwo
Oya Siwo
Northern Equatorial Current
Counter Current
N. Equatorial Current
Southern Equatorial Current
Peruvian Current
Guinea C.
Brazil Current
Benguela Current
Agulhas C.
N. E. Monsoon Drift
South Equatorial Current
Counter Current
Antarctic Drift

**July
Temperature
and
Ocean Currents**
(Northern Hemisphere—
Summer)

ACTUAL
SURFACE
TEMPERATURE
°C
30
20
10
0
-10

Warm Current
Cold Current

N. Pacific Current
Gulf Stream
Labrador
North Atlantic Drift
Oya Siwo
Kuro Siwo
Northern Equatorial Current
N. Equatorial Current
Counter Current
Southern Equatorial Current
Peruvian Current
Guinea C.
Brazil Current
Benguela Current
Agulhas C.
S.W. Monsoon Drift
South Equatorial Current
N. Equatorial Current
Counter Current
South Equatorial Current
Antarctic Drift

**Annual Range
of
Temperature**

°C
60
50
40
30
20
10
5
0

*The annual range of temperature
is the difference in degrees Celsius
between the warmest and coldest
months of the year.*

Projection: *Hammer Equal Area*

1:190 000 000

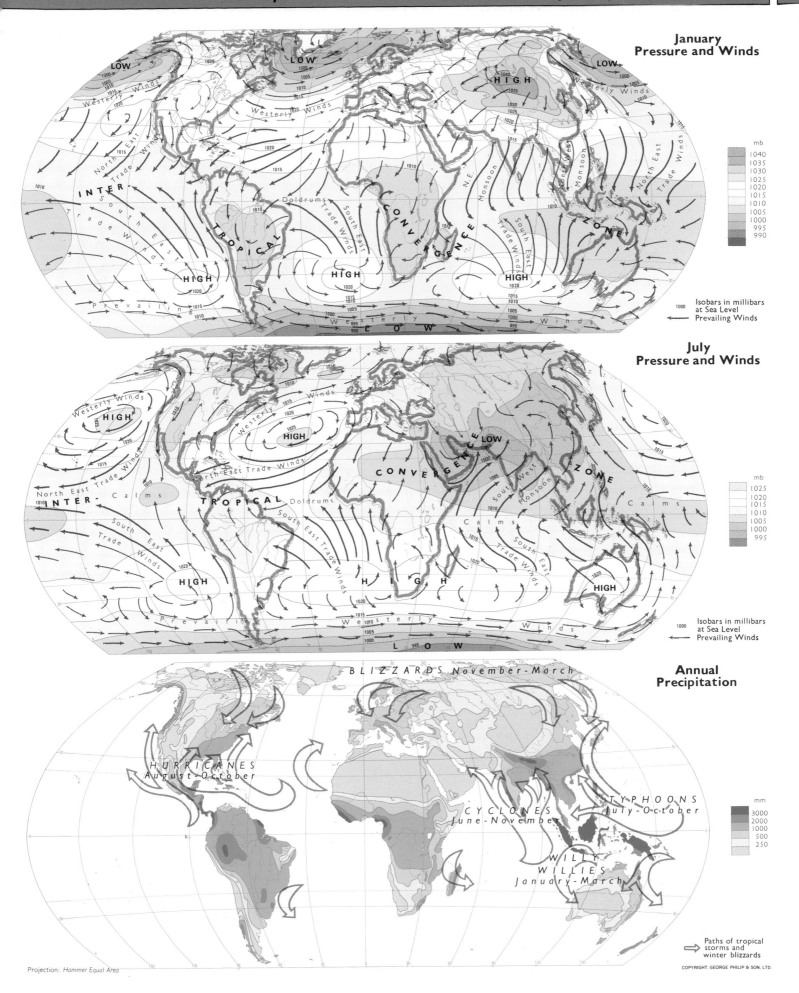

January
Pressure and Winds

mb
1040
1035
1030
1025
1020
1015
1010
1005
1000
995
990

1000 — Isobars in millibars
at Sea Level
Prevailing Winds

July
Pressure and Winds

mb
1025
1020
1015
1010
1005
1000
995

1000 — Isobars in millibars
at Sea Level
Prevailing Winds

Annual
Precipitation

BLIZZARDS November–March

HURRICANES
August–October

CYCLONES
June–November

TYPHOONS
July–October

WILLY
WILLIES
January–March

mm
3000
2000
1000
500
250

Paths of tropical
storms and
winter blizzards

Projection: Hammer Equal Area

COPYRIGHT. GEORGE PHILIP & SON, LTD.

1:190 000 000

These four pages give temperature and precipitation statistics for over 80 stations, which are arranged by listing the continents and the places within each continent in alphabetical order. The elevation of each station, in metres above mean sea level, is stated beneath its name. The average monthly temperature, in degrees Celsius, and the average monthly precipitation, in millimetres, are given. To the right, the average yearly rainfall, the average yearly temperature, and the annual range of temperature (the difference between the warmest and the coldest months) are also stated.

AFRICA

		Jan.	Feb.	Mar.	Apr.	May	June	July	Aug.	Sept.	Oct.	Nov.	Dec.	Year	Annual Range
Addis Ababa, Ethiopia	Precipitation	<3	3	25	135	213	201	206	239	102	28	<3	0	1 151	
2 450 m	Temperature	19	20	20	20	19	18	18	19	21	22	21	20	20	4
Cairo, Egypt	Precipitation	5	5	5	3	3	<3	0	0	<3	<3	3	5	28	
116 m	Temperature	13	15	18	21	25	28	28	28	26	24	20	15	22	15
Cape Town, South Africa	Precipitation	15	8	18	48	79	84	89	66	43	31	18	10	508	
17 m	Temperature	21	21	20	17	14	13	12	13	14	16	18	19	17	9
Casablanca, Morocco	Precipitation	53	48	56	36	23	5	0	<3	8	38	66	71	404	
50 m	Temperature	13	13	14	16	18	20	22	23	22	19	16	13	18	10
Johannesburg, South Africa	Precipitation	114	109	89	38	25	8	8	8	23	56	107	125	709	
1 665 m	Temperature	20	20	18	16	13	10	11	13	16	18	19	20	16	10
Khartoum, Sudan	Precipitation	<3	<3	<3	<3	3	8	53	71	18	5	<3	0	158	
390 m	Temperature	24	25	28	31	33	34	32	31	32	32	28	25	29	9
Kinshasa, Zaïre	Precipitation	135	145	196	196	158	8	3	3	31	119	221	142	1 354	
325 m	Temperature	26	26	27	27	26	24	23	24	25	26	26	26	25	4
Lagos, Nigeria	Precipitation	28	46	102	150	269	460	279	64	140	206	69	25	1 836	
3 m	Temperature	27	28	29	28	28	26	26	25	26	26	28	28	27	4
Lusaka, Zambia	Precipitation	231	191	142	18	3	<3	<3	0	<3	10	91	150	836	
1 277 m	Temperature	21	22	21	21	19	16	16	18	22	24	23	22	21	8
Monrovia, Liberia	Precipitation	31	56	97	216	516	973	996	373	744	772	236	130	5 138	
23 m	Temperature	26	26	27	27	26	25	24	25	25	25	26	26	26	3
Nairobi, Kenya	Precipitation	38	64	125	211	158	46	15	23	31	53	109	86	958	
1 820 m	Temperature	19	19	19	19	18	16	16	16	18	19	18	18	18	3
Tananarive, Madagascar	Precipitation	300	279	178	53	18	8	8	10	18	61	135	287	1 356	
1 372 m	Temperature	21	21	21	19	18	15	14	15	17	19	21	21	19	7
Timbuktu, Mali	Precipitation	<3	<3	3	<3	5	23	79	81	38	3	<3	<3	231	
301 m	Temperature	22	24	28	32	34	35	32	30	32	31	28	23	29	13
Tunis, Tunisia	Precipitation	64	51	41	36	18	8	3	8	33	51	48	61	419	
66 m	Temperature	10	11	13	16	19	23	26	27	25	20	16	11	18	17
Walvis Bay, South Africa	Precipitation	<3	5	8	3	3	<3	<3	3	<3	<3	<3	<3	23	
7 m	Temperature	19	19	19	18	17	16	15	14	14	15	17	18	18	5

AMERICA, NORTH

		Jan.	Feb.	Mar.	Apr.	May	June	July	Aug.	Sept.	Oct.	Nov.	Dec.	Year	Annual Range
Anchorage, Alaska, U.S.A.	Precipitation	20	18	15	10	13	18	41	66	66	56	25	23	371	
40 m	Temperature	−11	−8	−5	2	7	12	14	13	9	2	−5	−11	2	25
Cheyenne, Wyo., U.S.A.	Precipitation	10	15	25	48	61	41	53	41	31	25	13	13	376	
1 871 m	Temperature	−4	−3	1	5	10	16	19	19	14	7	1	−2	7	23
Chicago, Ill., U.S.A.	Precipitation	51	51	66	71	86	89	84	81	79	66	61	51	836	
251 m	Temperature	−4	−3	2	9	14	20	23	22	19	12	5	−1	10	27
Churchill, Man., Canada	Precipitation	15	13	18	23	32	44	46	58	51	43	39	21	402	
13 m	Temperature	−28	−26	−20	−10	−2	6	12	11	5	−2	−12	−22	−7	40

		Jan.	Feb.	Mar.	Apr.	May	June	July	Aug.	Sept.	Oct.	Nov.	Dec.	Year	Annual range
Edmonton, Alta., Canada															
	Precipitation	25	19	19	22	43	77	89	78	39	17	16	25	466	
676 m	Temperature	−15	−10	−5	4	11	15	17	16	11	6	−4	−10	3	32
Honolulu, Hawaii, U.S.A.															
	Precipitation	104	66	79	48	25	18	23	28	36	48	64	104	643	
12 m	Temperature	23	18	19	20	22	24	25	26	26	24	22	19	22	8
Houston, Tex., U.S.A.															
	Precipitation	89	76	84	91	119	117	99	99	104	94	89	109	1 171	
12 m	Temperature	12	13	17	21	24	27	28	29	26	22	16	12	21	17
Kingston, Jamaica															
	Precipitation	23	15	23	31	102	89	38	91	99	180	74	36	800	
34 m	Temperature	25	25	25	26	26	28	28	28	27	27	26	26	26	3
Los Angeles, Calif., U.S.A.															
	Precipitation	79	76	71	25	10	3	<3	<3	5	15	31	66	381	
95 m	Temperature	13	14	14	16	17	19	21	22	21	18	16	14	17	9
Mexico City, Mexico															
	Precipitation	13	5	10	20	53	119	170	152	130	51	18	8	747	
2 309 m	Temperature	12	13	16	18	19	19	17	18	18	16	14	13	16	7
Miami, Fla., U.S.A.															
	Precipitation	71	53	64	81	173	178	155	160	203	234	71	51	1 516	
8 m	Temperature	20	20	22	23	25	27	28	28	27	25	22	21	24	8
Montreal, Que., Canada															
	Precipitation	72	65	74	74	66	82	90	92	88	76	81	87	946	
57 m	Temperature	−10	−9	−3	−6	13	18	21	20	15	9	2	−7	6	31
New York, N.Y., U.S.A.															
	Precipitation	94	97	91	81	81	84	107	109	86	89	76	91	1 092	
96 m	Temperature	−1	−1	3	10	16	20	23	23	21	15	7	2	8	24
St. Louis, Mo., U.S.A.															
	Precipitation	58	64	89	97	114	114	89	86	81	74	71	64	1 001	
173 m	Temperature	0	1	7	13	19	24	26	26	22	15	8	2	14	26
San Francisco, Calif., U.S.A.															
	Precipitation	119	97	79	38	18	3	<3	<3	8	25	64	112	561	
16 m	Temperature	10	12	13	13	14	15	15	15	17	16	14	11	14	7
San José, Costa Rica															
	Precipitation	15	5	20	46	229	241	211	241	305	300	145	41	1 798	
1 146 m	Temperature	19	19	21	21	22	21	21	21	21	20	20	19	20	2
Vancouver, B.C., Canada															
	Precipitation	154	115	101	60	52	45	32	41	67	114	150	182	1113	
14 m	Temperature	3	5	6	9	12	15	17	17	14	10	6	4	10	14
Washington, D.C., U.S.A.															
	Precipitation	86	76	91	84	94	99	112	109	94	74	66	79	1 064	
22 m	Temperature	1	2	7	12	18	23	25	24	20	14	8	3	13	24

AMERICA, SOUTH

		Jan.	Feb.	Mar.	Apr.	May	June	July	Aug.	Sept.	Oct.	Nov.	Dec.	Year	Annual range
Antofagasta, Chile															
	Precipitation	0	0	0	<3	<3	3	5	3	<3	3	<3	0	13	
94 m	Temperature	21	21	20	18	16	15	14	14	15	16	18	19	17	7
Buenos Aires, Argentina															
	Precipitation	79	71	109	89	76	61	56	61	79	86	84	99	950	
27 m	Temperature	23	23	21	17	13	9	10	11	13	15	19	22	16	14
Caracas, Venezuela															
	Precipitation	23	10	15	33	79	102	109	109	107	109	94	46	836	
1 042 m	Temperature	19	19	20	21	22	21	21	21	21	21	20	20	21	3
Lima, Peru															
	Precipitation	3	<3	<3	<3	5	5	8	8	8	3	3	<3	41	
120 m	Temperature	23	24	24	22	19	17	17	16	17	18	19	21	20	8
Manaus, Brazil															
	Precipitation	249	231	262	221	170	84	58	38	46	107	142	203	1 811	
44 m	Temperature	28	28	28	27	28	28	28	28	29	29	29	28	28	2
Paraná, Brazil															
	Precipitation	287	236	239	102	13	<3	3	5	28	127	231	310	1 582	
260 m	Temperature	23	23	23	23	23	21	21	22	24	24	24	23	23	3
Quito, Ecuador															
	Precipitation	99	112	142	175	137	43	20	31	69	112	97	79	1 115	
2 879 m	Temperature	15	15	15	15	15	14	14	15	15	15	15	15	15	1
Rio de Janeiro, Brazil															
	Precipitation	125	122	130	107	79	53	41	43	66	79	104	137	1 082	
61 m	Temperature	26	26	25	24	22	21	21	21	21	22	23	25	23	5
Santiago, Chile															
	Precipitation	3	3	5	13	64	84	76	56	31	15	8	5	358	
520 m	Temperature	21	20	18	15	12	9	9	10	12	15	17	19	15	12

ASIA

		Jan.	Feb.	Mar.	Apr.	May	June	July	Aug.	Sept.	Oct.	Nov.	Dec.	Year	Annual range
Bahrain	Precipitation	8	18	13	8	<3	0	0	0	0	0	18	18	81	
5 m	Temperature	17	18	21	25	29	32	33	34	31	28	24	19	26	16
Bangkok, Thailand	Precipitation	8	20	36	58	198	160	160	175	305	206	66	5	1 397	
2 m	Temperature	26	28	29	30	29	29	28	28	28	28	26	25	28	5
Beirut, Lebanon	Precipitation	191	158	94	53	18	3	<3	<3	5	51	132	185	892	
34 m	Temperature	14	14	16	18	22	24	27	28	26	24	19	16	21	14
Bombay, India	Precipitation	3	3	3	<3	18	485	617	340	264	64	13	3	1 809	
11 m	Temperature	24	24	26	28	30	29	27	27	27	28	27	26	27	6
Calcutta, India	Precipitation	10	31	36	43	140	297	325	328	252	114	20	5	1 600	
6 m	Temperature	20	22	27	30	30	30	29	29	29	28	23	19	26	11
Colombo, Sri Lanka	Precipitation	89	69	147	231	371	224	135	109	160	348	315	147	2 365	
7 m	Temperature	26	26	27	28	28	27	27	27	27	27	26	26	27	2
Harbin, China	Precipitation	5	5	10	23	43	94	112	104	46	33	8	5	488	
160 m	Temperature	−18	−15	−5	6	13	19	22	21	14	4	−6	−16	3	40
Ho Chi Minh City, Vietnam	Precipitation	15	3	13	43	221	330	315	269	335	269	114	56	1 984	
9 m	Temperature	26	27	29	30	29	28	28	28	27	27	27	26	28	4
Jakarta, Indonesia	Precipitation	300	300	211	147	114	97	64	43	66	112	142	203	1 798	
8 m	Temperature	26	26	27	27	27	27	27	27	27	27	27	26	27	1
Hong Kong	Precipitation	33	46	74	137	292	394	381	361	257	114	43	31	2 162	
33 m	Temperature	16	15	18	22	26	28	28	28	27	25	21	18	23	13
Kabul, Afghanistan	Precipitation	31	36	94	102	20	5	3	3	<3	15	20	10	338	
1 815 m	Temperature	−3	−1	6	13	18	22	25	24	20	14	7	3	12	28
Karachi, Pakistan	Precipitation	13	10	8	3	3	18	81	41	13	<3	3	5	196	
4 m	Temperature	19	20	24	28	30	31	30	29	28	28	24	20	26	12
New Delhi, India	Precipitation	23	18	13	8	13	74	180	172	117	10	3	10	640	
218 m	Temperature	14	17	23	28	33	34	31	30	29	26	20	15	25	20
Shanghai, China	Precipitation	48	58	84	94	94	180	147	142	130	71	51	36	1 135	
7 m	Temperature	4	5	9	14	20	24	28	28	23	19	12	7	16	24
Singapore	Precipitation	252	173	193	188	173	173	170	196	178	208	254	257	2 413	
10 m	Temperature	26	27	28	28	28	28	28	27	27	27	27	27	27	2
Tehran, Iran	Precipitation	46	38	46	36	13	3	3	3	3	8	20	31	246	
1 220 m	Temperature	2	5	9	16	21	26	30	29	25	18	12	6	17	28
Tokyo, Japan	Precipitation	48	74	107	135	147	165	142	152	234	208	97	56	1 565	
6 m	Temperature	3	4	7	13	17	21	25	26	23	17	11	6	14	23
Ulan Bator, Mongolia	Precipitation	<3	<3	3	5	10	28	76	51	23	5	5	3	208	
1 325 m	Temperature	−26	−21	−13	−1	6	14	16	14	8	−1	−13	−22	−3	42

AUSTRALIA, NEW ZEALAND and ANTARCTICA

		Jan.	Feb.	Mar.	Apr.	May	June	July	Aug.	Sept.	Oct.	Nov.	Dec.	Year	Annual range
Alice Springs, Australia	Precipitation	43	33	28	10	15	13	8	8	8	18	31	38	252	
579 m	Temperature	29	28	25	20	15	12	12	14	18	23	26	28	21	17
Christchurch, New Zealand	Precipitation	56	43	48	48	66	66	69	48	46	43	48	56	638	
10 m	Temperature	16	16	14	12	9	6	6	7	9	12	14	16	11	10
Darwin, Australia	Precipitation	386	312	254	97	15	3	<3	3	13	51	119	239	1 491	
30 m	Temperature	29	29	29	29	28	26	25	26	28	29	30	29	28	5
Mawson, Antarctica	Precipitation	11	30	20	10	44	180	4	40	3	20	0	0	362	
14 m	Temperature	0	−5	−10	−14	−15	−16	−18	−18	−19	−13	−5	−1	−11	18

		Jan.	Feb.	Mar.	Apr.	May	June	July	Aug.	Sept.	Oct.	Nov.	Dec.	Year	Annual Range
Melbourne, Australia	Precipitation	48	46	56	58	53	53	48	48	58	66	58	58	653	
35 m	Temperature	20	20	18	15	13	10	9	11	13	14	16	18	15	11
Perth, Australia	Precipitation	8	10	20	43	130	180	170	149	86	56	20	13	881	
60 m	Temperature	23	23	22	19	16	14	13	13	15	16	19	22	18	10
Sydney, Australia	Precipitation	89	102	127	135	127	117	117	76	73	71	73	73	1 181	
42 m	Temperature	22	22	21	18	15	13	12	13	15	18	19	21	17	10

EUROPE and U.S.S.R.

		Jan.	Feb.	Mar.	Apr.	May	June	July	Aug.	Sept.	Oct.	Nov.	Dec.	Year	Annual Range
Archangel, U.S.S.R.	Precipitation	31	19	25	29	42	52	62	56	63	63	47	41	530	
13 m	Temperature	−16	−14	−9	0	7	12	15	14	8	2	−4	−11	0	31
Athens, Greece	Precipitation	62	37	37	23	23	14	6	7	15	51	56	71	402	
107 m	Temperature	10	10	12	16	20	25	28	28	24	20	15	11	18	18
Berlin, Germany	Precipitation	46	40	33	42	49	65	73	69	48	49	46	43	603	
55 m	Temperature	−1	0	4	9	14	17	19	18	15	9	5	1	9	20
Istanbul, Turkey	Precipitation	109	92	72	46	38	34	34	30	58	81	103	119	816	
114 m	Temperature	5	6	7	11	16	20	23	23	20	16	12	8	14	18
Kazalinsk, U.S.S.R.	Precipitation	10	10	13	13	15	5	5	8	8	10	13	15	125	
63 m	Temperature	−12	−11	−3	6	18	23	25	23	16	8	−1	−7	7	37
Lisbon, Portugal	Precipitation	111	76	109	54	44	16	3	4	33	62	93	103	708	
77 m	Temperature	11	12	14	16	17	20	22	23	21	18	14	12	17	12
London, U.K.	Precipitation	54	40	37	37	46	45	57	59	49	57	64	48	593	
5 m	Temperature	4	5	7	9	12	16	18	17	15	11	8	5	11	14
Málaga, Spain	Precipitation	61	51	62	46	26	5	1	3	29	64	64	62	474	
33 m	Temperature	12	13	15	17	19	29	25	26	23	20	16	13	18	17
Moscow, U.S.S.R.	Precipitation	39	38	36	37	53	58	88	71	58	45	47	54	624	
156 m	Temperature	−13	−10	−4	6	13	16	18	17	12	6	−1	−7	4	31
Odessa, U.S.S.R.	Precipitation	57	62	30	21	34	34	42	37	37	13	35	71	473	
64 m	Temperature	−3	−1	2	9	15	20	22	22	18	12	9	1	10	25
Omsk, U.S.S.R.	Precipitation	15	8	8	13	31	51	51	51	28	25	18	20	318	
85 m	Temperature	−22	−19	−12	−1	10	16	18	16	10	1	−11	−18	−1	40
Palma de Mallorca, Spain	Precipitation	39	34	51	32	29	17	3	25	55	77	47	40	449	
10 m	Temperature	10	11	12	15	17	21	24	25	23	18	14	11	17	15
Paris, France	Precipitation	56	46	35	42	57	54	59	64	55	50	51	50	619	
75 m	Temperature	3	4	8	11	15	18	20	19	17	12	7	4	12	17
Rome, Italy	Precipitation	71	62	57	51	46	37	15	21	63	99	129	93	744	
17 m	Temperature	8	9	11	14	18	22	25	25	22	17	13	10	16	17
Shannon, Irish Republic	Precipitation	94	67	56	53	61	57	77	79	86	86	96	117	929	
2 m	Temperature	5	5	7	9	12	14	16	16	14	11	8	6	10	11
Stavanger, Norway	Precipitation	93	56	45	70	49	84	93	118	142	129	125	126	1 130	
85 m	Temperature	1	1	3	6	10	13	15	15	13	9	6	3	8	14
Stockholm, Sweden	Precipitation	43	30	25	31	34	45	61	76	60	48	53	48	554	
44 m	Temperature	−3	−3	−1	5	10	15	18	17	12	7	3	0	7	21
Verkhoyansk, U.S.S.R.	Precipitation	5	5	3	5	8	23	28	25	13	8	8	5	134	
100 m	Temperature	−50	−45	−32	−15	0	12	14	9	2	−15	−38	−48	−17	64
Warsaw, Poland	Precipitation	27	32	27	37	46	69	96	65	43	38	31	44	555	
110 m	Temperature	−3	−3	2	7	14	17	19	18	14	9	3	0	8	22

CLIMATES — after Köppen

Climatic group	Climate		Temperature	Rainfall
A TROPICAL RAINY CLIMATES	**Af**	RAIN-FOREST CLIMATE	All mean monthly temperatures above 18°C	
	Am	MONSOON CLIMATE		
	Aw	SAVANNA CLIMATE		
B DRY CLIMATES	**BS**	STEPPE CLIMATE	Mean annual temperature. **h** = above 18°C **k** = below 18°C	
	BW	DESERT CLIMATE		
C WARM TEMPERATE RAINY CLIMATES	**Cw**	DRY WINTER CLIMATE	Mean temperature of the coldest month between −3°C to 18°C	
	Cs	DRY SUMMER CLIMATE (Mediterranean)		
	Cf	CLIMATE WITH NO DRY SEASON		
D COLD TEMPERATE RAINY CLIMATES	**Dw**	DRY WINTER CLIMATE	Mean temperature of the coldest month below −3°C	
	Df	CLIMATE WITH NO DRY SEASON		
E POLAR CLIMATES	**ET**	TUNDRA CLIMATE	Mean temperature of the hottest month between 0°C and 10°C	**H** More than 1500m above sea level
	EF	PERPETUAL FROST	Mean temperature of the hottest month between 0°C and 10°C	

a Mean temperature of hottest month above 22°C, and with more than 4 months of over 10°C

b Mean temperature of hottest month below 22°C and with more than 4 months of over 10°C

c Mean temperature of hottest month below 22°C, but with less than 4 months of over 10°C

d Mean temperature of hottest month below 22°C, and of the coldest month below −38°C

w dry winter — Rainfall of the driest month of the cold season is one-tenth or less of the rainfall of the wettest month of the hot season

s dry summer — Rainfall of the driest month of the hot season is less than one-third of the rainfall of the wettest month of the cold season and less than 40mm.

f with no dry season — Rainfall does not correspond to w or s climates

Temperature: All mean monthly temperatures above 18°C

Rainfall chart (Af, Am, Aw): Rainfall during the driest month (mm) vs Annual rainfall (mm) — 1000, 2000, 3000

Temperature chart: BW / BS — BW/BS Boundary, BS/Wet Climates Boundary, Wet Climates A, C, D. Mean annual temperature (°C) vs Annual rainfall (mm) — 200, 400, 600.
- - - - summer rainfall
——— winter rainfall
– · – · rainfall evenly distributed

SOIL REGIONS

1:240 000 000 — after Glinka, Stremme, Marbut, and others

- Tundra Soil
- Podzols
- Brown Forest Soil
- Lightly leached Dry Forest Soil
- Red and yellow Sub-tropical Forest Soil
- Reddish Savanna Soil and Tropical Red Earths
- Laterites
- Chernozem
- Degraded Chernozem
- Black Savanna Soil
- Chestnut Steppe Soil
- Grey, light brown and red brown Desert Steppe Soils
- Alluvium
- Mountain and High Plateau Soils
- Oases Soil
- Tropical and Mangrove Swamp

Projection: Interrupted Mollweide's Homolographic

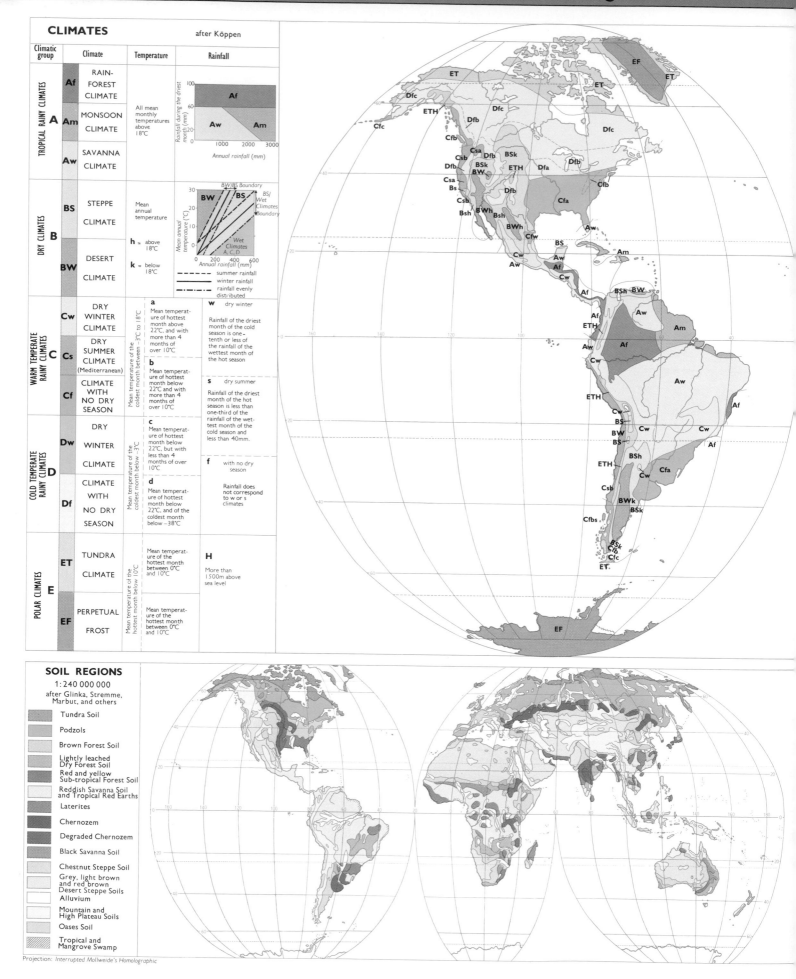

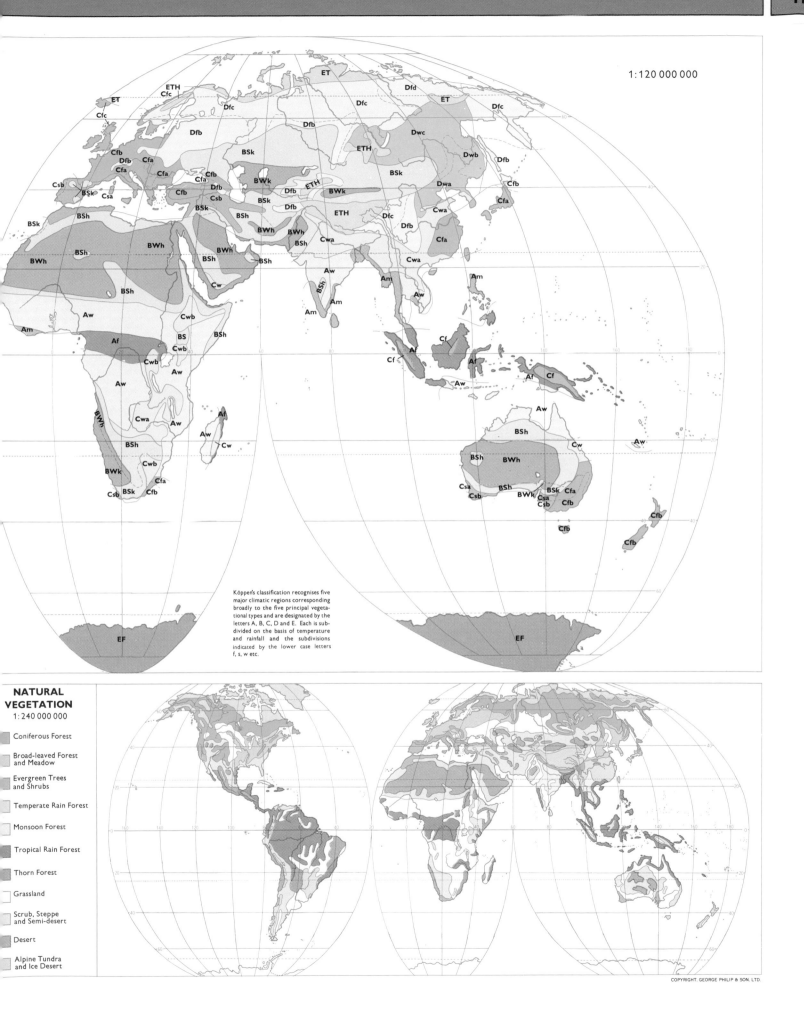

1:120 000 000

ET
ETH
Cfc
ET
Cfc
Dfd
Dfc
ET
Dfc
Dfb
Cfb
Dfb
ET
Dfb
BSk
Dwc
ETH
Cfb
Dfb
Dwb
Dfb
Cfb
Dfb
Cfa
Cfa
Cfb
BWk
BSk
Csb
Cfa
Cfa
Dfb
Dwa
Csb
BSk
Csa
Cfb
Csb
BSk
ETH
Cfa
Cwa
BSk
Dfb
BWk
BSk
Dfb
Dfc
BSh
Dfb
Cfa
BSk
BSh
ETH
Dfb
BWh
BSh
BWh
Cwa
BWh
BSh
BWh
BWh
BSh
Cwa
BSh
BSh
BSh
BSh
Cw
Am
Aw
Aw
Am
Aw
Am
Am
Cwb
Am
BSh
Cf
Af
Af
BS
Af
Cf
Cwb
Cf
Cwb
Aw
Aw
Af
Af
Aw
Aw
Aw
Cwa
Af
Cwb
Aw
Cw
BWh
Aw
BSh
Cwb
BSh
BWh
Cw
Aw
BWk
Cw
Csa
BSk
Cfa
Cfa
Csb
Cfb
BSh
Csb
Csb
BWk
BSk
Cfb
Cfb
Cfb
Cfb

Köppen's classification recognises five major climatic regions corresponding broadly to the five principal vegetational types and are designated by the letters A, B, C, D and E. Each is sub-divided on the basis of temperature and rainfall and the subdivisions indicated by the lower case letters f, s, w etc.

EF
EF

NATURAL VEGETATION

1:240 000 000

- Coniferous Forest
- Broad-leaved Forest and Meadow
- Evergreen Trees and Shrubs
- Temperate Rain Forest
- Monsoon Forest
- Tropical Rain Forest
- Thorn Forest
- Grassland
- Scrub, Steppe and Semi-desert
- Desert
- Alpine Tundra and Ice Desert

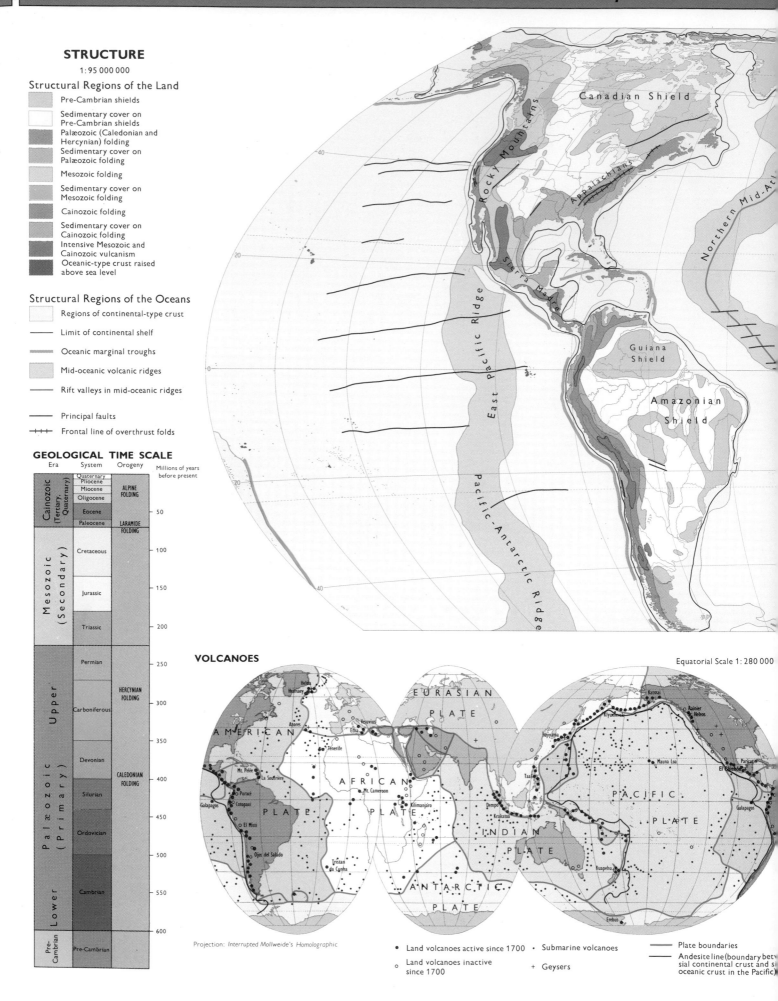

STRUCTURE

1 : 95 000 000

Structural Regions of the Land

- Pre-Cambrian shields
- Sedimentary cover on Pre-Cambrian shields
- Palæozoic (Caledonian and Hercynian) folding
- Sedimentary cover on Palæozoic folding
- Mesozoic folding
- Sedimentary cover on Mesozoic folding
- Cainozoic folding
- Sedimentary cover on Cainozoic folding
- Intensive Mesozoic and Cainozoic vulcanism
- Oceanic-type crust raised above sea level

Structural Regions of the Oceans

- Regions of continental-type crust
- Limit of continental shelf
- Oceanic marginal troughs
- Mid-oceanic volcanic ridges
- Rift valleys in mid-oceanic ridges
- Principal faults
- +++ Frontal line of overthrust folds

GEOLOGICAL TIME SCALE

Era	System	Orogeny	Millions of years before present
Cainozoic (Tertiary, Quaternary)	Quaternary		
	Pliocene	ALPINE FOLDING	
	Miocene		
	Oligocene		50
	Eocene		
	Paleocene	LARAMIDE FOLDING	
Mesozoic (Secondary)	Cretaceous		100
	Jurassic		150
	Triassic		200
Palæozoic (Primary) Upper	Permian		250
	Carboniferous	HERCYNIAN FOLDING	300
	Devonian		350
		CALEDONIAN FOLDING	400
Palæozoic (Primary) Lower	Silurian		
	Ordovician		450
	Cambrian		500
			550
Pre-Cambrian	Pre-Cambrian		600

VOLCANOES

Equatorial Scale 1 : 280 000

Projection: *Interrupted Mollweide's Homolographic*

- Land volcanoes active since 1700
- Land volcanoes inactive since 1700
- Submarine volcanoes
- + Geysers
- Plate boundaries
- Andesite line (boundary bet sial continental crust and s oceanic crust in the Pacific)

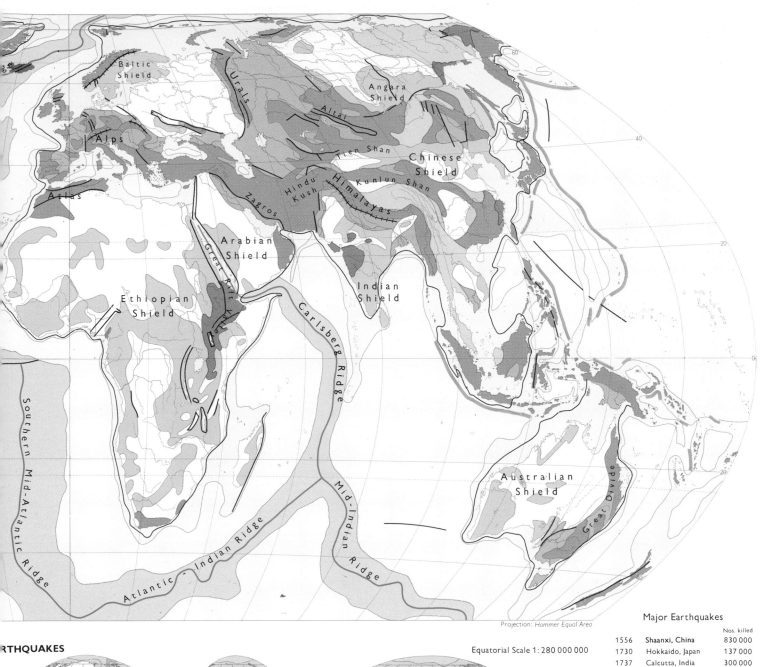

Baltic
Shield

Urals

Angara
Shield

Altai

Alps

Tien Shan

Chinese
Shield

Atlas

Hindu
Kush

Kunlun Shan

Himalayas

Zagros

Arabian
Shield

Great Rift Valley

Indian
Shield

Ethiopian
Shield

Carlsberg
Ridge

Southern Mid-Atlantic Ridge

Atlantic - Indian Ridge

Mid-Indian Ridge

Australian
Shield

Great Divide

Projection: *Hammer Equal Area*

Equatorial Scale 1: 280 000 000

ARTHQUAKES

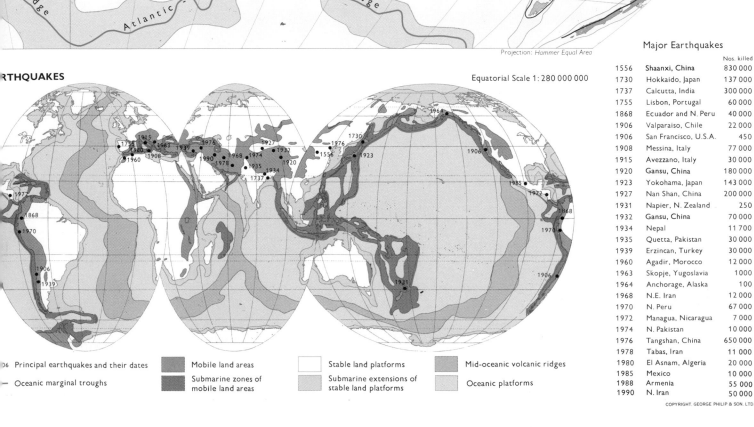

Principal earthquakes and their dates

Oceanic marginal troughs

Mobile land areas

Submarine zones of
mobile land areas

Stable land platforms

Submarine extensions of
stable land platforms

Mid-oceanic volcanic ridges

Oceanic platforms

Major Earthquakes

		Nos. killed
1556	**Shaanxi, China**	830 000
1730	Hokkaido, Japan	137 000
1737	Calcutta, India	300 000
1755	Lisbon, Portugal	60 000
1868	Ecuador and N. Peru	40 000
1906	Valparaiso, Chile	22 000
1906	San Francisco, U.S.A.	450
1908	Messina, Italy	77 000
1915	Avezzano, Italy	30 000
1920	**Gansu, China**	180 000
1923	Yokohama, Japan	143 000
1927	Nan Shan, China	200 000
1931	Napier, N. Zealand	250
1932	**Gansu, China**	70 000
1934	Nepal	11 700
1935	Quetta, Pakistan	30 000
1939	Erzincan, Turkey	30 000
1960	Agadir, Morocco	12 000
1963	Skopje, Yugoslavia	1000
1964	Anchorage, Alaska	100
1968	N.E. Iran	12 000
1970	N. Peru	67 000
1972	Managua, Nicaragua	7 000
1974	N. Pakistan	10 000
1976	Tangshan, China	650 000
1978	Tabas, Iran	11 000
1980	El Asnam, Algeria	20 000
1985	Mexico	10 000
1988	Armenia	55 000
1990	N. Iran	50 000

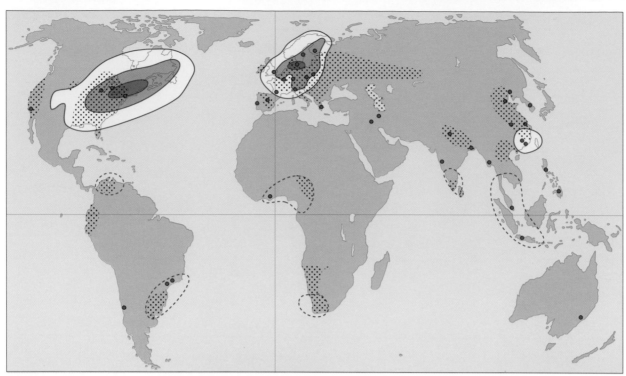

ACID RAIN

Acid rain is caused by high levels of sulphur and nitro in the atmosphere. They combine with water vapou and oxygen to form acids (H_2SO_4 and HNO_3) which fall as precipitation.

| | Main areas of sulph and nitrogen emiss (from the burning fossil fuels) |

| • | Major cities with hi levels of air polluti (including sulphur nitrogen emissions |

Areas of acid deposition

(pH numbers measure acidit normal rain is pH 5.6)

	pH less than 4.0 (most acidic)
	pH 4.0 - 4.5
	pH 4.5 - 5.0
⌐ ¬	Potential problem areas

GLOBAL WARMING

Global warming is caused by high levels of carbon dioxide and other gases in the atmosphere (the Greenhouse Effect). It is estimated that by 2020 the world could be approximately 1.3°C warmer than now.

Carbon dioxide (CO_2) emissions in tonnes per person per year

	Over 10 tonnes
	5 - 10 tonnes
	1 - 5 tonnes
	Under 1 tonne

Coastal areas vulnerable to rising sea levels caused by global warming

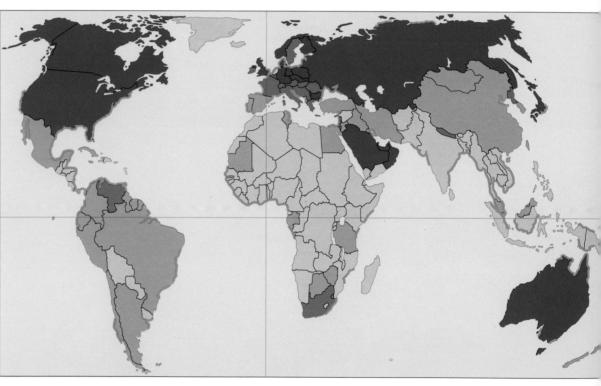

THE GREENHOUSE EFFECT

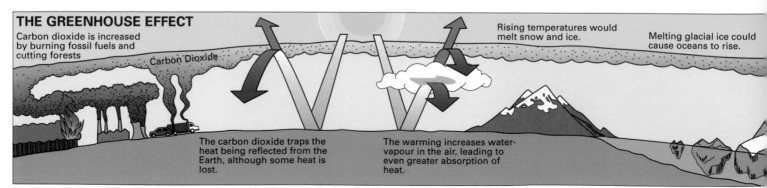

Carbon dioxide is increased by burning fossil fuels and cutting forests

Carbon Dioxide

Rising temperatures would melt snow and ice.

Melting glacial ice could cause oceans to rise.

The carbon dioxide traps the heat being reflected from the Earth, although some heat is lost.

The warming increases water-vapour in the air, leading to even greater absorption of heat.

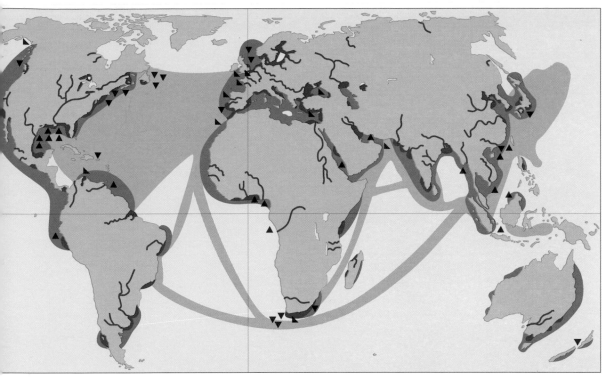

WATER POLLUTION

- Severely polluted sea areas and lakes
- Other polluted sea areas and lakes
- Sea areas of frequent oil pollution from shipping
- ▶ Major oil tanker spills
- ▲ Major oil rig blow-outs
- ▼ Offshore dumpsites for industrial and municipal waste
- —— Severely polluted rivers

SERTIFICATION

- Existing deserts
- as with a high risk of desertification
- s with a moderate k of desertification

FORESTATION THE TROPICS

- Former areas of rainforest
- Existing rainforest

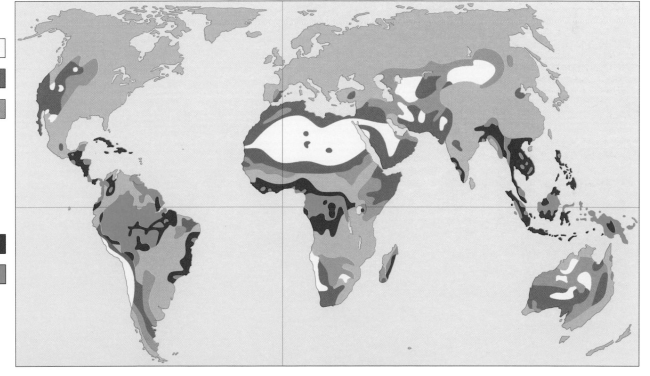

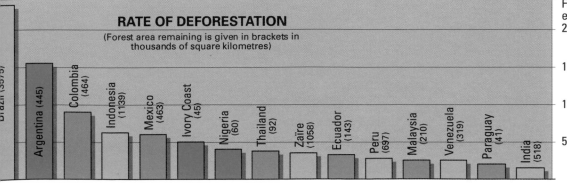

RATE OF DEFORESTATION

(Forest area remaining is given in brackets in thousands of square kilometres)

Forest area lost each year in the 1980s
20 000km²

Rate of deforestation (% each year)
- Over 2.5%
- 1.0 - 2.5%
- 0 - 1.0%

15 000km²

10 000km²

5 000km²

Countries: Argentina (445), Colombia (464), Indonesia (1139), Mexico (463), Ivory Coast (45), Nigeria (60), Thailand (92), Zaïre (1058), Ecuador (143), Peru (697), Malaysia (210), Venezuela (319), Paraguay (41), India (518)

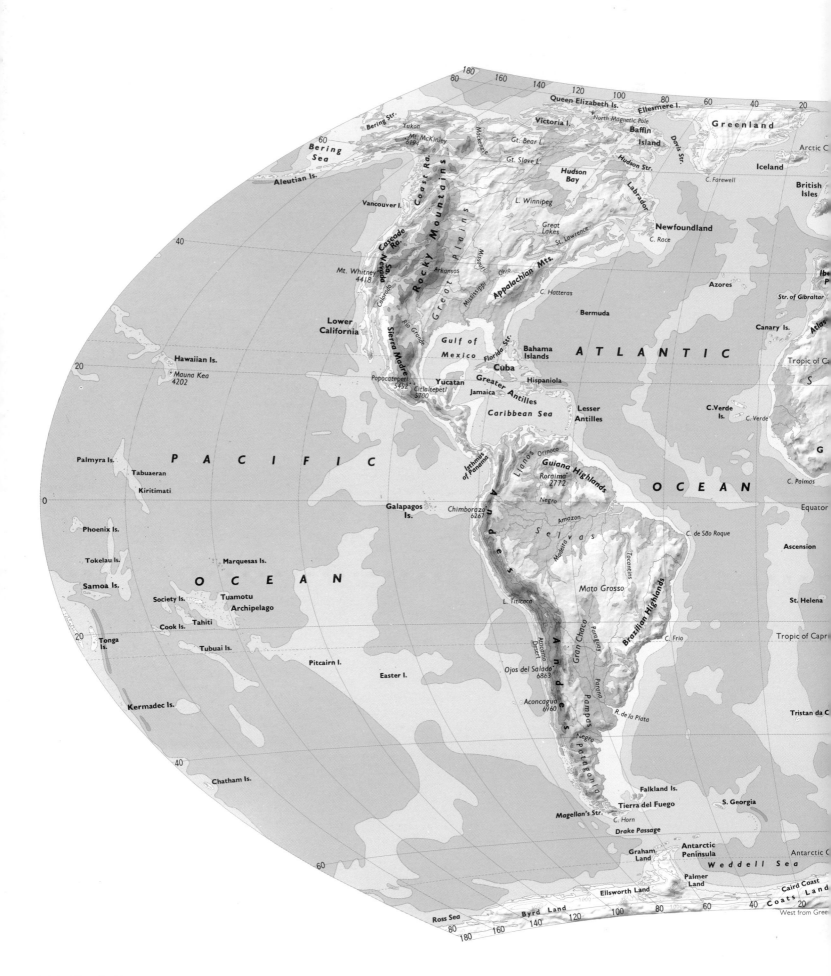

180
80 160 140 120 100 80 60 40 20

Queen Elizabeth Is.
Ellesmere I.
Victoria I.
North Magnetic Pole
Baffin
Island
Greenland

60
Bering Str.
Yukon
Mt. McKinley
6194
Mackenzie
Gt. Bear L.
Gt. Slave L.
Hudson Str.
Davis Str.
C. Farewell
Iceland
Arctic C

Bering
Sea
L. Winnipeg
Hudson
Bay
Labrador
British
Isles

Aleutian Is.
Vancouver I.
Coast Ra.
Rocky Mountains
Great
Lakes
St. Lawrence
Newfoundland
C. Race

40
Cascade Ra.
Sierra Nevada
Mt. Whitney
4418
Colorado
Arkansas
Missouri
Great Plains
Mississippi
Ohio
Appalachian Mts.
C. Hatteras
Azores
Ibe

Lower
California
Rio Grande
Sierra Madre
Gulf of
Mexico
Florida Str.
Bahama
Islands
Bermuda
ATLANTIC
Canary Is.
Str. of Gibraltar
Atlas

20
Hawaiian Is.
Mauna Kea
4202
Popocatepetl
5452
Citlaltepetl
5700
Yucatan
Cuba
Greater Antilles
Jamaica
Hispaniola
Lesser
Antilles
C. Verde
Is.
C. Verde
Tropic of Ca

Caribbean Sea
OCEAN
G

PACIFIC
Isthmus
of Panama
Orinoco
Llanos
Guiana Highlands
Roraima
2772
Negro
C. Palmas

Palmyra Is.
Tabuaeran
Kiritimati
Galapagos
Is.
Chimborazo
6267
Andes
Amazon
Selvas
Madeira
C. de São Roque
Ascension

0
Equator

Phoenix Is.
Tocantins
St. Helena

Tokelau Is.
Marquesas Is.
Mato Grosso
Brazilian Highlands

Samoa Is.
OCEAN
Society Is.
Tuamotu
Archipelago
L. Titicaca
Andes
Gran Chaco
Paraguay

Cook Is.
Tahiti
Atacama
Desert
Paraná
C. Frio
Tropic of Capri

20
Tonga
Is.
Tubuai Is.
Pitcairn I.
Easter I.
Ojos del Salado
6863
Paraná
Pampas

Kermadec Is.
Aconcagua
6960
R. de la Plata
Tristan da C

Negro
Patagonia
Falkland Is.

40
Chatham Is.
Tierra del Fuego
S. Georgia

Magellan's Str.
C. Horn
Drake Passage

Graham
Land
Antarctic
Peninsula
Palmer
Land
Antarctic C
Weddell Sea

60
Ellsworth Land
Coats Land
West from Gree

Ross Sea
Byrd Land
1000

80
180 160 140 120 100 80 60 40 20

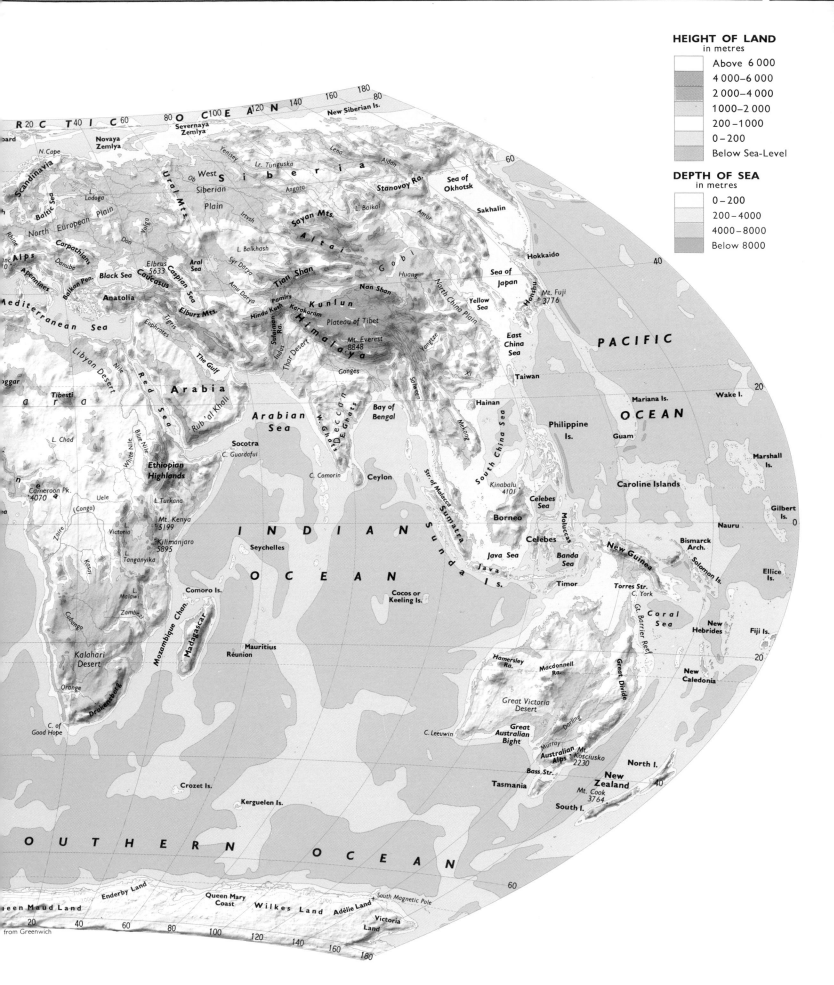

HEIGHT OF LAND
in metres
- Above 6 000
- 4 000–6 000
- 2 000–4 000
- 1000–2 000
- 200–1000
- 0–200
- Below Sea-Level

DEPTH OF SEA
in metres
- 0–200
- 200–4000
- 4000–8000
- Below 8000

ARCTIC OCEAN

New Siberian Is.
Severnaya Zemlya
N. Cape
Novaya Zemlya
Scandinavia
Baltic Sea
Ladoga
North European Plain
Rhine
Alps
Apennines
Carpathians
Danube
Balkan Pen.
Black Sea
Anatolia
Mediterranean Sea
Ural Mts.
West Siberian Plain
Ob
Yenisey
Lr. Tunguska
Lena
Angara
Irtysh
Siberia
Sayan Mts.
Altai
Stanovoy Ra.
Aldan
Amur
Sea of Okhotsk
Sakhalin
Hokkaido
L. Baikal
Gobi
Sea of Japan
Yellow Sea
Honshu
Mt. Fuji 3776
Elbrus 5633
Caucasus
Caspian Sea
Aral Sea
Syr Darya
Amu Darya
L. Balkhash
Tian Shan
Pamirs
Kunlun
Nan Shan
Huang
North China Plain
East China Sea
Elburz Mts.
Hindu Kush
Karakoram
Plateau of Tibet
Yangtze
Xi
Taiwan
PACIFIC OCEAN
Sulaiman Ra.
Indus
Thar Desert
Himalaya
Mt. Everest 8848
Ganges
Salween
Wake I.
Mariana Is.
Tigris
Euphrates
The Gulf
Arabia
Rub' al Khali
Deccan
W. Ghats
E. Ghats
Bay of Bengal
Mekong
Hainan
Philippine Is.
Guam
Libyan Desert
Nile
Red Sea
Arabian Sea
Socotra
C. Guardafui
Ceylon
C. Comorin
South China Sea
Caroline Islands
Marshall Is.
Tibesti
L. Chad
Cameroon Pk. 4070
Ethiopian Highlands
L. Turkana
Mt. Kenya 5199
Kilimanjaro 5895
Victoria
Uele
(Congo)
Zaire
Kasai
Seychelles
INDIAN OCEAN
Sumatra
Kinabalu 4101
Borneo
Celebes Sea
Celebes
Moluccas
Banda Sea
New Guinea
Bismarck Arch.
Solomon Is.
Nauru
Gilbert Is.
Ellice Is.
Fiji Is.
Java Sea
Java
Sunda Is.
Timor
Torres Str.
C. York
Coral Sea
New Hebrides
New Caledonia
Comoro Is.
Mozambique Chan.
Madagascar
Mauritius
Réunion
Cocos or Keeling Is.
Cubango
Zambezi
L. Malawi
L. Tanganyika
Kalahari Desert
Orange
Drakensberg
C. of Good Hope
Crozet Is.
Kerguelen Is.
Hamersley Ra.
Macdonnell Ra.
Great Divide
Great Victoria Desert
C. Leeuwin
Great Australian Bight
Murray
Darling
Australian Alps
Mt. Kosciusko 2230
Bass Str.
Tasmania
New Zealand
North I.
South I.
Mt. Cook 3764
SOUTHERN OCEAN
Enderby Land
Queen Mary Coast
Wilkes Land
Adélie Land
South Magnetic Pole
Green Maud Land
Victoria Land
from Greenwich

1:80 000 000

Copyright, George Philip & Son, Ltd.

Principal Air Routes
Distances in km

Polar Routes

Pacific Routes

Pacific Routes

GREENLAND

ICELAND

Queen Elizabeth Is.

Victoria I.

Baffin I.

Anchorage

Churchill

Hudson Bay

UNITED KINGDOM
IRELAND
Glasgo
Lon

Edmonton

Vancouver

Calgary

C A N A D A

Newfoundland

Seattle

Winnipeg

Quebec
Montreal
Toronto
Boston

FRA

PORTUGAL
Lisbon

Ma
SP

Chicago

Detroit

San Francisco

Denver
St. Louis

New York
Washington

Azores

UNITED STATES

Casablanca

MOROCCO

Los Angeles

Dallas

Canary Is.

W. SAHARA

A

Mexico

Houston

New Orleans

Gulf of Mexico

Miami

BAHAMAS

A T L A N T I C

Hawaiian Islands
(U.S.)

Tropic of Cancer

Havana

CUBA

West Indies

MAURITANIA

Mexico

JAMAICA

HAITI

DOMINICAN REP.

PUERTO RICO

C. Verde Is.

SENEGAL
GAMBIA
GUINEA-BISSAU

GUATEMALA
BELIZE
HONDURAS

Caribbean Sea

GUINEA

EL SALVADOR

NICARAGUA

COSTA RICA

PANAMA

Caracas

SIERRA LEONE
LIBERIA

IVORY COAST
BUR

Palmyra Is.
(U.S.)

Tabuaeran

Kiritimati

Equator

VENEZUELA

GUYANA

Bogota

COLOMBIA

SURINAM

FR. GUIANA

O C E A N

Galapagos Is.
(Ecuador)

Quito

ECUADOR

Manaus

Belém

Phoenix Is.

P A C I F I C

Ascension
(Br.)

Tokelau Is.
(N.Z.)

PERU

B R A Z I L

Recife

Lima

Samoan Is.

O C E A N

Brasilia

Salvador

St. Helena
(Br.)

Society Is.
(Fr.)

Tuamotu Archipelago
(Fr.)

La Paz

BOLIVIA

Tonga

Rio de Janeiro

PARAGUAY

Tubuai Is.
(Fr.)

Tropic of Capricorn

Asunción

São Paulo

Tristan da Cunha
(Br.)

Easter I.

A
R
G
E
N
T
I
N
A

C
H
I
L
E

URUGUAY

Kermadec Is.
(N.Z.)

Santiago

Montevideo

Buenos Aires

Chatham Is.
(N.Z.)

Falkland Is.

S. Georgia

Tierra del Fuego

FALKLAND IS. DEPENDENCIES (Br.)

ROSS DEPENDENCY

BRITISH ANTARCTIC TERRITORY

NORW

West from Greenwi

Projection: Hammer Equal Area

The maps of the Soviet Union and Yugoslavia show the situation at the time of going to press in December, 1991. Extra maps of the Republics and Nationalities of the Soviet Union and the Republics and Ethnic Groups of Yugoslavia are provided on p.161.

Principal Sea Routes
Distances in km

Pacific Routes

Pacific Routes

ARCTIC OCEAN

R 20 40 60 80 100 120 140 160 180 N

New Siberian Is.

Novaya Zemlya

Arkhangelsk

SOVIET UNION

Bering Sea

60

Yekaterinburg • Novosibirsk

NORWAY SWEDEN FINLAND
Helsinki
Oslo St. Petersburg (Leningrad)
Stockholm Moscow
Copenhagen
POLAND Warsaw
Berlin
Vienna Kiev
ROMANIA
Rome YUGOSLAVIA BULGARIA
Bucharest
ITALY GREECE Istanbul
Athens TURKEY
Tunis Mediterranean Sea
Tripoli
Alexandria
LIBYA EGYPT
Cairo

Irkutsk

Ulan Bator
MONGOLIA

Vladivostok
Sapporo

N. KOREA
Peking Dalian
S. JAPAN Tokyo
Pusan Osaka

Baku
Tashkent

Tehran
Baghdad
IRAN
SYRIA
IRAQ
ISRAEL JORDAN
KUWAIT

AFGHANISTAN
Kabul
Islamabad
Lahore

CHINA

Chungking
Shanghai

PACIFIC
Tropic of Cancer

40

20

SAUDI
ARABIA
Mecca
OMAN
BAHRAIN
U.A.E.
YEMEN
Red Sea

PAKISTAN
Karachi
Delhi
INDIA
BANGLA-DESH Dacca
Ahmadabad Calcutta
Bombay
Arabian Sea
Madras
Bay of Bengal

NEPAL
BURMA (MYANMAR)
Rangoon
Hanoi
LAOS
THAILAND
Bangkok
VIETNAM
CAM-BODIA
Phnom Penh
Ho Chi Minh City

Hong Kong

TAIWAN

Wake I. (U.S.)

OCEAN

Manila
PHILIPPINES

Northern Marianas

Marshall Is.

NIGER CHAD
Khartoum
Niamey Kano SUDAN
Ndjamena
NIGERIA
Lagos CENTRAL AFRICAN REPUBLIC
CAMEROON Douala
TORIAL GUINEA GABON CONGO
ZAIRE
CABINDA Kinshasa
Luanda
ANGOLA

DJIB.
Addis Ababa
ETHIOPIA SOMALI REP.
UGANDA KENYA
Nairobi
RWANDA
BURUNDI Mombasa
TANZANIA
Dar-es-Salaam

Colombo
SRI LANKA

MALAYSIA BRUNEI
Kuala Lumpur
Singapore
Padang Sumatra Borneo

Maldives

Seychelles

INDIAN

OCEAN

Maldives

INDONESIA

Jakarta Surabaya

Federated States of Micronesia

Kiribati

Equator

0

New Guinea PAPUA NEW GUINEA
Solomon Is.
Port Moresby
Tuvalu (Ellice Is.)

ZAMBIA
Harare
NAMIBIA ZIMBABWE
MOZAMBIQUE
BOTSWANA
SWAZ.
Johannesburg
SOUTH AFRICA LES.
Durban
Cape Town

MADAGASCAR
Antananarivo
Mauritius

Darwin

AUSTRALIA
Alice Springs

Coral Sea

Vanuatu
Fiji
New Caledonia (Fr.)

20

Tropic of Capricorn

Crozet Is. (Fr.)

Kerguelen Is. (Fr.)

Perth
Adelaide
Sydney
Canberra
Melbourne
Auckland

Tasmania
Hobart
NEW ZEALAND
Christchurch
Dunedin

40

SOUTHERN OCEAN

60

DEPENDENCY
20 40
from Greenwich

AUSTRALIAN DEPENDENCY
60 80 100 120

ADELIE LAND
140 160 80
180

1 : 80 000 000

Copyright, George Philip & Son, Ltd.

Country	Area in thousands of square km.	Population in thousands	Density of population per sq. km.	Capital Population in thousands
Afghanistan	652	15 510	28	Kābul (1 127)
Albania	29	3 140	108	Tiranë (216)
Algeria	2 382	23 840	10	Algiers (1 722)
Angola	1 247	9 480	8	Luanda (1 200)
Argentina	2 767	31 960	12	Buenos Aires (10 728)
Australia	7 687	16 530	2	Canberra (286)
Austria	84	7 600	92	Vienna (1 531)
Bangladesh	144	104 530	780	Dhaka (3 459)
Belgium	31	9 920	325	Brussels (970)
Belize	23	170	7	Belmopan (4)
Benin	113	4 450	40	Porto-Novo (208)
Bhutan	47	1 450	31	Thimphu (60)
Bolivia	1 099	6 990	6	Sucre (87)
				La Paz (993)
Botswana	582	1 210	2	Gaborone (111)
Brazil	8 512	144 430	17	Brasilia (1 577)
Brunei	6	240	45	Bandar Seri Begawan (58)
Bulgaria	111	8 990	81	Sofia (1 129)
Burkina Faso	274	8 510	31	Ouagadougou (375)
Burma (Myanmar)	677	39 970	61	Rangoon (2 459)
Burundi	28	5 150	198	Bujumbura (273)
Cambodia (Kampuchea)	181	7 870	44	Phnom Penh (500)
Cameroon	475	10 670	23	Yaoundé (654)
Canada	9 976	25 950	3	Ottawa (819)
Central African Rep.	623	2 770	4	Bangui (597)
Chad	1 284	5 400	4	Ndjamena (512)
Chile	757	12 750	17	Santiago (4 318)
China	9 597	1 104 000	118	Peking (9 750)
Colombia	1 139	30 240	29	Bogotá (3 975)
Congo	342	1 890	6	Brazzaville (596)
Costa Rica	51	2 850	56	San José (245)
Cuba	111	10 400	94	Havana (2 059)
Cyprus	9	690	75	Nicosia (165)
Czechoslovakia	128	15 620	125	Prague (1 211)
Denmark	43	5 130	122	Copenhagen (1 344)
Djibouti	23	380	17	Djibouti (290)
Dominican Republic	49	6 870	143	Santo Domingo (1 313)
Ecuador	284	10 200	37	Quito (1 110)
Egypt	1 001	51 900	52	Cairo (6 325)
El Salvador	21	5 110	243	San Salvador (884)
Equatorial Guinea	28	420	15	Rey Malabo (37)
Ethiopia	1 222	47 880	43	Addis Ababa (1 465)
Fiji	18	730	40	Suva (71)
Finland	338	4 950	16	Helsinki (987)
France	552	55 870	102	Paris (8 510)
French Guiana	90	86	1	Cayenne (38)
Gabon	268	1 090	4	Libreville (350)
Gambia, The	11	810	81	Banjul (146)
Germany	357	77 672	217	Bonn (291)
				Berlin (3 102)
Ghana	239	14 130	61	Accra (965)
Greece	132	10 010	76	Athens (3 027)
Greenland	2 176	54	0.2	Godthaab (11)
Guatemala	109	8 680	80	Guatemala (1 300)
Guinea	246	5 070	21	Conakry (705)
Guinea-Bissau	36	940	34	Bissau (125)
Guyana	215	1 010	5	Georgetown (188)
Haiti	28	5 520	197	Port-au-Prince (738)
Honduras	112	4 800	43	Tegucigalpa (598)
Hong Kong	1	5 680	5 680	Hong Kong (1 176)
Hungary	93	10 600	115	Budapest (2 105)
Iceland	103	250	3	Reykjavík (93)
India	3 288	786 600	268	Delhi (5 729)
Indonesia	1 905	174 950	97	Jakarta (6 503)
Iran	1 648	52 520	32	Tehrān (6 043)
Iraq	438	17 660	41	Baghdād (4 649)
Irish Republic	70	3 540	51	Dublin (921)
Israel	21	4 430	222	Jerusalem (483)
Italy	301	57 440	195	Rome (2 817)
Ivory Coast	322	11 610	37	Abidjan (1 850)
				Yamoussoukro (120)
Jamaica	11	2 450	223	Kingston (525)
Japan	378	122 610	330	Tōkyō (11 829)
Jordan	89	3 940	41	'Ammān (834)
Kenya	580	23 880	42	Nairobi (1 200)
Korea, North	121	21 900	183	Pyŏngyang (2 639)
Korea, South	99	41 970	428	Seoul (9 646)

Country	Area in thousands of square km.	Population in thousands	Density of population per sq. km.	Capital Population in thousands
Kuwait	18	1 960	109	Kuwait (189)
Laos	237	3 870	17	Vientiane (377)
Lebanon	10	2 830	285	Beirut (702)
Lesotho	30	1 680	56	Maseru (109)
Liberia	111	2 510	26	Monrovia (425)
Libya	1 760	4 230	2	Tripoli (980)
Luxembourg	3	368	142	Luxembourg (77)
Madagascar	587	11 240	19	Antananarivo (703)
Malawi	118	7 750	82	Lilongwe (99)
Malaysia	330	16 920	51	Kuala Lumpur (938)
Mali	1 240	8 920	7	Bamako (419)
Malta	0.3	345	1 150	Valletta (101)
Mauritania	1 026	1 920	2	Nouakchott (500)
Mauritius	2	1 100	579	Port Louis (139)
Mexico	1 958	82 730	43	Mexico City (18 748)
Mongolia	1 565	2 090	1	Ulan Bator (500)
Morocco	447	23 910	54	Rabat (893)
Mozambique	802	14 930	19	Maputo (883)
Namibia	824	1 760	2	Windhoek (115)
Nepal	141	18 230	133	Katmandu (235)
Netherlands	37	14 760	434	Amsterdam (1 031)
New Zealand	269	3 290	13	Wellington (325)
Nicaragua	130	3 620	30	Managua (615)
Niger	1 267	6 690	5	Niamey (399)
Nigeria	924	105 470	116	Lagos (1 097)
				Abuja
Norway	324	4 200	14	Oslo (643)
Oman	212	1 380	7	Muscat (80)
Pakistan	796	105 410	124	Islamabad (204)
Panama	77	2 320	31	Panamá (625)
Papua New Guinea	463	3 560	8	Port Moresby (152)
Paraguay	407	4 040	10	Asunción (708)
Peru	1 285	21 260	17	Lima (4 605)
Philippines	300	58 720	197	Manila (1 728)
Poland	313	37 860	120	Warsaw (1 671)
Portugal	92	10 410	113	Lisbon (1 612)
Puerto Rico	9	3 291	370	San Juan (1 816)
Romania	238	23 050	100	Bucharest (1 976)
Rwanda	26	6 750	270	Kigali (157)
Saudi Arabia	2 150	14 020	7	Riyadh (667)
Senegal	197	7 110	37	Dakar (1 382)
Sierra Leone	72	3 950	55	Freetown (470)
Singapore	0.6	2 650	4 417	Singapore (2 600)
Somali Republic	638	4 760	11	Mogadishu (1 000)
South Africa	1 221	33 750	28	Pretoria (739)
				Cape Town (1 491)
Spain	505	39 050	78	Madrid (3 101)
Sri Lanka	66	16 590	255	Colombo (1 412)
Sudan	2 506	23 800	10	Khartoum (476)
Surinam	163	386	3	Paramaribo (151)
Swaziland	17	740	44	Mbabane (38)
Sweden	450	8 440	20	Stockholm (1 471)
Switzerland	41	6 540	164	Bern (300)
Syria	185	11 340	62	Damascus (1 219)
Taiwan	36	19 800	550	Taipei (2 637)
Tanzania	945	24 000	27	Dodoma (85)
Thailand	513	54 540	107	Bangkok (5 468)
Togo	57	3 250	60	Lomé (366)
Trinidad and Tobago	5	1 240	244	Port of Spain (60)
Tunisia	164	7 810	50	Tunis (774)
Turkey	779	52 420	68	Ankara (2 252)
U.S.S.R.	22 402	283 680	13	Moscow (8 816)
Uganda	236	17 190	86	Kampala (458)
United Arab Emirates	84	1 500	18	Abu Dhabi (243)
United Kingdom	245	57 080	236	London (6 767)
U.S.A.	9 373	246 330	27	Washington (3 563)
Uruguay	177	3 060	18	Montevideo (1 248)
Venezuela	912	18 750	21	Caracas (3 185)
Vietnam	330	64 230	180	Hanoi (2 571)
Western Samoa	2.8	168	58	Apia (34)
Yemen, North	195	7 530	38	Sana' (278)
Yemen, South	333	2 510	8	Aden (264)
Yugoslavia	256	23 560	92	Belgrade (1 088)
Zaïre	2 345	33 460	15	Kinshasa (2 654)
Zambia	753	7 530	10	Lusaka (819)
Zimbabwe	391	8 880	23	Harare (681)

The population figures used are from censuses or more recent estimates and are given in thousands for towns and cities over 500,000 (over 1,000,000 in Brazil, China, India, Japan, U.S.A. and U.S.S.R.) Where possible the population of the metropolitan area is given e.g. Greater London, Greater New York etc.

AFRICA

ALGERIA (1983)
- Algiers 1 722
- Oran 664

ANGOLA (1988)
- Luanda 1 200

CAMEROON (1986)
- Douala 1 030
- Yaoundé 654

CENTRAL AFRICAN REPUBLIC (1988)
- Bangui 597

CHAD (1986)
- Ndjamena 512

CONGO (1985)
- Brazzaville 596

EGYPT (1986)
- Cairo 6 325
- Alexandria 2 893
- El Giza 1 671
- Shubra el Kheima 533

ETHIOPIA (1985)
- Addis Ababa 1 465

GHANA (1984)
- Accra 965

GUINEA (1983)
- Conakry 705

IVORY COAST (1982)
- Abidjan 1 850
- Bouaké 640

KENYA (1986)
- Nairobi 1 200

LIBYA (1982)
- Tripoli 980
- Benghazi 650

MADAGASCAR (1986)
- Antananarivo 703

MAURITANIA (1985)
- Nouakchott 500

MOROCCO (1982)
- Casablanca 2 158
- Rabat-Salé 893
- Fès 548

MOZAMBIQUE (1986)
- Maputo 883

NIGERIA (1983)
- Lagos 1 097
- Ibadan 1 060
- Ogbomosho 527

SENEGAL (1985)
- Dakar 1 382

SOMALI REP. (1986)
- Mogadishu 1 000

SOUTH AFRICA (1980)
- Johannesburg 1 726
- Cape Town 1 491
- Durban 961
- Pretoria 739
- Port Elizabeth 585

SUDAN (1983)
- Omdurman 526

TANZANIA (1985)
- Dar-es-Salaam 1 096

TUNISIA (1984)
- Tunis 774

ZAÏRE (1984)
- Kinshasa 2 654
- Lubumbashi 543

ZAMBIA (1987)
- Lusaka 819

ZIMBABWE (1983)
- Harare 681

ASIA

AFGHANISTAN (1982)
- Kābul 1 127

BANGLADESH (1982)
- Dacca 3 459
- Chittagong 1 388
- Khulna 623

BURMA (MYANMAR) (1983)
- Rangoon 2 459
- Mandalay 533
- Phnom Penh 500

CHINA (1986)
- Shanghai 12 320
- Beijing 9 750
- Tianjin 5 459
- Shenyang 4 285
- Wuhan 3 493
- Guangzhou 3 359
- Chongqing 2 832
- Harbin 2 668
- Chengdu 2 642
- Xi'an 2 387
- Zibo 2 329
- Nanchang 2 289
- Nanjing 2 289
- Lupanshui 2 247
- Taiyuan 1 929
- Changchun 1 908
- Dalian 1 682
- Zhaozhuang 1 612
- Zhengzhou 1 610
- Kunming 1 516
- Jinan 1 464
- Tangshan 1 410
- Guiyang 1 403
- Lanzhou 1 391
- Linyi 1 385
- Pingxiang 1 305
- Qiqihar 1 301
- Anshan 1 298
- Qingdao 1 273
- Xintao 1 272
- Hangzhou 1 271
- Fushun 1 270
- Yancheng 1 265
- Yulin 1 255
- Dongguang 1 230
- Chao'an 1 227
- Xiaogan 1 219
- Fuzhou, Fujian 1 205
- Suining 1 195
- Changsha 1 193
- Shijiazhuang 1 187
- Jilin 1 169
- Xintai 1 167
- Puyang 1 125
- Baotou 1 119
- Bozhou 1 112
- Zhongshan 1 073
- Luoyang 1 063
- Laiwu 1 054
- Leshan 1 039
- Ürümqi 1 038
- Ningbo 1 033
- Datong 1 020
- Huainan 1 019
- Heze 1 017
- Handan 1 014
- Linhai 1 012
- Macheng 1 010
- Changshu 1 004

HONG KONG (1986)
- Kowloon 2 302
- Hong Kong 1 176
- Tsuen Wan 654

INDIA (1981)
- Calcutta 9 194
- Bombay 8 243
- Delhi 5 729
- Madras 4 289
- Bangalore 2 922
- Ahmadabad 2 548
- Hyderabad 2 546
- Pune 1 686
- Kanpur 1 639
- Nagpur 1 302
- Jaipur 1 015
- Lucknow 1 008

INDONESIA (1980)
- Jakarta 6 503
- Surabaya 2 028
- Bandung 1 462
- Medan 1 379
- Semarang 1 026
- Palembang 787
- Ujung Pandang 709
- Malang 512

IRAN (1986)
- Tehrān 6 043
- Mashhad 1 464
- Esfahān 987
- Tabrīz 971
- Shīrāz 848
- Ahvāz 580
- Bākhtarān 561
- Qom 543

IRAQ (1985)
- Baghdād 4 649
- Basra 617
- Mosul 571

JAPAN (1985)
- Tōkyō 11 829
- Yokohama 2 993
- Ōsaka 2 636
- Nagoya 2 116
- Sapporo 1 543
- Kyōto 1 479
- Kobe 1 411
- Fukuoka 1 160
- Kawasaki 1 089
- Kitakyūshū 1 056
- Hiroshima 1 044

JORDAN (1986)
- 'Ammān 834

KOREA, NORTH (1984)
- Pyŏngyang 2 639
- Hamhung 775
- Chongjin 754
- Chinnamp'o 691
- Sinŭiju 500

KOREA, SOUTH (1985)
- Seoul 9 646
- Pusan 3 517
- Taegu 2 031
- Inchŏn 1 387
- Kwangju 906
- Taejon 866
- Ulsan 551

LEBANON (1980)
- Beirut 702

MALAYSIA (1980)
- Kuala Lumpur 938

MONGOLIA (1988)
- Ulan Bator 500

PAKISTAN (1981)
- Karachi 5 181
- Lahore 2 953
- Faisalabad 1 104
- Rawalpindi 795
- Hyderabad 752
- Multan 722
- Gujranwala 659
- Peshawar 556

PHILIPPINES (1984)
- Manila 1 728
- Quezon City 1 326
- Cebu 552
- Caloocan 524

SAUDI ARABIA (1974)
- Riyadh 667
- Jedda 561

SINGAPORE (1987)
- Singapore 2 600

SRI LANKA (1985)
- Colombo 1 412

SYRIA (1986)
- Damascus 1 219
- Aleppo 1 191

TAIWAN (1987)
- Taipei 2 637
- Kaohsiung 1 343
- Taichung 715
- Tainan 657
- Panchiao 506

THAILAND (1982)
- Bangkok 5 468

TURKEY (1985)
- İstanbul 5 495
- Ankara 2 252
- İzmir 1 490
- Adana 776
- Bursa 614

VIETNAM (1979)
- Ho Chi Minh City 3 420
- Hanoi 2 571
- Haiphong 1 279

EUROPE

AUSTRIA (1984)
- Vienna 1 531

BELGIUM (1988)
- Brussels 970

BULGARIA (1987)
- Sofia 1 129

CZECHOSLOVAKIA (1989)
- Prague 1 211

DENMARK (1988)
- Copenhagen 1 344

FINLAND (1988)
- Helsinki 987

FRANCE (1982)
- Paris 8 510
- Lyons 1 170
- Marseilles 1 080
- Lille 935
- Bordeaux 628
- Toulouse 523

GERMANY (1986-7)
- Berlin 3 102
- Hamburg 1 571
- Munich 1 275
- Cologne 914
- Essen 615
- Frankfurt 592
- Dortmund 568
- Stuttgart 565
- Düsseldorf 561
- Leipzig 552
- Bremen 522
- Dresden 520
- Duisburg 515
- Hanover 506

GREECE (1981)
- Athens 3 027
- Thessaloníki 871

HUNGARY (1988)
- Budapest 2 105

IRISH REPUBLIC (1986)
- Dublin 921

ITALY (1987)
- Rome 2 817
- Milan 1 479
- Naples 1 201
- Turin 1 025
- Palermo 729
- Genoa 722

NETHERLANDS (1988)
- Rotterdam 1 036
- Amsterdam 1 031
- The Hague 680
- Utrecht 521

NORWAY (1988)
- Oslo 643

POLAND (1988)
- Warsaw 1 671
- Łodz 845
- Kraków 745
- Wrocław 640
- Poznań 586

PORTUGAL (1981)
- Lisbon 1 612
- Oporto 1 315

ROMANIA (1985)
- Bucharest 1 976

SPAIN (1987)
- Madrid 3 101
- Barcelona 1 704
- Valencia 732
- Seville 655
- Zaragoza 575
- Málaga 566

SWEDEN (1988)
- Stockholm 1 471
- Göteborg 720

SWITZERLAND (1986)
- Zürich 840

U.S.S.R. (1987)
- Moscow 8 816
- Leningrad 4 948
- Kiev 2 544
- Tashkent 2 124
- Baku 1 741
- Kharkov 1 587
- Minsk 1 543
- Gorki 1 425
- Novosibirsk 1 423
- Sverdlovsk 1 331
- Kuybyshev 1 280
- Tbilisi 1 194
- Dnepropetrovsk 1 182
- Yerevan 1 168
- Odessa 1 141
- Omsk 1 134
- Chelyabinsk 1 119
- Alma-Ata 1 108
- Ufa 1 092
- Donetsk 1 090
- Perm 1 075
- Kazan 1 068
- Rostov 1 004

UNITED KINGDOM (1985)
- London 6 767
- Birmingham 1 007
- Glasgow 734
- Liverpool (1981) 510

YUGOSLAVIA (1981)
- Belgrade 1 088
- Zagreb 650

NORTH AMERICA

CANADA (1986)
- Toronto 3 427
- Montréal 2 921
- Vancouver 1 381
- Ottawa 819
- Edmonton 785
- Calgary 671
- Winnipeg 625
- Québec 603
- Hamilton 557

CUBA (1987)
- Havana 2 059

DOMINICAN REP. (1981)
- Santo Domingo 1 313

EL SALVADOR (1983)
- San Salvador 884

GUATEMALA (1983)
- Guatemala 1 300

HAITI (1984)
- Port-au-Prince 738

HONDURAS (1986)
- Tegucigalpa 598

JAMAICA (1982)
- Kingston 525

MEXICO (1986)
- Mexico 18 748
- Guadalajara 2 587
- Monterrey 2 335
- Puebla 1 218
- León 947
- Torreón 730
- San Luis Potosi 602
- Ciudad Juárez 596
- Mérida 580
- Culiacán Rosales 560
- Mexicali 511

NICARAGUA (1981)
- Managua 615

PANAMA (1984)
- Panama 625

PUERTO RICO (1984)
- San Juan 1 816

UNITED STATES (1987)
- New York 17 968
- Los Angeles 13 075
- Chicago 8 111
- San Francisco 5 878
- Philadelphia 5 833
- Detroit 4 611
- Boston 4 059
- Dallas 3 655
- Houston 3 635
- Washington 3 563
- Miami 2 912
- Cleveland 2 766
- Atlanta 2 561
- St. Louis 2 438
- Pittsburgh 2 316
- Minneapolis-St. Paul 2 295
- Seattle 2 285
- Baltimore 2 280
- San Diego 2 201
- Tampa 1 914
- Phoenix 1 885
- Denver 1 847
- Cincinnati 1 690
- Milwaukee 1 552
- Kansas City (Mo.) 1 518
- Portland (Or.) 1 364
- New Orleans 1 334
- Norfolk 1 309
- Columbus (Oh.) 1 299
- Sacramento 1 291
- San Antonio 1 275
- Indianapolis 1 213
- Buffalo 1 187
- Charlotte 1 065

OCEANIA

AUSTRALIA (1986)
- Sydney 3 431
- Melbourne 2 942
- Brisbane 1 171
- Perth 1 025
- Adelaide 993

NEW ZEALAND (1988)
- Auckland 842

SOUTH AMERICA

ARGENTINA (1985)
- Buenos Aires 10 728
- Córdoba 1 055
- Rosario 1 016
- Mendoza 668
- La Plata 611
- San Miguel de Tucumán 571

BOLIVIA (1985)
- La Paz 993

BRAZIL (1985)
- São Paulo 10 099
- Rio de Janeiro 5 615
- Belo Horizonte 2 122
- Salvador 1 811
- Fortaleza 1 589
- Brasilia 1 577
- Nova Iguaçu 1 325
- Recife 1 290
- Curitiba 1 285
- Pôrto Alegre 1 275
- Belém 1 221

CHILE (1985)
- Santiago 4 318

COLOMBIA (1985)
- Bogotá 3 975
- Medellin 1 419
- Cali 1 324
- Barranquilla 897

ECUADOR (1982)
- Guayaquil 1 301
- Quito 1 110

PARAGUAY (1983)
- Asunción 708

PERU (1988)
- Lima 4 605
- Arequipa 592

URUGUAY (1985)
- Montevideo 1 248

VENEZUELA (1986)
- Caracas 3 185
- Maracaibo 1 261
- Valencia 1 089
- Maracay 826
- Barquisimento 696

AGE DISTRIBUTION PYRAMIDS

The bars represent the percentage of the total population (males plus females) in the age group shown. Males are on the left, females on the right.

■ 1990   — 2020

World

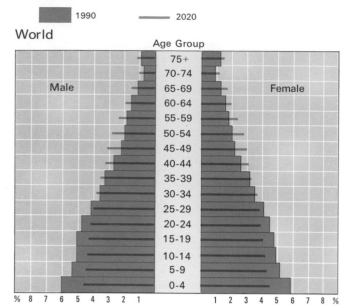

Developed Countries

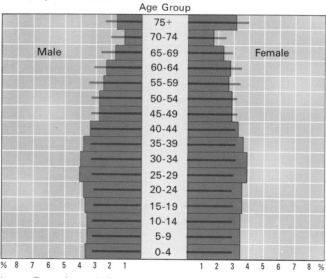

Less Developed Countries

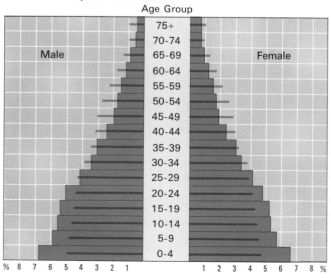

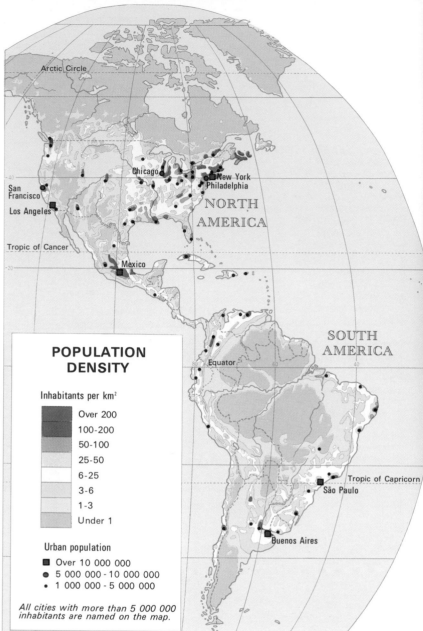

POPULATION DENSITY

Inhabitants per km²

- Over 200
- 100-200
- 50-100
- 25-50
- 6-25
- 3-6
- 1-3
- Under 1

Urban population

- ■ Over 10 000 000
- ● 5 000 000 - 10 000 000
- • 1 000 000 - 5 000 000

All cities with more than 5 000 000 inhabitants are named on the map.

Projection: *Mollweide's Interrupted Homolographic*

POPULATION CHANGE 1930-2020   Population totals are in millions

Figures in italics represent the percentage average annual increase for the period show

	1930	1930–1960	1960	1960–1990	1990	1990–2020	2020
World	2013	*1.4%*	3019	*1.9%*	5292	*1.4%*	8062
Africa	155	*2.0%*	281	*2.8%*	648	*2.7%*	1441
North America	135	*1.3%*	199	*1.1%*	276	*0.6%*	327
Latin America*	129	*1.8%*	218	*2.4%*	448	*1.6%*	719
Asia	1073	*1.5%*	1669	*2.1%*	3108	*1.4%*	4680
Europe	355	*0.6%*	425	*0.5%*	498	*0.1%*	514
Oceania	10	*1.4%*	16	*1.7%*	27	*1.1%*	37
U.S.S.R.	176	*0.7%*	214	*1.0%*	288	*0.6%*	343

* *South America plus Central America, Mexico and the West Indies*

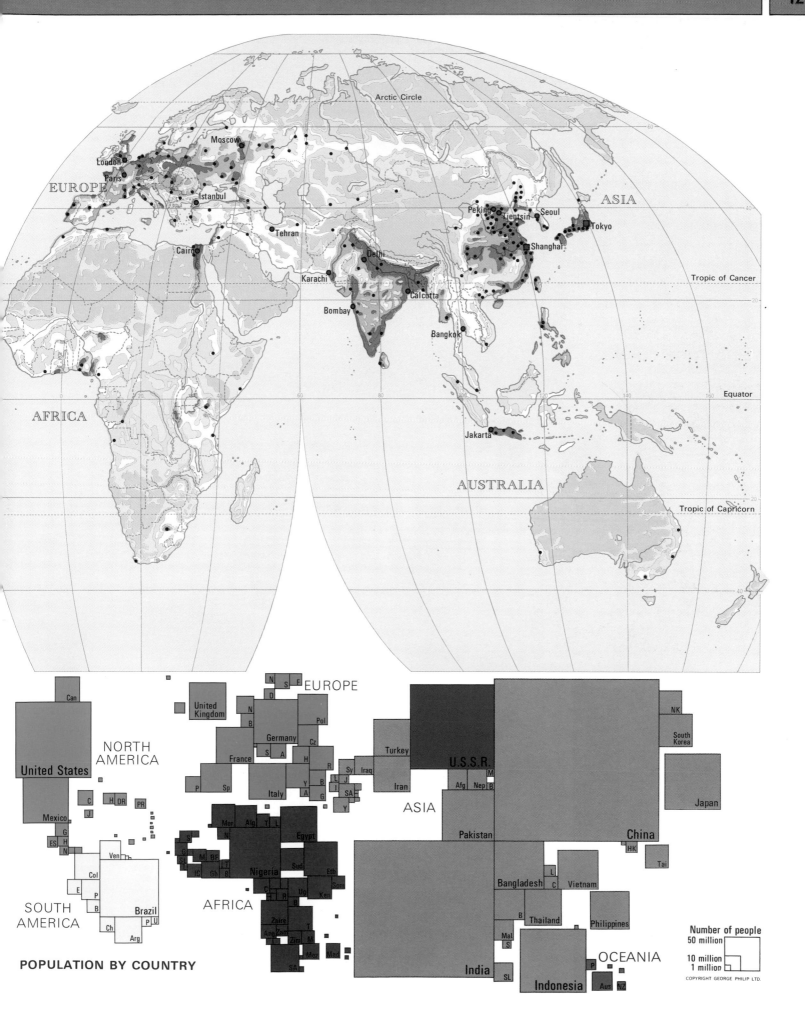

Arctic Circle

EUROPE

Moscow
London
Paris
Istanbul

Tehran

Cairo

ASIA

Peking
Tientsin
Seoul
Tokyo
Shanghai

Karachi
Delhi

Bombay
Calcutta

Tropic of Cancer

Bangkok

AFRICA

Jakarta

Equator

AUSTRALIA

Tropic of Capricorn

POPULATION BY COUNTRY

EUROPE

Can

United Kingdom

NORTH AMERICA

N S F
D
N
B
Germany
Pol
Cz
France
S A H
R
Sy Iraq
Turkey
U.S.S.R.
NK
South Korea

United States

C H DR PR
J

Mexico
G
ES H
N
Ven
Col

P Sp
Italy
Y B J
SA
Y
G

ASIA

Iran

Afg Nep B M
Japan

China
HK
Tai

E
P
B
Brazil
P U

SOUTH AMERICA

Ch Arg

Mor Alg T L
NI
S
M BF
IC Gh B
Egypt
Sud
Eth
Som

Pakistan

Bangladesh
L
C
Vietnam

AFRICA

Nigeria
C
R
B
Ug
Ken

B
Thailand
Philippines

Zaire
Ang Zam
Zim M
Mad

Mal
S

India
SL
OCEANIA

SA

Indonesia
Aus NZ

Number of people
50 million
10 million
1 million

COPYRIGHT GEORGE PHILIP LTD.

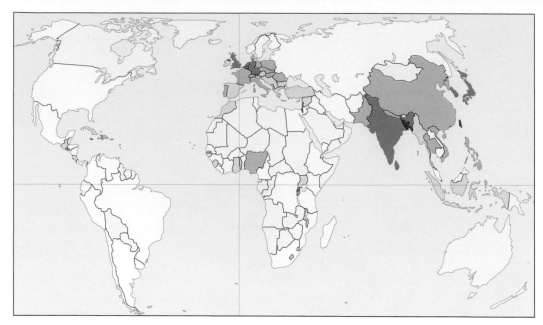

POPULATION DENSITY BY COUNTRY

Density of people per square kilometre

- Over 500 people per km²
- 200-500 people per km²
- 100-200 people per km²
- 50-100 people per km²
- 10-50 people per km²
- Under 10 people per km²

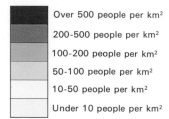

Top 5 countries		Bottom 5 countries	
Macau	19 600 per km²	Greenland	0.2 per km²
Hong Kong	5 533 per km²	Western Sahara	0.6 per km²
Singapore	4 310 per km²	French Guiana	0.9 per km²
Bangladesh	751 per km²	Mongolia	1.2 per km²
Taiwan	532 per km²	Mauritania	1.9 per km²

U.K. 235 per km²

POPULATION CHANGE 1986-2000

Expected percentage population change between 1986 and 2000

- Over 60% population gain
- 40-60% population gain
- 20-40% population gain
- 0-20% population gain
- No change or population loss

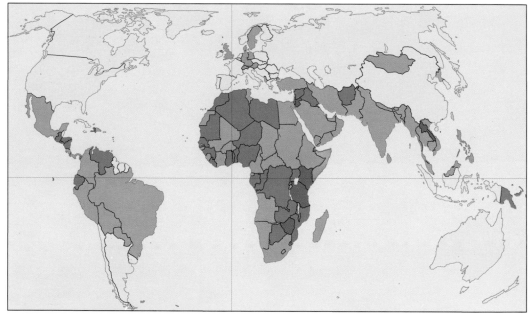

Top 5 countries		Bottom 5 countries	
Haiti	+84%	Andorra	−15%
Kenya	+82%	Switzerland	−10%
El Salvador	+77%	Oman	−5%
Jordan	+75%	Sweden	−4%
Tanzania	+74%	West Germany	−2%

U.K. − 0.9%

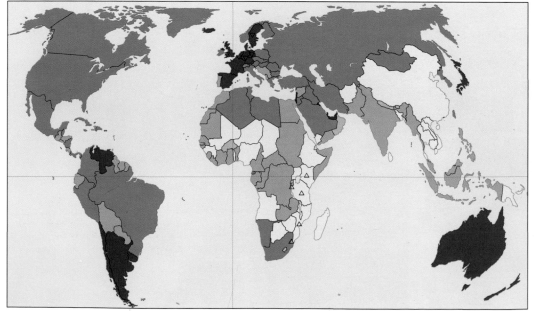

URBAN POPULATION

Percentage of total population living in towns and cities

- Over 75% urban
- 50-75% urban
- 25-50% urban
- 10-25% urban
- Under 10% urban

Most urbanized 1990		Least urbanized 1990	
Singapore	100%	Bhutan	5%
Belgium	97%	Burundi	7%
Kuwait	96%	Rwanda	8%
Hong Kong	93%	Burkina Faso	9%
U.K.	93%	Nepal	10%

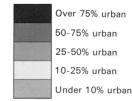

△ Fastest urbanization per annum		▽ Slowest urbanization per annum	
Tanzania	+9.6%	Sweden	+0.1%
Mozambique	+9.0%	West Germany	+0.1%
Burundi	+8.3%	Belgium	+0.2%
Swaziland	+8.0%	U.K.	+0.3%
Kenya	+7.8%	East Germany	+0.3%

CHILD MORTALITY

The number of babies who die
under the age of one, per 1000 births

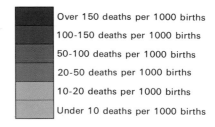

Over 150 deaths per 1000 births
100-150 deaths per 1000 births
50-100 deaths per 1000 births
20-50 deaths per 1000 births
10-20 deaths per 1000 births
Under 10 deaths per 1000 births

Highest child mortality		Lowest child mortality	
Mozambique	172 deaths	Iceland	3 deaths
Afghanistan	171 deaths	Japan	5 deaths
Mali	168 deaths	Sweden	6 deaths
Ethiopia	153 deaths	Finland	6 deaths
Sierra Leone	153 deaths	Switzerland	7 deaths

U.K.   8 deaths

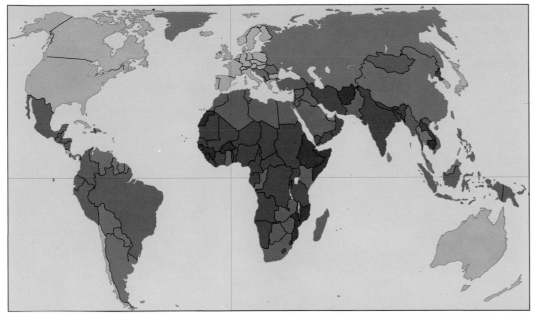

LIFE EXPECTANCY

Average expected lifespan in years

Over 70 years
60-70 years
50-60 years
40-50 years
Below 40 years

Highest life expectancy		Lowest life expectancy	
Japan	77.3 years	Burkina Faso	31.6 years
Iceland	77.1 years	Chad	32.0 years
Sweden	76.9 years	Sierra Leone	34.0 years
Netherlands	76.3 years	Cent. African Rep.	34.5 years
Switzerland	76.1 years	Gabon	35.0 years

U.K.   75 years

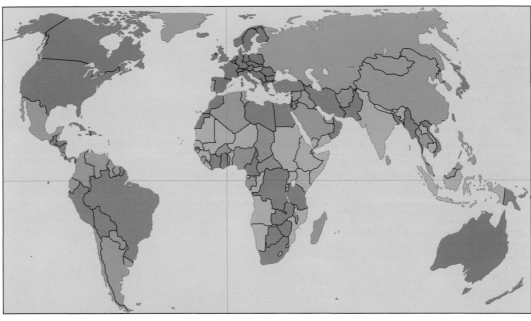

FAMILY SIZE

The average number of children a woman
can expect to bear during her lifetime

6 children or more
5 children or more
4 children or more
3 children or more
2 children or more
1 child

*In the U.K. the average family size is 1.8
children per family, whilst in Kenya
the average size is 5 children.*

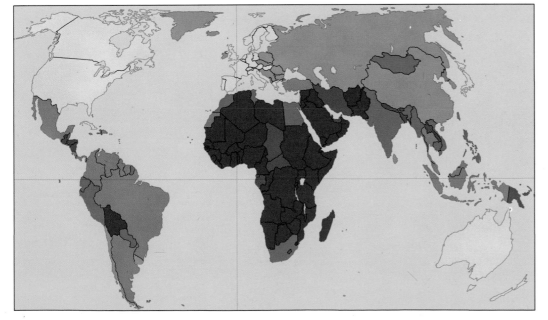

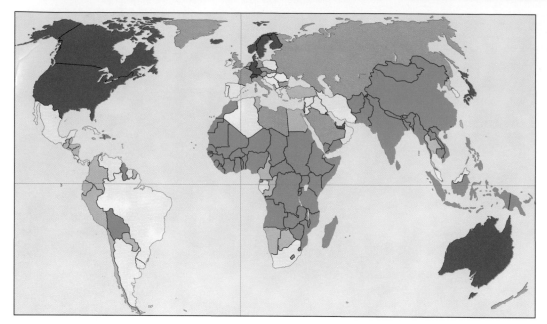

WEALTH

The value of total production
divided by population
(The Gross National Product per capita)

Over 400% of World average

200-400% of World average

100-200% of World average

World average wealth per person £1991

50-100% of World average

25-50% of World average

Under 25% of World average

Richest 5 countries 1988		Poorest 5 countries 1988	
Switzerland	£15 075	Mozambique	£55
Japan	£11 635	Ethiopia	£66
Iceland	£11 148	Bhutan	£87
Norway	£11 071	Chad	£87
U.S.A.	£10 938	Malawi	£90
	U.K.	£7 078	

AID

Aid provided or received,
divided by total population
(3 years average 1985-7)

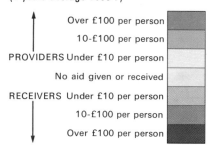

Over £100 per person

10-£100 per person

PROVIDERS Under £10 per person

No aid given or received

RECEIVERS Under £10 per person

10-£100 per person

Over £100 per person

Top 5 providers 1988		Top 5 receivers 1988	
Norway	£130	Israel	£507
Sweden	£100	Botswana	£224
Denmark	£99	Jordan	£198
Netherlands	£84	Papua N.Guinea	£192
Saudi Arabia	£83	Mauritania	£173
U.K.	£26		

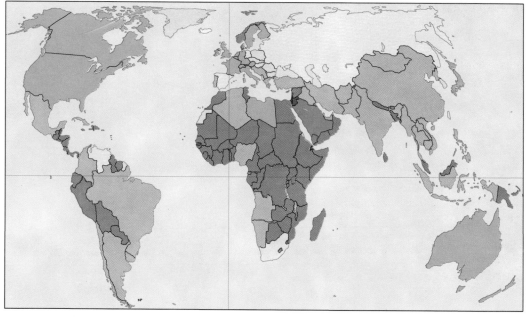

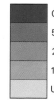

ILLITERACY

Percentage of total
population unable
to read or write

Over 75% of population illiterate

50-75% of population illiterate

25-50% of population illiterate

10-25% of population illiterate

Under 10% of population illiterate

5 most illiterate countries		5 least illiterate countries	
Somalia	88%	Iceland	0.1%
Niger	86%	U.S.S.R.	0.2%
Burkina Faso	86%	Tonga	0.4%
Mali	83%	U.S.A.	0.5%
Mauritania	83%	Barbados	0.7%
	U.K.	1%	

THE IMPORTANCE OF AGRICULTURE

The percentage of the total population who depend on agriculture

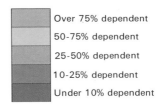

Over 75% dependent

50-75% dependent

25-50% dependent

10-25% dependent

Under 10% dependent

Top 5 countries		Bottom 5 countries	
Burundi	92%	Singapore	1.2%
Rwanda	92%	Kuwait	1.4%
Bhutan	91%	Hong Kong	1.5%
Nepal	91%	Qatar	1.8%
Burkina Faso	90%	U.K.	2.2%

DAILY FOOD CONSUMPTION

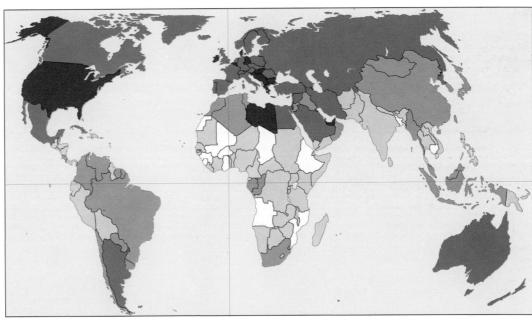

Average daily food intake in Kilocalories* per person

Over 3 500 K. cal per person

3 000-3 500 K. cal per person

2 500-3 000 K. cal per person

2 000-2 500 K. cal per person

Under 2 000 K. cal per person

A unit of the energy value of food

Top 5 countries 1988		Bottom 5 countries 1988	
E Germany	3 814K. cal	Central Africa	1 040K. cal
U.A.E.	3 733K. cal	Mozambique	1 595K. cal
Greece	3 688K. cal	Chad	1 717K. cal
U.S.A.	3 645K. cal	Ethiopia	1 749K. cal
Bulgaria	3 642K. cal	Ghana	1 759K. cal
		U.K.	3 256K. cal

HEALTH CARE

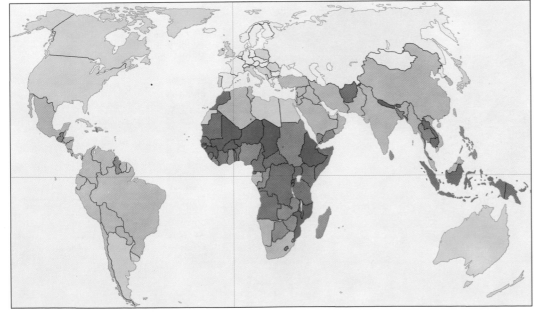

Number of people per doctor

Over 25 000 people per doctor

10 000-25 000 people per doctor

5 000-10 000 people per doctor

1 000- 5 000 people per doctor

500-1 000 people per doctor

Under 500 people per doctor

Most people per doctor 1988		Fewest people per doctor 1988	
Ethiopia	77 356	Italy	234
Guinea	57 390	U.S.S.R.	270
Burkina Faso	57 183	Czechoslovakia	277
Niger	38 775	Bulgaria	277
Chad	38 358	Hungary	307
		U.K.	611

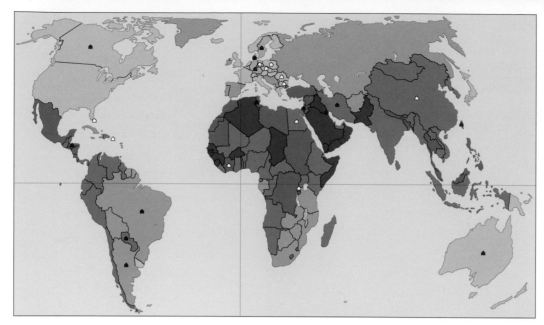

HOUSING

Number of people per household
(latest available year)

Over 6 people per household

6 people per household

5 people per household

4 people per household

3 people per household

Under 3 people per household

Expenditure on housing and energy as a
percentage of total consumer spending

▲ Over 20% spent

△ Under 5% spent

WATER SUPPLY

Percentage of total population
with access to safe drinking water
(latest available year)

Over 90% with safe water

75 - 90% with safe water

60 - 75% with safe water

45 - 60% with safe water

30 - 45% with safe water

Under 30% with safe water

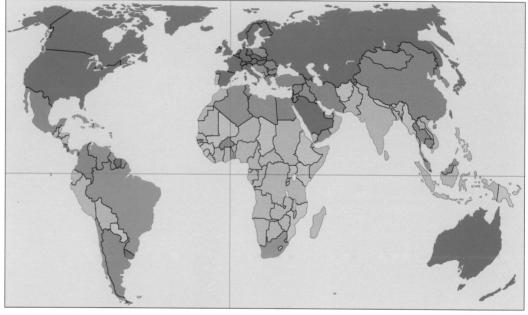

CAR OWNERSHIP

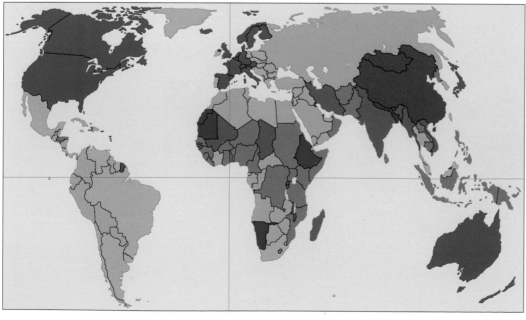

Number of people per car
(latest available year)

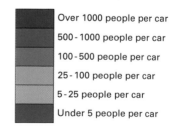

Over 1000 people per car

500 - 1000 people per car

100 - 500 people per car

25 - 100 people per car

5 - 25 people per car

Under 5 people per car

Most people per car		Most cars (millions)	
China	4300	U.S.A.	140.7
Mauritania	3400	Japan	30.8
Bangladesh	2053	W. Germany	29.2
Nepal	2000	France	27.0
Togo	1237	Italy	23.5

TYPE OF WORK

Percentage of total workforce employed
in agriculture* (latest available year)

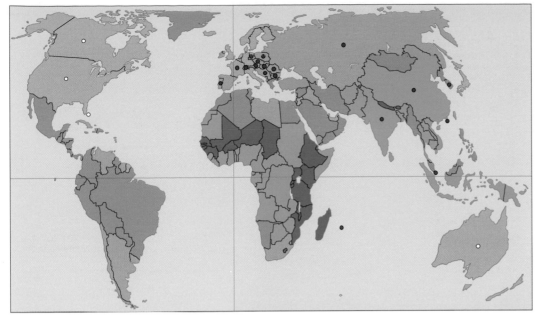

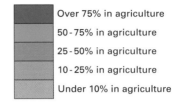

Over 75% in agriculture

50-75% in agriculture

25-50% in agriculture

10-25% in agriculture

Under 10% in agriculture

● Over 25% of total workforce
employed in manufacturing

○ Over 75% of total workforce
employed in service industries
(work in offices, shops, tourism,
transport, construction and
government)

* Includes forestry and fishing

WOMEN IN THE WORKFORCE

Working women as a percentage of
the total workforce (latest available year)

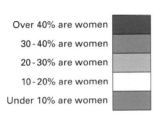

Over 40% are women

30-40% are women

20-30% are women

10-20% are women

Under 10% are women

Most women in the workforce		Fewest women in the workforce	
Burundi	48%	U.A.E.	6%
U.S.S.R.	48%	Saudi Arabia	7%
Mozambique	48%	Bangladesh	7%
Tanzania	48%	Qatar	7%
Benin	48%	Algeria	8%
		U.K.	39%

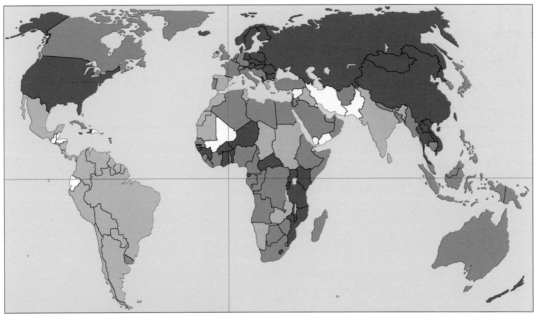

SELF SUFFICIENCY IN FOOD

Balance of trade in food products as
a percentage of total trade in food
products 1988

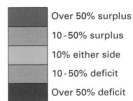

Over 50% surplus

10-50% surplus

10% either side

10-50% deficit

Over 50% deficit

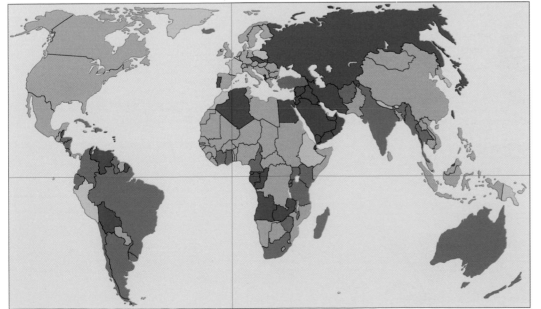

Wheat

The most important grain crop in the temperate regions though it is also grown in a variety of climates e.g. in Monsoon lands as a winter crop.

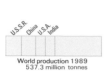

World production 1989
537.3 million tonnes

Oats

Widely grown in temperate regions with the limit fixed by early autumn frosts. Mainly fed to cattle. The best quality oats are used for oatmeal, porridge and breakfast foods.

World production 1989
42.6 million tonnes

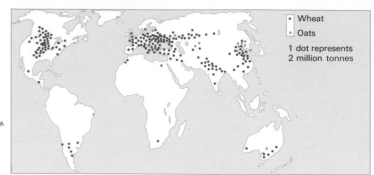

Rye

The hardiest of cereals and more resistant to cold, pests and disease than wheat. An important foodstuff in Central and E. Europe and the U.S.S.R.

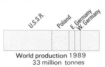

World production 1989
33 million tonnes

Maize (or Corn)

Needs plenty of sunshine, summer rain or irrigation and frost free for 6 months. Important as animal feed and for human food in Africa, Latin America and as a vegetable and breakfast cereal.

World production 1989
470.6 million tonnes

Barley

Has the widest range of cultivation requiring only 8 weeks between seed time and harvest. Used mainly as animal-feed and by the malting industry.

World production 1989
171.3 million tonnes

Rice

The staple food of half the human race. The main producing areas are the flood plains and hill terraces of S. and E. Asia where water is abundant in the growing season.

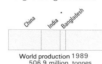

World production 1989
506.9 million tonnes

Millets

The name given to a number of related members of the grass family, of which sorghum is one of the most important. They provide nutritious grain.

World production 1989
88.7 million tonnes

Potatoes

An important food crop though less nutritious weight for weight than grain crops. Requires a temperate climate with a regular and plentiful supply of rain.

World production 1989
279.4 million tonnes

Vegetable oilseeds and oils

Despite the increasing use of synthetic chemical products and animal and marine fats, vegetable oils extracted from these crops grow in quantity, value and importance. Food is the major use- in margarine and cooking fats.

Groundnuts are also a valuable subsistence crop and the meal is used as animal feed. Soya-bean meal is a growing source of protein for humans and animals. The Mediterranean lands are the prime source of olive oil.

Groundnut · Sunflower · Soya bean

Tea and cacao

Tea requires plentiful rainfall and well-drained, sloping ground, whereas cacao prefers a moist heavy soil. Both are grown mainly for export.

Coffee

Prefers a hot climate, wet and dry seasons and an elevated location. It is very susceptible to frost, drought and market fluctuations.

Brazil Colombia Mexico Indonesia
World production 1989
5.7 million tonnes

- Tea
- Cacao
- Coffee

1 dot represents
100 000 tonnes

Sugar beet

Requires a deep, rich soil and a temperate climate. Europe produces over 90% of the world's beets mainly for domestic consumption.

U.S.S.R. France U.S.A. W.Germany
World production 1989
296.2 million tonnes

Sugar cane

Also requires deep and rich soil but a tropical climate. It produces a much higher yield per hectare than beet and is grown primarily for export.

Brazil India Cuba China
World production 1989
1002.5 million tonnes

- Sugar beet
- Sugar cane

1 dot represents
10 million tonnes

Fruit

With the improvements in canning, drying and freezing, and in transport and marketing, the international trade and consumption of deciduous and soft fruits, citrus fruits and tropical fruits has greatly increased. Recent developments in the use of the peel will give added value to some of the fruit crops.

Fish

Commercial fishing requires large shoals of fish of one species within reach of markets. Freshwater fishing is also important. A rich source of protein, fish will become an increasingly valuable food source.

Japan U.S.S.R. China
World catch 1987
92.7 million tonnes

- Temperate fruit
- Citrus fruit
- Principal fishing grounds

Beef cattle

Australia, New Zealand and Argentina provide the major part of international beef exports. Western U.S.A. and Europe have considerable production of beef for their local high demand.

U.S.A. U.S.S.R. Argentina
World production 1989
50.8 million tonnes

Dairy cattle

The need of herds for a rich diet and for nearby markets result in dairying being characteristic of densely-populated areas of the temperate zones – U.S.A., N.W. Europe, and S.E. Australia.

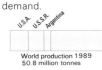

U.S.S.R. U.S.A. France W.Germany
World production 1989
473.8 million tonnes

- Cattle

1 dot represents
10 million head

- Dairy produce

Sheep

Raised mostly for wool and meat, their skins and the cheese from their milk are important products in some countries. The merino yields a fine wool and crossbreeds are best for meat.

Australia U.S.S.R. China New Zealand
World production 1989
1178 million head

Pigs

Can be reared in most climates from monsoon to cool temperate. They are abundant in China, the Corn Belt of the U.S.A. N.W. and C. Europe, Brazil and U.S.S.R.

China U.S.S.R. U.S.A.
World production 1989
67.2 million tonnes

- Sheep
- Pigs

1 dot represents
10 million head

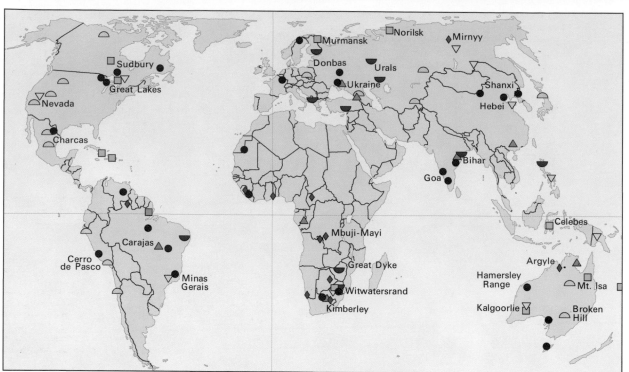

Some countries are highly
dependent upon minerals.
The following are depende
on metals and minerals for
over 50% of the value of
their exports:
Zambia 93%,
New Caledonia 81%,
Zaire 55%.

● Iron Fe   ■ Nickel Ni   ◗ Chrome Cr   ▲ Manganese Mn   ▽ Gold Au   ◠ Silver Ag   ◆ Diamonds

Top 5 producers for each mineral with percentage of World production 1989

Iron		*Nickel*		*Chrome*		*Manganese*		*Gold*		*Silver*		*Diamonds*	
U.S.S.R.	29%	U.S.S.R.	30%	South Africa	35%	U.S.S.R.	40%	South Africa	30%	Mexico	16%	Australia	38%
China	17%	Canada	27%	U.S.S.R.	27%	South Africa	15%	U.S.S.R.	14%	U.S.A.	14%	Zaire	20%
Brazil	16%	Australia	10%	Albania	7%	Brazil	11%	U.S.A.	13%	Peru	14%	Botswana	15%
Australia	11%	New Caledonia	8%	India	7%	Gabon	10%	Australia	10%	U.S.S.R.	11%	U.S.S.R.	12%
U.S.A.	6%	Cuba	6%	Zimbabwe	5%	China	7%	Canada	8%	Canada	10%	South Africa	9%

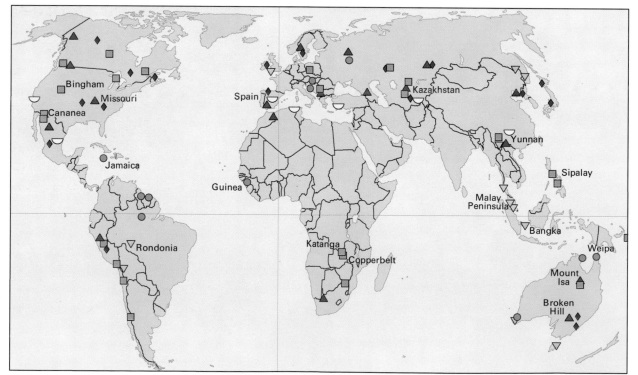

■ Copper Cu   ▲ Lead Pb   ● Bauxite Al   ▽ Tin Sn   ◆ Zinc Zn   ◡ Mercury Hg

Top 5 producers for each mineral with percentage of World production 1989

Copper		*Lead*		*Bauxite*		*Tin*		*Zinc*		*Mercury*	
Chile	19%	Australia	16%	Australia	38%	Brazil	23%	Canada	19%	U.S.S.R.	28%
U.S.A.	18%	U.S.S.R.	15%	Guinea	17%	Malaysia	15%	U.S.S.R.	13%	Spain	26%
Canada	9%	U.S.A.	14%	Jamaica	9%	Indonesia	15%	Australia	12%	China	15%
U.S.S.R.	8%	Canada	9%	Brazil	8%	China	13%	Peru	9%	Algeria	13%
China	6%	China	9%	U.S.S.R.	7%	U.S.S.R.	7%	China	7%	Mexico	6%

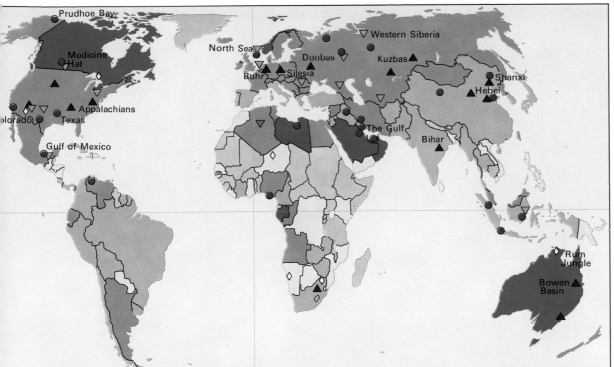

ENERGY PRODUCTION

Primary energy production expressed as kg of coal per person

	Over 10 000 kg per person
	1000-10 000 kg per person
	100-1000 kg per person
	10-100 kg per person
	Under 10 kg per person

Primary energy sources include coal, lignite, peat, oil, natural gas, plus hydro-, nuclear and geothermally generated electricity.

In developing countries traditional fuels are still very important. Sometimes called biomass fuels, they include wood, charcoal and dried dung. The pie graph for Nigeria at the foot of the page shows their importance to even the eleventh highest oil producer in the World.

● Oil	▽ Natural Gas	▲ Coal and Lignite	◇ Uranium *(the fuel used to generate nuclear power)*

Top 5 producers for each primary energy source with percentage of World production 1989

Oil		Natural Gas		Coal		Lignite		Uranium		Nuclear Power		Hydro-Electricity	
U.S.S.R.	20%	U.S.S.R.	38%	China	30%	East Germany	20%	Canada	23%	U.S.A.	32%	U.S.A.	14%
U.S.A.	14%	U.S.A.	26%	U.S.A.	19%	U.S.A.	19%	U.S.S.R.	13%	France	13%	Canada	12%
Saudi Arabia	8%	Canada	5%	U.S.S.R.	16%	U.S.S.R.	11%	East Germany	12%	Japan	10%	U.S.S.R.	11%
	5%	Netherlands	3%	India	6%	West Germany	7%	U.S.A.	10%	West Germany	7%	Brazil	9%
Mexico	5%	Algeria	2%	Poland	6%	Czechoslovakia	6%	Australia	7%	Canada	4%	China	6%

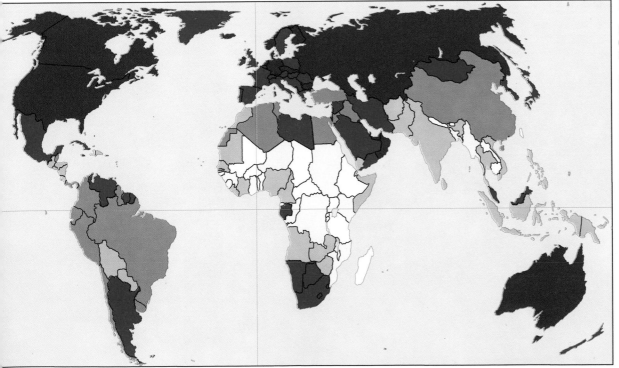

ENERGY CONSUMPTION

Primary energy consumption expressed as kg of coal per person

	Over 5 000 kg per person
	1000-5 000 kg per person
	500-1 000 kg per person
	100-500 kg per person
	50-100 kg per person
	Under 50 kg per person

Energy consumption by continent 1989

		(Change 1988-9)
North America	27.7%	(+1.4%)
Asia	23.0%	(+6.3%)
Europe	22.3%	(−0.6%)
U.S.S.R.	17.3%	(−0.0%)
South America	5.7%	(+4.1%)
Africa	2.7%	(+2.1%)
Australasia	1.3%	(+8.7%)

World total 12 019.9 million tonnes

TYPE OF ENERGY CONSUMED BY SELECTED COUNTRIES

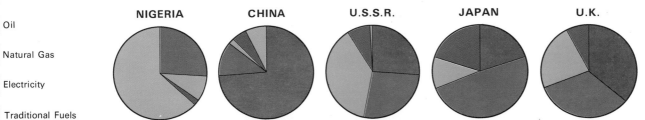

	Coal and Lignite
	Oil
	Natural Gas
	Electricity
	Traditional Fuels

NIGERIA CHINA U.S.S.R. JAPAN U.K.

DEPENDENCE ON TRADE

Value of exports as a percentage
of G.D.P. (Gross Domestic Product)
1988

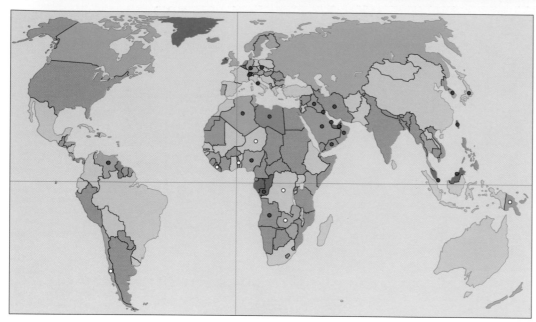

Over 50% G.D.P.

40-50% G.D.P.

30-40% G.D.P.

20-30% G.D.P.

10-20% G.D.P.

Under 10% G.D.P.

● Most dependent on industrial
exports (over 75% of total exports)

● Most dependent on fuel exports
(over 75% of total exports)

○ Most dependent on metal and
mineral exports (over 75% of total
exports)

BALANCE OF TRADE

Value of exports in proportion to
the value of imports 1988

Exports exceed
imports by:

More than 50%

10-50%

10% either side

10-50%

Imports exceed
exports by:

More than 50%

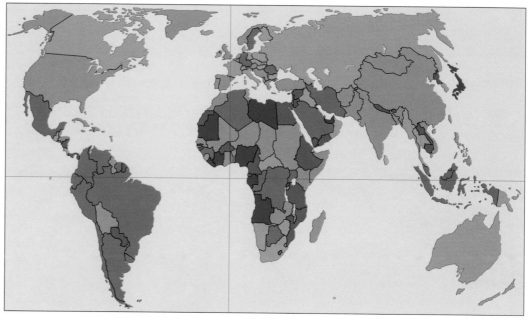

SHARE OF WORLD TRADE

Percentage share of total world
exports by value 1988

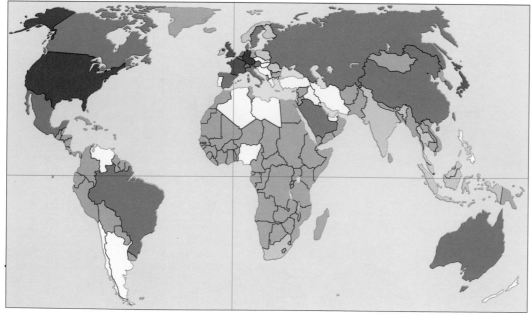

Over 10% of world trade

5-10% of world trade

1-5% of world trade

0.5-1% of world trade

0.25-0.5% of world trade

Under 0.25% of world trade

SHIPPING

Freight unloaded in
millions of tonnes 1988

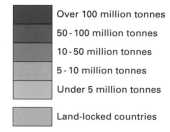

Over 100 million tonnes

50 - 100 million tonnes

10 - 50 million tonnes

5 - 10 million tonnes

Under 5 million tonnes

Land-locked countries

Major Seaports

- Handling over 100 million tonnes p.a.
- ○ Handling 50-100 million tonnes p.a.

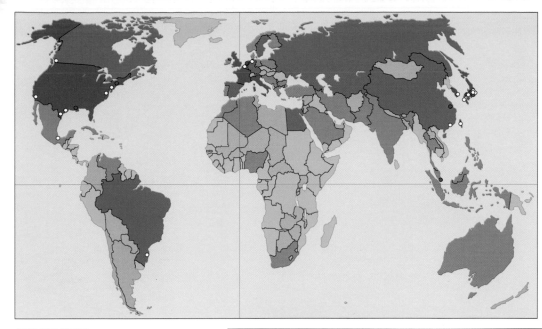

AIR TRAVEL

Passenger kilometres flown 1988*

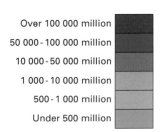

Over 100 000 million

50 000 - 100 000 million

10 000 - 50 000 million

1 000 - 10 000 million

500 - 1 000 million

Under 500 million

Major airports (handling over
20 million passengers in 1988) ○

* Passenger kilometres are the number of
passengers (international and domestic)
multiplied by the distance flown by each
passenger from the airport of origin.

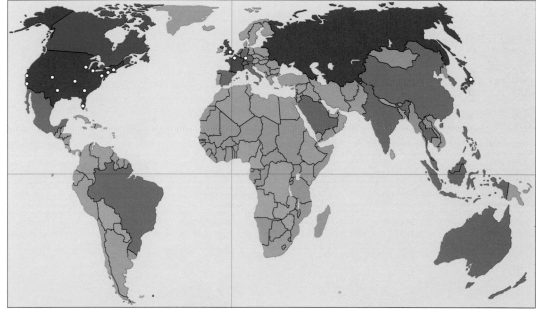

TOURISM

Tourism receipts as a percentage of
G.N.P. (Gross National Product) 1988

Over 10% of G.N.P. from tourism

5 - 10% of G.N.P. from tourism

2.5 - 5% of G.N.P. from tourism

1 - 2.5% of G.N.P. from tourism

0.5 - 1% of G.N.P. from tourism

Under 0.5% of G.N.P. from tourism

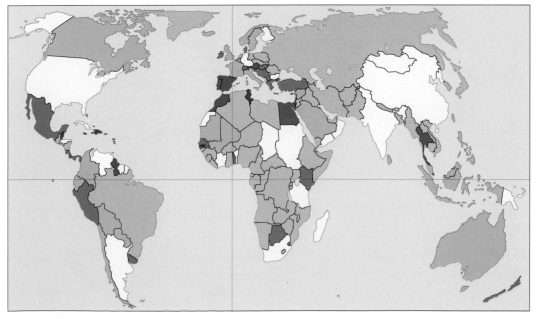

Largest percentage share of total world spending on tourism 1988		Largest percentage share of total world receipts from tourism 1988	
West Germany	16%	U.S.A.	10%
U.S.A.	14%	Spain	9%
U.K.	8%	Italy	8%
Japan	7%	France	8%
France	6%	U.K.	6%

THE WORLD: *languages and religion*

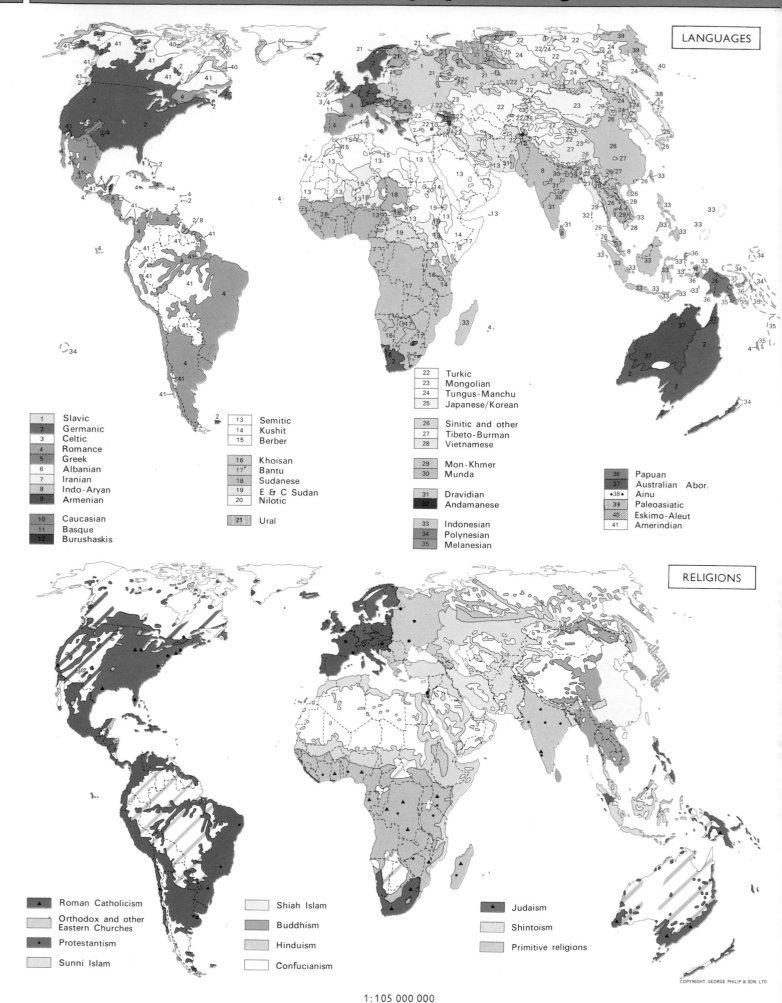

LANGUAGES

1	Slavic
2	Germanic
3	Celtic
4	Romance
5	Greek
6	Albanian
7	Iranian
8	Indo-Aryan
9	Armenian

10	Caucasian
11	Basque
12	Burushaskis

13	Semitic
14	Kushit
15	Berber

16	Khoisan
17	Bantu
18	Sudanese
19	E & C Sudan
20	Nilotic

21	Ural

22	Turkic
23	Mongolian
24	Tungus-Manchu
25	Japanese/Korean

26	Sinitic and other
27	Tibeto-Burman
28	Vietnamese

29	Mon-Khmer
30	Munda

31	Dravidian
32	Andamanese

33	Indonesian
34	Polynesian
35	Melanesian

36	Papuan
37	Australian Abor.
38	Ainu
39	Paleoasiatic
40	Eskimo-Aleut
41	Amerindian

RELIGIONS

▲	Roman Catholicism
	Orthodox and other Eastern Churches
•	Protestantism
	Sunni Islam

	Shiah Islam
	Buddhism
	Hinduism
	Confucianism

★	Judaism
	Shintoism
	Primitive religions

COPYRIGHT. GEORGE PHILIP & SON. LTD.

1:105 000 000

UNITED NATIONS

Created in 1945 to promote peace and cooperation and based in New York, the United Nations is the world's largest international organisation, with 159 members and an annual budget of over two billion US dollars. Each member of the General Assembly has one vote, while the permanent members of the 15-nation Security Council - USA, USSR, China, UK and France - hold a veto. The Economic and Social Council comprises 54 members responsible for economic, social, cultural, educational, health and related matters. The Secretariat is the UN's chief administrative arm; the only territory now administered by the Trusteeship Council is Belau (by the USA). The UN has 24 specialised agencies - based in Canada, France, Switzerland and Italy as well as the USA - which help members in fields such as economic development (UNDP), education (UNESCO), agriculture (FAO) and medicine (WHO).

The Secretariat (civil servants who run the UN)

Security Council (tries to keep the peace between countries)

Trusteeship Council (looks after Trust Terr.)

Economic & Social Council (looks after UN agencies)

International Court of Justice

U.N AGENCIES: IAEA, ILO, FAO, UNESCO, IMF, UNDP, WHO, ICAO, WMO, GATT, UNICEF, UNIDO, UNFPA, ITU

[The International Court of Justice is based in The Hague]

Membership: There are 17 independent states who are not members of the UN - Andorra, Estonia, Kiribati, Latvia, Liechtenstein, Lithuania, Micronesia, N. Korea, S. Korea, Monaco, Nauru, San Marino, Switzerland, Taiwan, Tonga, Tuvalu and Vatican City. The UN's 159 members include two who are not independent nations - the Soviet republics of Byelorussia and Ukraine. There were 51 members in 1945. Official languages are Chinese, English, French, Russian, Spanish and Arabic.

Funding: The UN budget for 1988-1989 was US $ 1,788,746,000. Contributions are assessed by members' ability to pay, with the maximum 25% of the total, the minimum 0.01%. Contributions for 1988-1989 were: USA 25%, Japan 11.38%, USSR 9.99%, W. Germany 8.08%, France 6.25%, UK 4.86%, Italy 3.99%, Canada 3.09%, Spain 1.95%, Netherlands 1.65% (others 23.75%).

Peacekeeping: The UN has been involved in 18 peacekeeping operations worldwide since 1945, five of which (Afghanistan/Pakistan, Iran/Iraq, Angola, Namibia and Honduras) were initiated in 1988-1989. In June 1991 UN personnel totalling over 11,000 were working in eight separate areas.

EFTA: European Free Trade Association (formed 1960). Portugal left the 'Seven' in 1989 to join the EEC.
ACP: African-Caribbean-Pacific (1963).
OIEC: Organisation for International Economic Cooperation (1991). It was formed from the defunct Communist trade bloc COMECON.

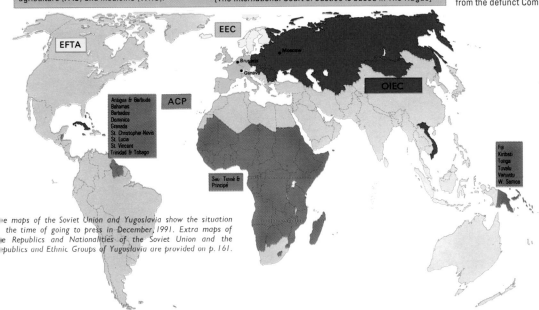

EFTA · EEC · ACP · OIEC

Antigua & Barbuda, Bahamas, Barbados, Dominica, Grenada, St. Christopher-Nevis, St. Lucia, St. Vincent, Trinidad & Tobago

Sao Tomé & Príncipe

Fiji, Kiribati, Tonga, Tuvalu, Vanuatu, W. Samoa

Moscow · Brussels · Geneva

*e maps of the Soviet Union and Yugoslavia show the situation
the time of going to press in December, 1991. Extra maps of
e Republics and Nationalities of the Soviet Union and the
publics and Ethnic Groups of Yugoslavia are provided on p.161.*

EFTA · EEC · OIEC

Moscow · Brussels · Geneva

EEC: European Economic Community (1957). The 'Common Market' aims to integrate economies, coordinate social developments and bring about political union. Members of what is now the world's biggest market share agricultural and industrial policies and tariffs on trade.

NATO: North Atlantic Treaty Organisation (formed 1949). It continues after 1991 despite the winding up of the Warsaw Pact.
OAU: Organisation of African Unity (1963). Its 52 members present over 90% of Africa's population.
ASEAN: Association of South-East Asian Nations (1967).
OAS: Organisation of American States (1949). It aims to promote social and economic cooperation between developed countries of North America and eveloping nations of Latin America.
LAIA: Latin American Integration Association (1980).
OECD: Organisation for Economic Cooperation and Development (1961). The 24 major Western free-market economies plus Yugoslavia as associate member.
COMMONWEALTH: The Commonwealth of Nations evolved from the British Empire; it comprises 18 nations recognising the British monarch as head of state and 32 with their own heads of state.
OPEC: Organisation of Petroleum Exporting Countries (1960). It controls about three-quarters of the world's oil supply.

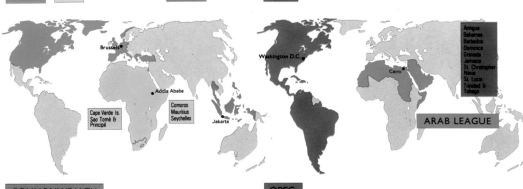

NATO · OAU · ASEAN · OAS · ARAB LEAGUE

Brussels · Addis Ababa · Washington D.C. · Cairo · Jakarta

Cape Verde Is. · Sao Tomé & Príncipe · Comoros · Mauritius · Seychelles

Antigua, Bahamas, Barbados, Dominica, Grenada, Jamaica, St. Christopher-Nevis, St. Lucia, Trinidad & Tobago

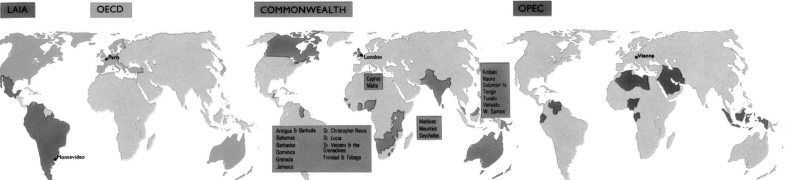

LAIA · OECD · COMMONWEALTH · OPEC

Paris · Montevideo · London · Vienna

Cyprus, Malta

Antigua & Barbuda, Bahamas, Barbados, Dominica, Grenada, Jamaica, St. Christopher-Nevis, St. Lucia, St. Vincent & the Grenadines, Trinidad & Tobago

Maldives, Mauritius, Seychelles

Kiribati, Nauru, Solomon Is., Tonga, Tuvalu, Vanuatu, W. Samoa

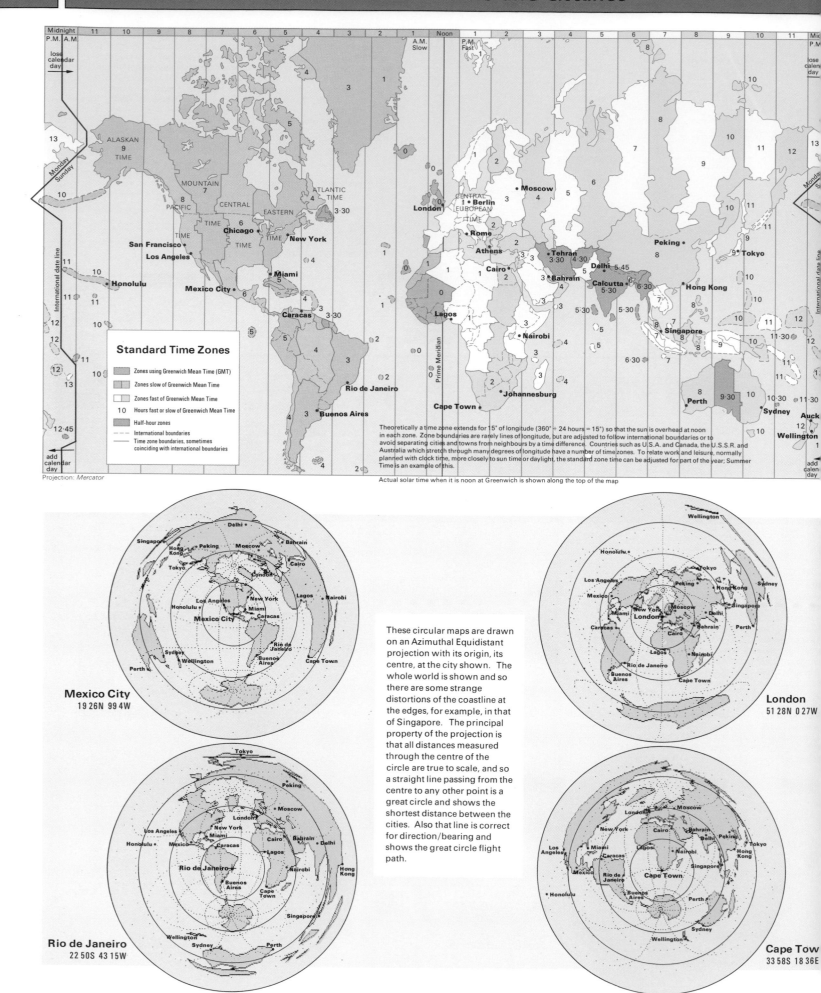

Standard Time Zones

- Zones using Greenwich Mean Time (GMT)
- Zones slow of Greenwich Mean Time
- Zones fast of Greenwich Mean Time
- 10 Hours fast or slow of Greenwich Mean Time
- Half-hour zones
- --- International boundaries
- — Time zone boundaries, sometimes coinciding with international boundaries

Theoretically a time zone extends for 15° of longitude (360° ÷ 24 hours = 15°) so that the sun is overhead at noon in each zone. Zone boundaries are rarely lines of longitude, but are adjusted to follow international boundaries or to avoid separating cities and towns from neighbours by a time difference. Countries such as U.S.A. and Canada, the U.S.S.R. and Australia which stretch through many degrees of longitude have a number of time zones. To relate work and leisure, normally planned with clock time, more closely to sun time or daylight, the standard zone time can be adjusted for part of the year; Summer Time is an example of this.

Actual solar time when it is noon at Greenwich is shown along the top of the map

Projection: *Mercator*

Mexico City
19 26N 99 4W

London
51 28N 0 27W

Rio de Janeiro
22 50S 43 15W

Cape Town
33 58S 18 36E

These circular maps are drawn on an Azimuthal Equidistant projection with its origin, its centre, at the city shown. The whole world is shown and so there are some strange distortions of the coastline at the edges, for example, in that of Singapore. The principal property of the projection is that all distances measured through the centre of the circle are true to scale, and so a straight line passing from the centre to any other point is a great circle and shows the shortest distance between the cities. Also that line is correct for direction/bearing and shows the great circle flight path.

These distances are in kilometres and are the great circle distances between the cities (international airports). Great circle distances are the shortest distances between two points on the globe. They are the normal flight paths for aircraft where they are free from the restrictions of air corridors or national airspace.

	Bahrain	Buenos Aires	Cairo	Cape Town	Caracas	Delhi	Hong Kong	Honolulu	Lagos	London	Los Angeles	Mexico	Miami	Moscow	Nairobi	New York	Peking	Perth	Rio de Janeiro	Singapore	Sydney	Tokyo
Buenos Aires	13 291																					
Cairo	1 927	11 845																				
Cape Town	7 496	6 880	7 246																			
Caracas	12 121	5 124	10 200	10 254																		
Delhi	2 618	15 784	4 400	9 278	14 186																	
Hong Kong	6 387	18 442	8 121	11 852	16 340	3 768																
Honolulu	13 882	12 158	14 195	18 555	9 671	11 984	8 911															
Lagos	5 454	7 932	3 926	4 783	7 722	8 071	11 832	16 286														
London	5 089	11 128	3 528	9 672	7 465	6 726	9 637	11 617	4 998													
Los Angeles	13 210	9 854	12 206	16 067	5 813	12 863	11 634	4 105	12 408	8 752												
Mexico	13 962	7 391	12 360	13 701	3 572	14 651	12 121	6 096	11 043	8 898	2 498											
Miami	12 182	7 113	10 441	12 334	2 190	13 495	14 430	7 806	9 045	7 102	3 759	2 050										
Moscow	3 466	13 488	2 909	10 150	9 900	4 359	7 148	11 289	6 250	2 505	9 748	10 682	9 191									
Nairobi	3 398	10 413	3 542	4 096	11 545	5 413	8 750	17 255	3 828	6 835	15 560	14 812	12 771	6 365								
New York	10 613	8 526	9 009	12 551	3 402	11 747	12 956	8 000	8 437	5 535	3 968	3 361	1 751	7 476	11 828							
Peking	6 180	19 273	7 526	12 956	14 356	3 804	1 985	8 124	11 452	8 146	10 030	12 426	12 475	5 789	9 217	10 971						
Perth	9 467	12 562	11 256	8 684	17 610	7 874	6 030	10 886	12 517	14 495	14 986	16 247	18 281	12 236	8 889	18 699	8 000					
Rio de Janeiro	11 462	1 990	9 897	6 080	4 522	14 054	17 688	13 330	6 022	9 248	10 132	7 659	6 713	11 528	8 937	7 724	17 306	13 527				
Singapore	6 319	15 860	8 246	9 650	18 332	4 148	2 581	10 789	11 149	10 867	14 099	16 593	16 951	8 437	7 446	15 330	4 489	3 909	15 729			
Sydney	12 502	11 760	14 391	10 982	15 341	10 424	7 370	8 163	15 514	17 005	12 052	12 973	15 012	14 501	12 125	16 001	8 956	3 274	13 512	6 294		
Tokyo	8 271	18 338	9 552	14 710	14 154	5 852	2 874	6 185	13 475	9 584	8 806	11 304	11 991	7 487	11 243	10 869	2 089	7 896	18 557	5 300	7 809	
Wellington	14 678	9 943	16 503	11 287	13 119	12 647	9 424	7 508	16 047	18 816	10 787	11 099	13 054	16 547	13 643	14 406	10 782	5 246	11 865	8 521	2 226	9 258

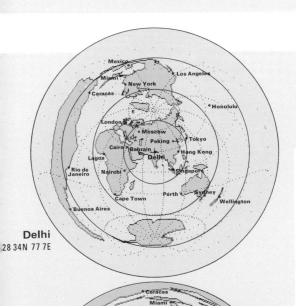

Delhi
28 34N 77 7E

Tokyo
35 33N 139 46E

The three circles are drawn at radius 5 000, 10 000 and 15 000 km from the central city

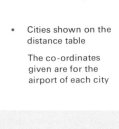

• Cities shown on the distance table

The co-ordinates given are for the airport of each city

Singapore
1 21N 103 54E

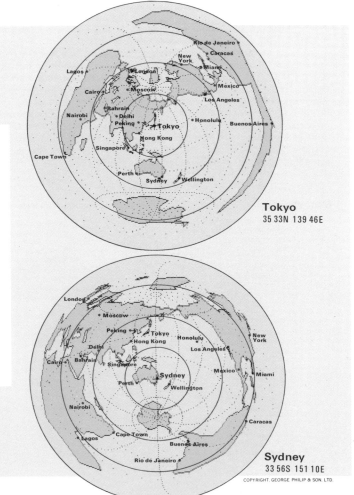

Sydney
33 56S 151 10E

The number in bold type which follows each name in the index refers to the number of the page where that feature or place will be found.

The geographical co-ordinates which follow the place name are sometimes only approximate but are close enough for the place name to be located.

An open square □ signifies that the name refers to an administrative division of a country while a solid square ■ follows the name of a country.

Rivers have been indexed to their mouth or to their confluence.

The alphabetical order of names composed of two or more words is governed primarily by the first word and then by the second. This is an example of the rule:

> *West Wyalong*
> *West Yorkshire*
> *Westbourne*
> *Westbury*
> *Westbury-on-Severn*
> *Western Australia*

Names composed of a proper name (Gibraltar) and a description (Strait of) are positioned alphabetically by the proper name. All river names are followed by ➤. If the same word occurs in the name of a town and a geographical feature, the town name is listed first followed by the name or names of the geographical features.

Names beginning with M', Mc are all indexed as if they were spelled Mac.

If the same place name occurs twice or more in the index and the places are in different countries they will be followed by the country names and the latter in alphabetical order.

> *Sydney, Australia*
> *Sydney, Canada*

In the index each placename is followed by its geographical co-ordinates which allow the reader to find the place on the map. These co-ordinates give the latitude and longitude of a particular place.

The latitude (or parallel) is the distance of a point north or south of the Equator measured as an angle with the centre of the earth. The Equator is latitude 0°, the North Pole is 90°N and the South Pole 90°S. On a globe the lines could be drawn as concentric circles parallel to the Equator, decreasing in diameter from the Equator until they become a point at the Poles. On the maps these lines of latitude are usually represented as lines running across the map from East to West in smooth curves. They are numbered on the sides of the map; north of the Equator the numbers increase northwards, to the south they increase southwards. The degree interval between them depends on the scale of the map. On a large scale map (for example, 1:2 000 000) the interval is one degree, but on a small scale (for example 1:50 000 000) it will be ten degrees.

Lines of longitude (or meridians) cut the latitude lines at right angles on the globe and intersect with one another at the Poles. Longitude is measured by the angle at the centre of the earth between it and the meridian of origin which runs through Greenwich (0°). It may be a measurement East or West of this line and from 0° to 180° in each direction. The longitude line of 180° runs North – South through the Pacific Ocean. On a particular map the interval between the lines of longitude is always the same as that between the lines of latitude and normally they are drawn vertically. They are numbered in the top and bottom margins and a note states East or West from Greenwich.

The unit of measurement for latitude and longitude is the degree and it is subdivided into 60 minutes. An index entry states the position of a place in degrees and minutes, a space being left between the degrees and minutes. The latitude is followed by N(orth) or S(outh) and the longitude by E(ast) or W(est).

The diagram illustrates how the reader has to estimate the required distance from the nearest line of latitude or longitude. In the diagram there is one degree, or 60 minutes between the lines and so to find the position of Calais an estimate has to be made, 57 parts of 60 north of the 50 degree latitude line and 50 parts of 60, or 50 minutes east of the one degree longitude line.

Where the map is smaller in scale it is more difficult to calculate the position of a place because there are five or ten degree intervals between the lines.

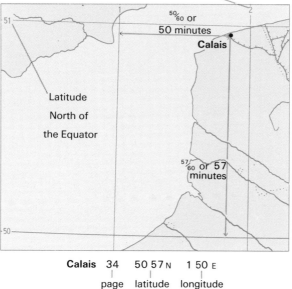

Scale 1:2 000 000   Longitude East from Greenwich

Calais   34   50 57 N   1 50 E
         page   latitude   longitude

The following is a list of the principal abbreviations used in the Index.

A.S.S.R. – Autonomous Soviet Socialist Republic	Col. – Colombia	I. – Island (Isle, Ile, Isla)	P.N.G. – Papua New Guinea
Afg. – Afghanistan	Cont. – Continent	Ill. – Illinois	P.R. – Puerto Rico
Afr. – Africa	Cr. – Creek	Ind. – Indies	Pac. Oc. – Pacific Ocean
Alb. – Albania	Cur. – Curaçao	Kor. – Korea	Pan. – Panama
Alg. – Algeria	Dom. – Dominica	Kuw. – Kuwait	Par. – Paraguay
Am. – America	Dom. Rep. – Dominican Republic	L. – Lake (Lac, Loch, Lough, Lago)	Pen. – Peninsula
Ant. – Antarctica	E. – East	Leb. – Lebanon	Pk. – Peak
Arch. – Archipelago	Eq. Guin. – Equatorial Guinea	Les. – Lesotho	Pt. – Point (Pointe, Punta)
Arg. – Argentina	Eth. – Ethiopia	Lib. – Liberia	Ra. – Range
Atl. Oc. – Atlantic Ocean	Falk. – Falkland Is.	Mart. – Martinique	Rom. – Romania
B. – Bay	Fr. – France	Mass. – Massachusetts	S. – South
B. Faso – Burkina Faso	Fr. G. – French Guiana	Maurit. – Mauritania	S. Oc. – Southern Ocean
Barb. – Barbados	G. – Gulf (Golf, Golfo)	Minn. – Minnesota	Sd. – Sound
Berm. – Bermuda	Ga. – Georgia	Miss. – Mississippi	Sene. – Senegal
Bol. – Bolivia	Ger. – Germany	Mong. – Mongolia	Si. Arab. – Saudi Arabia
Bots. – Botswana	Gr. – Great	Mor. – Morocco	Som. – Somalia
Bulg. – Bulgaria	Green. – Greenland	Mt. – Mountain (Mount, Mont, Monte, Monti, Montana)	St. L. – St. Lucia
Bur. – Burma	Gren. – Grenada		Str. – Strait
C. – Cape (Cap, Cabo)	Guad. – Guadeloupe	N. – North	Swaz. – Swaziland
C.A.R. – Central African Republic	Guat. – Guatemala	N. Cal. – New Caledonia	Tanz. – Tanzania
C.R. – Costa Rica	Guin. – Guinea	Nam. – Namibia	U.A.E. – United Arab Emirates
Cam. – Cameroon	Guy. – Guyana	Nic. – Nicaragua	Ven. – Venezuela
Carib. – Caribbean Sea	Hond. – Honduras	Nig. – Nigeria	W. – West
Chan. – Channel	Hr. – Harbour	Nor. – Norway	Yem. – Yemen
	Hts. – Heights	Oc. – Oceania	Zam. – Zambia
			Zim. – Zimbabwe

The maps of the Soviet Union and Yugoslavia show the situation at the time of going to press in December, 1991. Extra maps of the Republics and Nationalities of the Soviet Union and the Republics and Ethnic Groups of Yugoslavia are provided on p. 161.

* Renamed Rybinsk

★ *Renamed Naberezhnyye Chelny*

Dargaville

Gelsenkirchen

150 INDEX

Jersey City

Jersey City, *U.S.A.* 93 40 41N 74 8W
Jerusalem, *Asia* 57 31 47N 35 10 E
Jervaulx, *U.K.* 19 54 19N 1 41W
Jervis Bay, *Austral.* 70 35 8S 150 43 E
Jhansi, *India* 58 25 30N 78 36 E
Jhelum →, *Pak.* 58 31 20N 72 10 E
Jiamusi, *China* 61 46 40N 130 26 E
Ji'an, *China* 61 27 6N 114 59 E
Jiangsu □, *China* 61 33 0N 120 0 E
Jiangxi □, *China* 61 27 30N 116 0 E
Jilin, *China* 61 43 44N 126 30 E
Jilin □, *China* 61 44 0N 124 0 E
Jima, *Eth.* 79 7 40N 36 47 E
Jinan, *China* 61 36 38N 117 1 E
Jinja, *Uganda* 80 0 25N 33 12 E
Jinzhou, *China* 61 41 5N 121 3 E
Jixi, *China* 61 45 20N 130 50 E
João Pessoa, *Brazil* 101 7 10S 34 52W
Johannesburg, *S. Afr.* 81 26 10S 28 2 E
John o' Groats, *U.K.* 23 58 39N 3 3W
Johnstone, *U.K.* 20 55 50N 4 31W
Johnstown, *U.S.A.* 92 40 19N 78 53W
Johor Baharu, *Malay.* 63 1 28N 103 46 E
Jönköping, *Swed.* 45 57 45N 14 10 E
Jonquière, *Canada* 93 48 27N 71 14W
Jordan ■, *Asia* 57 31 0N 36 0 E
Jordan →, *Asia* 57 31 48N 35 32 E
Jos, *Nig.* 78 9 53N 8 51 E
Joseph Bonaparte G., *Austral.* 66 14 35S 128 50 E
Jotunheimen, *Nor.* 44 61 35N 8 25 E
Juan de Fuca Str., *Canada* 90 48 15N 124 0W
Juàzeiro do Norte, *Brazil* 101 7 10S 39 18W
Juiz de Fora, *Brazil* 101 21 43S 43 19W
Juliaca, *Peru* 100 15 25S 70 10W
Julianehåb, *Green.* 89 60 43N 46 0W
Jullundur, *India* 58 31 20N 75 40 E
Jundiaí, *Brazil* 102 24 30S 47 0W
Juneau, *U.S.A.* 88 58 20N 134 20W
Jura, *U.K.* 20 56 0N 5 50W
Jura, Mts., *Europe* 42 46 40N 6 5 E
Jura, Paps of, *U.K.* 20 55 55N 6 0W
Jura, Sd. of, *U.K.* 20 55 57N 5 45W
Jurby Hd., *U.K.* 18 54 23N 4 31W
Juruá →, *Brazil* 100 2 37S 65 44W
Jutland = Jylland, *Den.* 45 56 25N 9 30 E
Jylland, *Den.* 45 56 25N 9 30 E
Jyväskylä, *Fin.* 44 62 14N 25 50 E

K

Kābul, *Afg.* 57 34 28N 69 11 E
Kabwe, *Zam.* 81 14 30S 28 29 E
Kaduna, *Nig.* 78 10 30N 7 21 E
Kaesŏng, *N. Kor.* 61 37 58N 126 35 E
Kagoshima, *Jap.* 62 31 35N 130 33 E
Kaifeng, *China* 61 34 49N 114 30 E
Kaiserslautern, *Ger.* 36 49 30N 7 43 E
Kaitaia, *N.Z.* 71 35 8S 173 17 E
Kajaani, *Fin.* 44 64 17N 27 46 E
Kakinada, *India* 59 16 57N 82 11 E
Kalahari, *Africa* 81 24 0S 21 30 E
Kalamazoo, *U.S.A.* 92 42 20N 85 35W
Kalemie, *Zaïre* 80 5 55S 29 9 E
Kalgoorlie-Boulder, *Austral.* 66 30 40S 121 22 E
Kalimantan, *Indon.* 63 0 0 114 0 E
* Kalinin, *U.S.S.R.* 46 56 55N 35 55 E
Kaliningrad, *U.S.S.R.* 46 54 42N 20 32 E
Kaluga, *U.S.S.R.* 46 54 35N 36 10 E
Kamchatka Pen., *U.S.S.R.* 49 57 0N 160 0 E
Kamensk Uralskiy, *U.S.S.R.* 48 56 25N 62 2 E
Kames, *U.K.* 20 55 53N 5 15W
Kamina, *Zaïre* 80 8 45S 25 0 E
Kamloops, *Canada* 88 50 40N 120 20W
Kampala, *Uganda* 80 0 20N 32 30 E
Kampuchea = Cambodia ■, *Asia* 63 12 15N 105 0 E
Kananga, *Zaïre* 80 5 55S 22 18 E
Kanazawa, *Jap.* 62 36 30N 136 38 E
Kanchenjunga, *Nepal* 59 27 50N 88 10 E
Kandy, *Sri L.* 58 7 18N 80 43 E
Kangaroo I., *Austral.* 67 35 45S 137 0 E
Kanin, Pen., *U.S.S.R.* 46 68 0N 45 0 E
Kankan, *Guin.* 78 10 23N 9 15W
Kano, *Nig.* 78 12 2N 8 30 E
Kanpur, *India* 58 26 28N 80 20 E
Kansas □, *U.S.A.* 90 38 40N 98 0W
Kansas City, *Kans., U.S.A.* 91 39 0N 94 40W
Kansas City, *Mo., U.S.A.* 91 39 3N 94 30W
Kansk, *U.S.S.R.* 49 56 20N 95 37 E
Kanturk, *Ire.* 25 52 10N 8 55W
Kaohsiung, *Taiwan* 61 22 35N 120 16 E
Kaolack, *Sene.* 78 14 5N 16 8W
Kara Bogaz Gol, Zaliv, *U.S.S.R.* 47 41 0N 53 30 E
Kara Kalpak A.S.S.R. □, *U.S.S.R.* 48 43 0N 60 0 E
Kara Kum, *U.S.S.R.* 48 39 30N 60 0 E
Kara Sea, *U.S.S.R.* 48 75 0N 70 0 E
Karachi, *Pak.* 58 24 53N 67 0 E
Karaganda, *U.S.S.R.* 48 49 50N 73 10 E

* *Renamed Tver*

Karakoram Ra., *Asia* 58 35 30N 77 0 E
Karbalā, *Iraq* 56 32 36N 44 3 E
* Karl-Marx-Stadt, *Ger.* 42 50 50N 12 55 E
Karlskrona, *Swed.* 45 56 10N 15 35 E
Karlsruhe, *Ger.* 42 49 3N 8 23 E
Karlstad, *Swed.* 45 59 23N 13 30 E
Karratha, *Austral.* 66 20 53S 116 40 E
Karsakpay, *U.S.S.R.* 48 47 55N 66 40 E
Karshi, *U.S.S.R.* 48 38 53N 65 48 E
Kāshān, *Iran* 56 34 5N 51 30 E
Kashi, *China* 60 39 30N 76 2 E
Kassala, *Sudan* 79 16 0N 36 0 E
Kassel, *Ger.* 42 51 19N 9 32 E
Katmandu, *Nepal* 59 27 45N 85 20 E
Katoomba, *Austral.* 70 33 41S 150 19 E
Katowice, *Pol.* 43 50 17N 19 5 E
Katrine, L., *U.K.* 20 56 15N 4 30W
Katsina, *Nig.* 78 13 0N 7 32 E
Kattegatt, *Den.* 45 57 0N 11 20 E
Kauai, *U.S.A.* 90 22 0N 159 30W
Kaunas, *Lithuania* 46 54 54N 23 54 E
Kaválla, *Greece* 41 40 57N 24 28 E
Kawagoe, *Jap.* 62 35 55N 139 29 E
Kawasaki, *Jap.* 62 35 35N 139 42 E
Kawthoolei □, *Burma* 59 18 0N 97 30 E
Kayes, *Mali* 78 14 25N 11 30W
Kayseri, *Turk.* 47 38 45N 35 30 E
Kazakhstan □, *U.S.S.R.* 48 50 0N 70 0 E
Kazan, *U.S.S.R.* 46 55 48N 49 3 E
Kea, *U.K.* 16 50 13N 5 4W
Keady, *U.K.* 24 54 15N 6 42W
Keal, Loch na, *U.K.* 20 56 30N 6 5W
Kecskemét, *Hung.* 43 46 57N 19 42 E
Kediri, *Indon.* 63 7 51S 112 1 E
Keelby, *U.K.* 19 53 34N 0 15W
Keele, *U.K.* 18 53 0N 2 17W
Keeper Hill, *Ire.* 25 52 46N 8 17W
Keewatin, *Canada* 88 49 46N 94 34W
Kefallinía, *Greece* 41 38 20N 20 30 E
Keflavík, *Ice.* 44 64 2N 22 35W
Kegworth, *U.K.* 14 52 50N 1 17W
Keighley, *U.K.* 18 53 52N 1 54W
Keith, *U.K.* 23 57 33N 2 58W
Keld, *U.K.* 18 54 24N 2 11W
Kellerberrin, *Austral.* 66 31 36S 117 38 E
Kells = Ceanannus Mor, *Ire.* 24 53 42N 6 53W
Kells, Rhinns of, *U.K.* 20 55 9N 4 22W
Kelowna, *Canada* 88 49 50N 119 25W
Kelsale, *U.K.* 15 52 15N 1 30 E
Kelsall, *U.K.* 18 53 14N 2 44W
Kelso, *U.K.* 21 55 36N 2 27W
Kelvedon, *U.K.* 15 51 50N 0 43 E
Kemble, *U.K.* 14 51 40N 2 1W
Kemerovo, *U.S.S.R.* 48 55 20N 86 5 E
Kemi, *Fin.* 44 65 44N 24 34 E
Kempsey, *U.K.* 14 52 8N 2 11W
Kempston, *U.K.* 15 52 7N 0 30W
Ken, L., *U.K.* 21 55 0N 4 8W
Kendal, *U.K.* 18 54 19N 2 44W
Kenilworth, *U.K.* 14 52 22N 1 35W
Kenitra, *Mor.* 78 34 15N 6 40W
Kenmare, *Ire.* 25 51 52N 9 35W
Kenmare →, *Ire.* 25 51 40N 10 0W
Kennet →, *U.K.* 14 51 24N 0 58W
Kenninghall, *U.K.* 15 52 26N 1 0 E
Kenora, *Canada* 88 49 47N 94 29W
Kent □, *U.K.* 15 51 12N 0 40 E
Kentisbeare, *U.K.* 16 50 51N 3 18W
Kenton, *U.K.* 16 50 37N 3 28W
Kentucky □, *U.S.A.* 91 37 20N 85 0W
Kenya ■, *Africa* 80 1 0N 38 0 E
Kerala □, *India* 58 11 0N 76 15 E
Kerch, *U.S.S.R.* 47 45 20N 36 20 E
Kérkira, *Greece* 41 39 38N 19 50 E
Kermān, *Iran* 57 30 15N 57 1 E
Kerrera I., *U.K.* 20 56 24N 5 32W
Kerry □, *Ire.* 25 52 7N 9 35W
Kerry Hd., *Ire.* 25 52 26N 9 56W
Kessingland, *U.K.* 15 52 25N 1 41 E
Keswick, *U.K.* 18 54 35N 3 9W
Ketchikan, *U.S.A.* 88 55 25N 131 40W
Kettering, *U.K.* 15 52 24N 0 44W
Kettle Ness, *U.K.* 19 54 32N 0 41W
Kettlewell, *U.K.* 18 54 8N 2 2W
Keweenaw Pen., *U.S.A.* 92 47 30N 88 0W
Kexby, *U.K.* 19 53 21N 0 41W
Key West, *U.S.A.* 91 24 33N 82 0W
Keyingham, *U.K.* 19 53 42N 0 7W
Keymer, *U.K.* 15 50 55N 0 5W
Keynsham, *U.K.* 14 51 25N 2 30W
Keyworth, *U.K.* 14 52 52N 1 8W
Khabarovsk, *U.S.S.R.* 49 48 30N 135 5 E
Khaniá, *Greece* 41 35 30N 24 4 E
Kharagpur, *India* 59 22 20N 87 25 E
Kharkov, *U.S.S.R.* 47 49 58N 36 20 E
Khartoum, *Sudan* 79 15 31N 32 35 E
Khaskovo, *Bulg.* 41 41 56N 25 30 E
Kherson, *U.S.S.R.* 47 46 35N 32 35 E
Khíos, I., *Greece* 41 38 20N 26 0 E
Khorrāmshahr, *Iran* 56 30 29N 48 15 E
Khouribga, *Mor.* 78 32 58N 6 57W
Khulna, *Bangla.* 59 22 45N 89 34 E
Khulna □, *Bangla.* 59 22 25N 89 35 E
Khurasan, *Iran* 57 34 0N 57 0 E
Kibworth Beauchamp, *U.K.* 15 52 33N 0 59W
Kicking Horse Pass, *Canada* 88 51 28N 116 16W
Kidderminster, *U.K.* 14 52 24N 2 13W
Kidlington, *U.K.* 14 51 49N 1 18W

* *Renamed Chemnitz*

Kidsgrove, *U.K.* 18 53 6N 2 15W
Kidstones, *U.K.* 18 54 15N 2 2W
Kidwelly, *U.K.* 17 51 44N 4 20W
Kiel, *Ger.* 42 54 16N 10 8 E
Kielce, *Pol.* 43 50 52N 20 42 E
Kielder, *U.K.* 21 55 14N 2 35W
Kiev, *U.S.S.R.* 47 50 30N 30 28 E
Kigali, *Rwanda* 80 1 59S 30 4 E
Kigoma-Ujiji, *Tanz.* 80 4 55S 29 36 E
Kikládhes, *Greece* 41 37 20N 24 30 E
Kikwit, *Zaïre* 80 5 5S 18 45 E
Kilbirnie, *U.K.* 20 55 46N 4 42W
Kilbrannan Sd., *U.K.* 20 55 40N 5 23W
Kilcreggan, *U.K.* 20 55 59N 4 50W
Kildare, *Ire.* 25 53 10N 6 50W
Kildare □, *Ire.* 25 53 10N 6 50W
Kildonan, *U.K.* 23 58 10N 3 50W
Kilfinan, *U.K.* 20 55 57N 5 19W
Kilham, *U.K.* 19 54 4N 0 22W
Kilimanjaro, *Tanz.* 80 3 7S 37 20 E
Kilkee, *Ire.* 25 52 41N 9 40W
Kilkeel, *U.K.* 24 54 4N 6 0W
Kilkenny, *Ire.* 25 52 40N 7 17W
Kilkenny □, *Ire.* 25 52 35N 7 15W
Kilkhampton, *U.K.* 16 50 53N 4 30W
Kilkieran B., *Ire.* 25 53 18N 9 45W
Killala, *Ire.* 24 54 13N 9 12W
Killala B., *Ire.* 24 54 20N 9 12W
Killaloe, *Ire.* 25 52 48N 8 28W
Killarney, *Ire.* 25 52 2N 9 30W
Killarney, Lakes of, *Ire.* 25 52 0N 9 30W
Killary Harbour, *Ire.* 24 53 38N 9 52W
Killchianaig, *U.K.* 20 56 2N 5 48W
Killean, *U.K.* 20 55 38N 5 40W
Killiecrankie, Pass of, *U.K.* 23 56 44N 3 46W
Killin, *U.K.* 20 56 28N 4 20W
Killinghall, *U.K.* 19 54 1N 1 33W
Killybegs, *Ire.* 24 54 38N 8 26W
Kilmacolm, *U.K.* 20 55 54N 4 39W
Kilmarnock, *U.K.* 20 55 36N 4 30W
Kilmartin, *U.K.* 20 56 8N 5 29W
Kilmaurs, *U.K.* 20 55 37N 4 33W
Kilmelford, *U.K.* 20 56 16N 5 30W
Kilninver, *U.K.* 20 56 20N 5 30W
Kilrenny, *U.K.* 21 56 15N 2 40W
Kilrush, *Ire.* 25 52 39N 9 30W
Kilsby, *U.K.* 14 52 20N 1 11W
Kilsyth, *U.K.* 21 55 58N 4 3W
Kilwinning, *U.K.* 20 55 40N 4 41W
Kimberley, *Austral.* 66 16 20S 127 0 E
Kimberley, *S. Afr.* 81 28 43S 24 46 E
Kimbolton, *U.K.* 15 52 17N 0 23W
Kincardine, *U.K.* 21 56 4N 3 43W
Kindu, *Zaïre* 80 2 55S 25 50 E
Kineton, *U.K.* 14 52 10N 1 30W
King Frederick VI Coast, *Green.* 89 63 0N 43 0W
King Sd., *Austral.* 66 16 50S 123 20 E
Kingarth, *U.K.* 20 55 45N 5 2W
Kinghorn, *U.K.* 21 56 4N 3 10W
King's Lynn, *U.K.* 15 52 45N 0 25 E
King's Sutton, *U.K.* 14 52 1N 1 16W
King's Worthy, *U.K.* 14 51 6N 1 18W
Kingsbarns, *U.K.* 21 56 18N 2 40W
Kingsbridge, *U.K.* 16 50 17N 3 46W
Kingsbury, *U.K.* 14 52 33N 1 41W
Kingscourt, *Ire.* 24 53 55N 6 48W
Kingskerswell, *U.K.* 16 50 30N 3 34W
Kingsland, *U.K.* 14 52 15N 2 49W
Kingsteignton, *U.K.* 16 50 32N 3 35W
Kingston, *Canada* 92 44 14N 76 30W
Kingston, *Jam.* 94 18 0N 76 50W
Kingston, *U.K.* 14 51 18N 1 40W
Kingston-upon-Hull, *U.K.* 19 53 45N 0 20W
Kingston-upon-Thames, *U.K.* 15 51 23N 0 20W
Kingstown, *St. Vinc.* 94 13 10N 61 10W
Kingswear, *U.K.* 16 50 21N 3 33W
Kingswood, *U.K.* 14 51 26N 2 31W
Kington, *U.K.* 14 52 12N 3 2W
Kingussie, *U.K.* 23 57 5N 4 2W
Kinlochewe, *U.K.* 22 57 37N 5 20W
Kinlochleven, *U.K.* 22 56 42N 4 59W
Kinnairds Hd., *U.K.* 23 57 40N 2 0W
Kinneret, Lake, *Isr.* 57 32 45N 35 35 E
Kinross, *U.K.* 21 56 13N 3 25W
Kinsale, *Ire.* 25 51 42N 8 31W
Kinsale, Old Hd. of, *Ire.* 25 51 37N 8 32W
Kinshasa, *Zaïre* 80 4 20S 15 15 E
Kintyre, *U.K.* 20 55 30N 5 35W
Kintyre, Mull of, *U.K.* 20 55 17N 5 55W
Kippen, *U.K.* 20 56 8N 4 12W
Kippure, *Ire.* 25 53 11N 6 23W
Kirensk, *U.S.S.R.* 49 57 50N 107 55 E
Kirgizia □, *U.S.S.R.* 48 42 0N 75 0 E
Kirgiziya Steppe, *U.S.S.R.* 47 50 0N 55 0 E
Kiribati ■, *Pac. Oc.* 65 1 0N 176 0 E
Kirk Michael, *U.K.* 18 54 17N 4 35W
Kirkbean, *U.K.* 21 54 56N 3 35W
Kirkbride, *U.K.* 18 54 54N 3 13W
Kirkburton, *U.K.* 19 53 36N 1 42W
Kirkby, *U.K.* 18 53 29N 2 54W
Kirkby-in-Ashfield, *U.K.* 19 53 6N 1 15W
Kirkby Lonsdale, *U.K.* 18 54 13N 2 36W
Kirkby Malzeard, *U.K.* 19 54 10N 1 38W
Kirkby Stephen, *U.K.* 18 54 27N 2 23W
Kirkby Thore, *U.K.* 18 54 38N 2 34W
Kirkbymoorside, *U.K.* 19 54 16N 0 56W

Kirkcaldy, *U.K.* 21 56 7N 3 10W
Kirkcolm, *U.K.* 20 54 59N 5 4W
Kirkconnel, *U.K.* 21 55 23N 4 0W
Kirkcowan, *U.K.* 20 54 53N 4 38W
Kirkcudbright, *U.K.* 21 54 50N 4 3W
Kirkcudbright B., *U.K.* 21 54 46N 4 0W
Kirkham, *U.K.* 18 53 47N 2 52W
Kirkinner, *U.K.* 20 54 49N 4 28W
Kirkintilloch, *U.K.* 21 55 57N 4 10W
Kirkland Lake, *Canada* 92 48 9N 80 2W
Kirkliston, *U.K.* 21 55 55N 3 27W
Kirkoswald, *U.K.* 18 54 46N 2 41W
Kirkoswold, *U.K.* 20 55 19N 4 48W
Kirkstone P., *U.K.* 18 54 29N 2 55W
Kirkūk, *Iraq* 56 35 30N 44 21 E
Kirkwall, *U.K.* 23 58 59N 2 59W
Kirkwhelpington, *U.K.* 21 55 9N 2 0W
† Kirov, *U.S.S.R.* 46 58 35N 49 40 E
* Kirovabad, *U.S.S.R.* 47 40 45N 46 20 E
†† Kirovograd, *U.S.S.R.* 47 48 35N 32 20 E
Kirovsk, *U.S.S.R.* 46 48 35N 38 30 E
Kirriemuir, *U.K.* 23 56 41N 3 0W
Kirtling, *U.K.* 15 52 11N 0 27 E
Kirtlington, *U.K.* 14 51 54N 1 9W
Kirton, *U.K.* 19 52 56N 0 3W
Kirton-in-Lindsey, *U.K.* 19 53 29N 0 35W
Kiruna, *Swed.* 44 67 52N 20 15 E
Kisangani, *Zaïre* 80 0 35N 25 15 E
Kishinev, *U.S.S.R.* 47 47 0N 28 50 E
Kismayu, *Som.* 73 0 22S 42 32 E
Kisumu, *Kenya* 80 0 3S 34 45 E
Kitakyūshū, *Jap.* 62 33 50N 130 50 E
Kitchener, *Canada* 92 43 27N 80 29W
Kíthira, *Greece* 41 36 9N 23 0 E
Kitikmeot □, *Canada* 88 70 0N 110 0W
Kitimat, *Canada* 88 54 3N 128 38W
Kitwe, *Zam.* 81 12 54S 28 13 E
Klagenfurt, *Austria* 42 46 38N 14 20 E
Klerksdorp, *S. Afr.* 81 26 51S 26 38 E
Klondike, *Canada* 88 64 0N 139 26W
Knapdale, *U.K.* 20 55 55N 5 30W
Knaresborough, *U.K.* 19 54 1N 1 29W
Knebworth, *U.K.* 15 51 52N 0 11W
Knighton, *U.K.* 17 52 21N 3 2W
Knockmealdown Mts., *Ire.* 25 52 16N 8 0W
Knossos, *Greece* 41 35 16N 25 10 E
Knott End, *U.K.* 18 53 55N 3 0W
Knottingley, *U.K.* 19 53 42N 1 15W
Knowle, *U.K.* 14 52 23N 1 43W
Knoxville, *U.S.A.* 91 35 58N 83 57W
Knutsford, *U.K.* 18 53 18N 2 22W
Kōbe, *Jap.* 62 34 45N 135 10 E
København = Copenhagen, *Den.* 45 55 41N 12 34 E
Koblenz, *Ger.* 36 50 21N 7 36 E
Kodiak I., *U.S.A.* 88 57 30N 152 45W
Koforidua, *Ghana* 78 6 3N 0 17W
Kokand, *U.S.S.R.* 48 40 30N 70 57 E
Kokchetav, *U.S.S.R.* 48 53 20N 69 25 E
Kokkola, *Fin.* 44 63 50N 23 8 E
Kola Pen., *U.S.S.R.* 46 67 30N 38 0 E
Kolding, *Den.* 45 55 30N 9 29 E
Kolguyev, I., *U.S.S.R.* 46 69 20N 48 30 E
Kolomna, *U.S.S.R.* 46 55 8N 38 45 E
Kolwezi, *Zaïre* 80 10 40S 25 25 E
Kolyma →, *U.S.S.R.* 49 69 30N 161 0 E
Kolyma Ra., *U.S.S.R.* 49 63 0N 157 0 E
Komandorskiye, Is., *U.S.S.R.* 49 55 0N 167 0 E
Komsomolets I., *U.S.S.R.* 49 80 30N 95 0 E
Komsomolsk, *U.S.S.R.* 49 50 30N 137 0 E
Konya, *Turk.* 47 37 52N 32 35 E
Kópavogur, *Ice.* 44 64 6N 21 55W
Korce, *Alb.* 41 40 37N 20 50 E
Korea, North ■, *Asia* 61 40 0N 127 0 E
Korea, South ■, *Asia* 61 36 0N 128 0 E
Korea Strait, *Asia* 61 34 0N 129 30 E
Kōriyama, *Jap.* 62 37 24N 140 23 E
Korla, *China* 60 41 45N 86 4 E
Kortrijk, *Belg.* 36 50 50N 3 17 E
Koryak Range, *U.S.S.R.* 49 61 0N 171 0 E
Kos, *Greece* 41 36 50N 27 15 E
Košice, *Czech.* 43 48 42N 21 15 E
Kôstî, *Sudan* 79 13 8N 32 43 E
Kostroma, *U.S.S.R.* 46 57 50N 40 58 E
Kota, *India* 58 25 14N 75 49 E
Kota Baharu, *Malay.* 63 6 7N 102 14 E
Kota Kinabalu, *Malay.* 63 6 0N 116 4 E
Kotka, *Fin.* 45 60 28N 26 58 E
Kra, Isthmus of, *Thai.* 63 10 15N 99 30 E
Kragujevac, *Yug.* 41 44 2N 20 56 E
Krakatau, *Indon.* 63 6 10S 105 20 E
Kraków, *Pol.* 43 50 4N 19 57 E
Krasnodar, *U.S.S.R.* 47 45 5N 39 0 E
Krasnoturinsk, *U.S.S.R.* 46 59 46N 60 12 E
Krasnovodsk, *U.S.S.R.* 48 40 0N 52 52 E
Krasnoyarsk, *U.S.S.R.* 49 56 8N 93 0 E
Krefeld, *Ger.* 36 51 20N 6 32 E
Kremenchug, *U.S.S.R.* 47 49 5N 33 25 E
Krishna →, *India* 59 15 57N 80 59 E
Kristiansand, *Nor.* 45 58 9N 8 1 E
Kristianstad, *Swed.* 45 56 2N 14 9 E
Kristiansund, *Nor.* 44 63 7N 7 45 E
Krivoy Rog, *U.S.S.R.* 47 47 51N 33 20 E
Kroonstad, *S. Afr.* 81 27 43S 27 19 E
Krung Thep = Bangkok, *Thai.* 63 13 45N 100 35 E
Kruševac, *Yug.* 41 43 35N 21 28 E
Kuala Lumpur, *Malay.* 63 3 9N 101 41 E

† *Renamed Vyatka*
* *Renamed Gyandzha*
†† *Renamed Yelizavetgrad*

N

Staffa

T

✱ *Renamed Yekaterinburg*

Zug

YUGOSLAVIA

Population 1981 census by ethnic group

Serbs	8,140,452
Croats	4,428,005
Moslems	1,999,957
Slovenes	1,753,554
Macedonians	1,339,729
Montenegrins	579,023
Albanians	1,730,364
Hungarians	426,866

Total Population (1990 est) 24,107,000

SLOVENIA
Population 1988 1,940,000
(Slovenes 90.5%)
Capital: Ljubljana

BOSNIA & HERZEGOVINA
Population 1988 4,440,000
(Moslems 39.5%, Serbs 32.0%, Croats 18.4%)
Capital: Sarajevo

SERBIA
Population 1988 9,760,000
(Serbs 66.4%)
Capital: Belgrade

CROATIA
Population 1988 4,680,000
(Croats 75.1%, Serbs 11.5%)
Capital: Zagreb

MONTENEGRO
Population 1988 632,000
(Montenegrins 68.5%, Moslems 13.4%)
Capital: Titograd

MACEDONIA
Population 1988 2,090,000
(Macedonians 67.0%, Albanians 19.7%)
Capital: Skoplje

LITHUANIA (independent 1991)
Population 1990 3.7 million
Area 65,000 km²
Capital: Vilnius

LATVIA (independent 1991)
Population 1990 2.7 million
Area 64,000 km²
Capital: Riga

ESTONIA (independent 1991)
Population 1990 2.7 million
Area 45,000 km²
Capital: Tallinn

BYELORUSSIA
Population 1990 10.3 million
Area 208,000 km²
Capital: Minsk

MOLDAVIA
Population 1990 4.4 million
Area 34,000 km²
Capital: Kishinev

UKRAINE
Population 1990 51.8 million
Area 604,000 km²
Capital: Kiev

RUSSIAN FEDERATION
Population 1990 148.0 million
Area 17,075,000 km²
Capital: Moscow

GEORGIA
Population 1990 5.5 million
Area 70,000 km²
Capital: Tbilisi

KAZAKHSTAN
Population 1990 16.7 million
Area 2,717,000 km²
Capital: Alma-Ata

ARMENIA
Population 1990 3.3 million
Area 30,000 km²
Capital: Yerevan

UZBEKISTAN
Population 1990 20.3 million
Area 447,000 km²
Capital: Tashkent

AZERBAIJAN
Population 1990 7.1 million
Area 87,000 km²
Capital: Baku

TURKMENISTAN
Population 1990 3.6 million
Area 488,000 km²
Capital: Ashkhabad

KIRGIZIA
Population 1990 4.4 million
Area 199,000 km²
Capital: Bishkek

TADZHIKISTAN
Population 1990 5.3 million
Area 143,000 km²
Capital: Dushanbe

NATIONALITIES OF SOVIET UNION

Total population 1989 census
286.7 million

Russians	145.2 million
Ukrainians	44.2 million
Uzbeks	16.7 million
Belorussians	10.0 million
Kazakhs	8.1 million
Azerbaijanians	6.8 million
Tatars	6.6 million
Armenians	4.6 million
Georgians	4.0 million
Moldavians	3.4 million
Tajiks	3.2 million
Lithuanians	3.0 million
Turkmenians	2.7 million
Kirghiz	2.5 million
Germans	2.0 million
Chuvashes	1.8 million
Latvians	1.5 million
Bashkirs	1.5 million
Jews	1.4 million
Mordovians	1.2 million
Poles	1.1 million
Estonians	1.0 million

MAP PROJECTIONS

MAP PROJECTIONS

A map projection is the systematic depiction on a plane surface of the imaginary lines of latitude or longitude from a globe of the earth. This network of lines is called the graticule and forms the framework upon which an accurate depiction of the earth is made. The map graticule, which is the basis of any map, is constructed sometimes by graphical means, but often by using mathematical formulae to give the intersections of the graticule plotted as x and y co-ordinates. The choice between projections is based upon which properties the cartographer wishes the map to possess, the map scale and also the extent of the area to be mapped. Since the globe is three dimensional, it is not possible to depict its surface on a two dimensional plane without distortion. Preservation of one of the basic properties listed below can only be secured at the expense of the others and the choice of projection is often a compromise solution.

Correct Area

In these projections the areas from the globe are to scale on the map. For example, if you look at the diagram at the top right, areas of 10° x 10° are shown from the equator to the poles. The proportion of this area at the extremities are approximately 11:1. An equal area projection will retain that proportion in its portrayal of those areas. This is particularly useful in the mapping of densities and distributions. Projections with this property are termed **Equal Area, Equivalent or Homolographic.**

Correct Distance

In these projections the scale is correct along the meridians, or in the case of the Azimuthal Equidistant scale is true along any line drawn from the centre of the projection. They are called **Equidistant.**

Correct Shape

This property can only be true within small areas as it is achieved only by having a uniform scale distortion along both x and y axes of the projection. The projections are called **Conformal** or **Orthomorphic.**

In order to minimise the distortions at the edges of some projections, central portions of them are often selected for atlas maps. Below are listed some of the major types of projection.

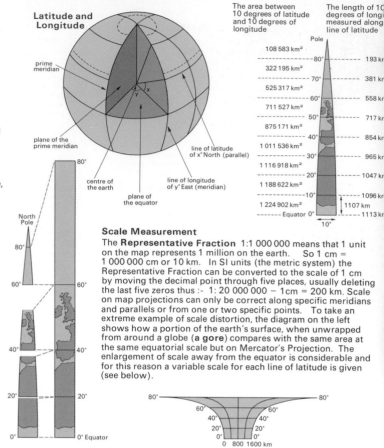

Latitude and Longitude

prime meridian

plane of the prime meridian

centre of the earth

plane of the equator

line of latitude of x° North (parallel)

line of longitude of y° East (meridian)

North Pole

The area between 10 degrees of latitude and 10 degrees of longitude

The length of 10 degrees of longitude measured along line of latitude

	Pole	
80°	108 583 km²	193 km
70°	322 195 km²	381 km
60°	525 317 km²	558 km
50°	711 527 km²	717 km
40°	875 171 km²	854 km
30°	1 011 536 km²	965 km
20°	1 116 918 km²	1047 km
10°	1 188 622 km²	1096 km
Equator 0°	1 224 902 km²	1107 km / 1113 km

Scale Measurement

The **Representative Fraction** 1:1 000 000 means that 1 unit on the map represents 1 million on the earth. So 1 cm = 1 000 000 cm or 10 km. In SI units (the metric system) the Representative Fraction can be converted to the scale of 1 cm by moving the decimal point through five places, usually deleting the last five zeros thus :- 1: 20 000 000 − 1cm = 200 km. Scale on map projections can only be correct along specific meridians and parallels or from one or two specific points. To take an extreme example of scale distortion, the diagram on the left shows how a portion of the earth's surface, when unwrapped from around a globe (**a gore**) compares with the same area at the same equatorial scale but on Mercator's Projection. The enlargement of scale away from the equator is considerable and for this reason a variable scale for each line of latitude is given (see below).

0 800 1600 km

AZIMUTHAL OR ZENITHAL PROJECTIONS

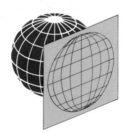

These are constructed by the projection of part of the graticule from the globe onto a plane tangential to any single point on it. This plane may be tangential to the equator (**equatorial case**), the poles (**polar case**) or any other point (**oblique case**). Any straight line drawn from the point at which the plane touches the globe is the shortest distance from that point and is known as a **great circle.** In its **Gnomonic** construction *any* straight line on the map is a great circle, but there is great exaggeration towards the edges and this reduces its general uses. There are five different ways of transferring the graticule onto the plane and these are shown on the right. The central diagram below shows how the graticules vary, using the polar case as the example.

Equidistant   Equal-Area   Orthographic   Gnomonic   Stereographic (conformal)

Oblique Case

The plane touches the globe at any point between the equator and poles. The oblique orthographic uses the distortion in azimuthal projections away from the centre to give a graphic depiction of the earth as seen from any desired point in space. It can also be used in both Polar and Equatorial cases. It is used not only for the earth but also for the moon and planets.

Polar Case

The polar case is the simplest to construct and the diagram below shows the differing effects of all five methods of construction comparing their coverage, distortion etc., using North America as the example.

Equatorial Case

The example shown here is Lambert's Equivalent Azimuthal It is the only projection which is both equal area and where bearing is true from the centre.

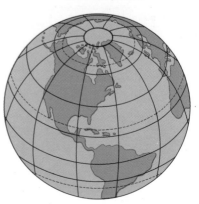

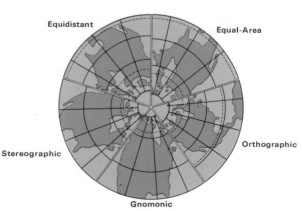

Equidistant   Equal-Area

Stereographic   Orthographic

Gnomonic

CONICAL PROJECTIONS

These use the projection of the graticule from the globe onto a cone which is tangential to a line of latitude (termed the **standard parallel**). This line is always an arc and scale is always true along it. Because of its method of construction it is used mainly for depicting the temperate latitudes around the standard parallel i.e. where there is least distortion. To reduce the distortion and include a larger range of latitudes, the projection may be constructed with the cone bisecting the surface of the globe so that there are two standard parallels each of which is true to scale. The distortion is thus spread more evenly between the two chosen parallels.

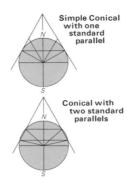

Simple Conical with one standard parallel

Conical with two standard parallels

Bonne

This is a modification of the simple conic whereby the true scale along the meridians is sacrificed to enable the accurate representation of areas. However scale is true along each parallel but shapes are distorted at the edges.

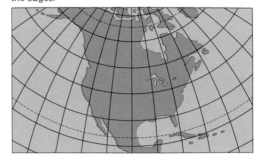

Simple Conic

Scale is correct not only along the standard parallel but also along all meridians. The selection of the standard parallel used is crucial because of the distortion away from it. The projection is usually used to portray regions or continents at small scales.

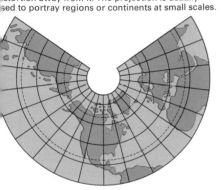

Lambert's Conformal Conic

This projection uses two standard parallels but instead of being equal area as Albers, it is Conformal. Because it has comparatively small distortion, direction and distances can be readily measured and it is therefore used for some navigational charts.

Albers Conical Equal Area

This projection uses two standard parallels and once again the selection of the two specific ones relative to the land area to be mapped is very important. It is equal area and is especially useful for large land masses oriented East-West, for example the U.S.A.

CYLINDRICAL AND OTHER WORLD PROJECTIONS

This group of projections are those which permit the whole of the Earth's surface to be depicted on one map. They are a very large group of projections and the following are only a few of them. Cylindrical projections are constructed by the projection of the graticule from the globe onto a cylinder tangential to the globe. In the examples shown here the cylinder touches the equator, but it can be moved through 90° so it touches the poles - this is called the **Transverse Aspect**. If the cylinder is twisted so that it touches anywhere between the equator and poles it is called the **Oblique Aspect**. Although cylindrical projections can depict all the main land masses, there is considerable distortion of shape and area towards the poles. One cylindrical projection, **Mercator** overcomes this shortcoming by possessing the unique navigational property that any straight drawn on it is a line of constant bearing (**loxodrome**), i.e. a straight line route on the globe crosses the parallels and meridians on the map at the same angles as on the globe. It is used for maps and charts between 15° either side of the equator. Beyond this enlargement of area is a serious drawback, although it is used for navigational charts at all latitudes.

Cylindrical with two standard parallels

Simple Cylindrical

Mercator

Mollweide

Sanson-Flamsteed

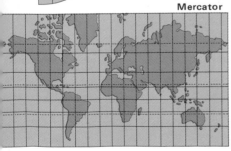

Hammer

This is not a cylindrical projection, but is developed from the Lambert Azimuthal Equal Area by doubling all the East-West distances along the parallels from the central meridian. Like both Sanson–Flamsteed and Mollweide it is distorted towards its edges but has curved parallels to lessen the distortion.

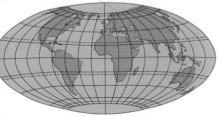

Mollweide and Sanson-Flamsteed

Both of these projections are termed **pseudo-cylindrical**. They are basically cylindrical projections where parallels have been progressively shortened and drawn to scale towards the poles. This allows them to overcome the gross distortions exhibited by the ordinary cylindrical projections and they are in fact Equal Area, Mollweide's giving a slightly better shape. To improve the shape of the continents still further they, like some other projections can be **Interrupted** as can be seen below, but this is at the expense of contiguous sea areas. These projections can have any central meridian and so can be 'centred' on the Atlantic, Pacific, Asia, America etc. In this form both projections are suitable for any form of mapping statistical distributions.

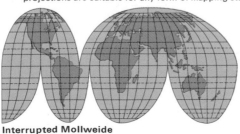

Interrupted Mollweide

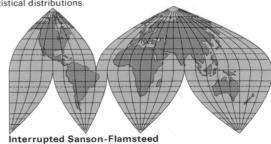

Interrupted Sanson-Flamsteed